ELIZABETH HEYRICK

Elizabeth Heyrick

The Making of an Anti-Slavery Campaigner

Jocelyn Robson

PEN & SWORD HISTORY
AN IMPRINT OF PEN & SWORD BOOKS LTD.
YORKSHIRE – PHILADELPHIA

First published in Great Britain in 2024 by
PEN AND SWORD HISTORY
An imprint of
Pen & Sword Books Ltd
Yorkshire – Philadelphia

ISBN 978 1 39906 838 3

A CIP catalogue record for this book is available from the British Library.

Typeset in Times New Roman 11/13.5 by
SJmagic DESIGN SERVICES, India.
Printed and bound in the UK by CPI Group (UK) Ltd.

Pen & Sword Books Limited incorporates the imprints of Atlas, Archaeology,
Aviation, Discovery, Family History, Fiction, History, Maritime, Military,
Military Classics, Politics, Select, Transport, True Crime, Air World, Frontline
Publishing, Leo Cooper, Remember When, Seaforth Publishing, The Praetorian
Press, Wharncliffe Local History, Wharncliffe Transport, Wharncliffe True Crime
and White Owl.

For a complete list of Pen & Sword titles please contact
PEN & SWORD BOOKS LIMITED
George House, Units 12 & 13, Beevor Street, Off Pontefract Road,
Barnsley, South Yorkshire, S71 1HN, England
E-mail: enquiries@pen-and-sword.co.uk
Website: www.pen-and-sword.co.uk

or

PEN AND SWORD BOOKS
1950 Lawrence Rd, Havertown, PA 19083, USA
E-mail: uspen-and-sword@casematepublishers.com
Website: www.penandswordbooks.com

MIX
Paper | Supporting
responsible forestry
FSC® C013604

Contents

List of Plates vii

Acknowledgements ix

Timeline in the Fight for the Abolition of British Slavery xi

Key Characters xiii

Searching for Elizabeth Heyrick xix

Backdrop xxiv

PART I: 1760–1770

Chapter 1 '.....in hopeless disaccord' 2

Chapter 2 'I will not be trifled with' 8

Chapter 3 '...the prettiest and the ugliest of the litter should both be preserved' 18

PART II: 1780–1790

Chapter 4 'No Presbyterians, no machines' 28

Chapter 5 'Never daring even to think of it' 36

Chapter 6 'All the work of a moment' 48

PART III: 1790–1800

Chapter 7 '...an emblem of the Wise' 62

Chapter 8 'If we purchase the commodity, we participate in the crime' 73

Chapter 9 'Peace – when there is no peace' 81

PART IV: 1800–1820

Chapter 10 'The Rights of the Poor' 94

Chapter 11 'A War with beggars! An exterminating crusade against the poor and miserable!' 102

Chapter 12 '...by a train of most exquisite reasoning' 111

PART V: 1820–1830

Chapter 13 'Let compensation be made in the first place where it is most due' 124

Chapter 14 'Finish the great work' 130

Chapter 15 'A burning passion for justice' 140

Endnotes 151

Select Bibliography 189

Appendix 1 Pamphlets by Elizabeth Heyrick (née Coltman) 191

Appendix 2 *Immediate not gradual abolition; or an inquiry into the shortest, safest, and most effectual means of getting rid of West Indian slavery* by Elizabeth Heyrick (1824) 193

Index 216

List of Plates

1. A plan of Leicester.
   Published by T. Coombe 1802/Reproduced by permission of the Record Office for Leicestershire, Leicester and Rutland.
2. Shambles Lane, Leicester.
   Drawing by John Flowers/Reproduced by permission of the Record Office for Leicestershire, Leicester and Rutland.
3. Portrait of Elizabeth's mother, also named Elizabeth.
   Unknown artist/Reproduced by permission of the Record Office for Leicestershire, Leicester and Rutland.
4. Portrait of Elizabeth's father, John.
   Unknown artist/Reproduced by permission of the Record Office for Leicestershire, Leicester and Rutland.
5. Elizabeth's older brother John.
   Unknown artist/Reproduced by permission of the Record Office for Leicestershire, Leicester and Rutland.
6. Elizabeth's youngest brother, Rowland.
   E. Coltman/Unknown artist/Reproduced by permission of the Record Office for Leicestershire, Leicester and Rutland.
7. Maria at Moulines, by Angelica Kauffman (1741-1807).
   Private Collection/Bridgeman Images
8. John Coltman's collection of Roman coins. From: John Throsby (1791, '*The History and Antiquities of the Ancient Town of Leicester*' (Leicester, Cengage Gale) facing p. 21.
9. St Nicholas Church.
   From: John Throsby (1791, '*The History and Antiquities of the Ancient Town of Leicester*' (Leicester, Cengage Gale) p. 232.
10. The Jewry Wall, in front of St Nicholas Church.
    Author's photo.
11. Views of Rothley Temple in Leicestershire, which were published in 1893 in *The Illustrated London News*.
    Look and Learn

12. 'Taste in High Life'.
Universal History Archive/UIG/Bridgeman Images.
13. Framework Knitters workshop in Bonsall.
Author's photo.
14. Bull stone, Bonsall.
Author's photo.
15. Reverend Robert Throsby.
From 'Scrapbook' compiled by Susanna Watts/*Reproduced by permission of the Record Office for Leicestershire, Leicester and Rutland.*
16. The Art of Stocking Framework Knitting.
Engraving from Universal Magazine 1750/Reproduced by permission of the Record Office for Leicestershire, Leicester and Rutland.
17. 'Am I not a Man and a Brother?'
Grainger/Bridgeman Images
18. 'Am I not a woman and a Sister?'
Grainger/Bridgeman Images
19. The Slave ship 'Brookes' of Liverpool.
Private Collection @ Michael Graham-Stewart/Bridgeman Images
20. Britannia giving freedom to Poor African Slaves.
Engraved by J. Bridgens after W. Green/Wilberforce House, Hull City Museums and Art Galleries UK, Wilberforce House Museum/ Bridgeman Images.
21. The Retreat.
Private Collection/Bridgeman Images.
22. Women preaching at a meeting of Quakers.
Private Collection, Look and Learn/Bridgeman Images.
23. Elizabeth's letter to Mary Lloyd in 1806.
Copyright Britain Yearly Meeting of the Society of Friends (Quakers).
24. Original silhouette of Elizabeth Heyrick.
Private Collection/reproduced with permission.
25. The copied silhouette of Elizabeth Heyrick.
Copyright Britain Yearly Meeting of the Society of Friends (Quakers).

Appendix 2: 'Immediate not Gradual Abolition or, an inquiry into the shortest, safest, and most effectual means of getting rid of West India Slavery' (London, 1824). E. Heyrick/*Reproduced by permission of the Record Office for Leicestershire, Leicester and Rutland.*

Acknowledgements

I came to the eighteenth century from a standing start. Its history and its people were new to me and Elizabeth's story has brought me into contact with numerous individuals who have kindly shared their knowledge and expertise. In Leicester, professional genealogist John Pretty constructed Elizabeth's family tree for me, and I was able to fill significant gaps in the Coltmans' story. I was also able to find their descendant, Tony Clarke, who has been generous in facilitating my research. I have had unrestricted access to the artefacts and precious family records that his father Geoffrey Clarke had left in his care. Here was the original text of the first letter hand-written by Elizabeth's father-to-be to her mother-to-be in 1763 and carefully preserved ever since. Here, too, was the original and delicate cardboard silhouette of Elizabeth, made in the 1820s and saved for posterity by her sister.

Other memorable moments have included a trip to Derbyshire, to the village of Bonsall, where Elizabeth began her activism with a direct challenge to the cruel practices of bull-baiting. Crouched under a front pew in the local church, I found the huge bull stone that had been used to tie the bull down during its torment. In the Framework Knitters Museum in Wigston, it was the deafening noise of working machines used in hosiery factories like those owned by the Coltman family that stayed with me. And in the Victoria and Albert Museum in London I was shown archival collections of eighteenth-century scissor art, silhouettes of people but also tiny, feathery images of landscapes, animals and flowers, like those Elizabeth's mother had created in her younger days.

Visits to locations that I could link with Elizabeth's story were rewarding. Yet inevitably most of my time has been spent in libraries and archives where I have been assisted by many skilful people including librarians, historians and archivists at the University of Leicester, the Library of the Society of Friends in London, and the Record Office for Leicestershire, Leicester and Rutland in Wigston Magna. I am particularly grateful also to staff at the London Library for pursuing numerous enquiries on my behalf and to the Society of Authors for professional guidance. Other organisations I am indebted to include the Bonsall History Group, Dr William's Library, the National Portrait Gallery, the Victoria and Albert Museum, the British Library, the Leicester Museum and Art Gallery, the Library of Birmingham, the Bodleian Library in Oxford, the Great Meeting Unitarian Chapel in Leicester, Borthwick Institute for Archives at the University of York, Wigston Framework Knitters Museum, Friends of Welford Road Cemetery, St James the Apostle's Church in Derbyshire, and the Wirksworth Team Ministry Office, also in Derbyshire.

I am also grateful to a small group of experts and knowledgeable friends. Special mentions to the following who have kept me sane and encouraged my efforts when I was flagging: Ann Harris for a trip to the Bronte Museum in Yorkshire, Rosmond Kinsey Milner for advice on the art and portraiture of the Georgian period, Liz Philipson for historical insights, Paula Lanning for her calm support, Elaine Whitlock for her interest and enthusiasm, Philip Philippou for technical help, Laura Hirst, Charlotte Mitchell and Beverley Adams for editorial support and Karl French of the Literary Consultancy. Finally, sincere thanks to my three readers, who ploughed through various drafts of various chapters at different stages and still managed to remain positive about a long and complicated story. Bill Bailey, Merryn Hutchings and Jess Jenkins drew on their considerable knowledge and diverse expertise to advise and assist me and I owe them much. Over the last six years, they have spent time with me, lent resources, read drafts, offered advice and listened as I attempted to unravel the confusions and ambiguities that arose during my research and writing. I am most grateful to them for their patience, insights and guidance.

Timeline in the Fight for the Abolition of British Slavery

1562	First English slaving expedition is carried out by Sir John Hawkins, who takes Africans to Spanish plantations in the Americas.
1672	Royal Africa Company is founded to control British slave trade.
1769	Birth of Elizabeth Heyrick.
1772	In the Somerset case, Granville Sharp wins a ruling prohibiting the forcible removal of slaves from England.
1776-83	War of American Independence
1778	Slavery is made illegal in Scotland.
1787	'Society for Effecting the Abolition of the Slave Trade' is founded in London.
1781	The Zong massacre takes place.
1789	French Revolution begins.
1790	First bill for the Abolition of the Slave Trade fails in the British parliament.
1791	*Rights of Man* by Thomas Paine is published. The radical William Fox calls for boycott of slave-grown sugar in 'An Address to the People of Great Britain on the Propriety of Abstaining from West India Sugar and Rum'.
1792	House of Lords rejects an Abolition Bill passed by the House of Commons.
1794	France abolishes slavery in all its territories.
1797	Death of Olaudah Equiano.
1807	An Act for the Abolition of the Slave Trade is passed in Britain, prohibiting the slave trade in the British Empire. It does not abolish the practice of slavery.

1813	Death of Granville Sharp.
1823	Slave revolt in Demerara (Guyana). Founding of 'The London Society for Mitigating and Gradually Abolishing the State of Slavery Throughout the British Dominions'.
1824	Politicians Ellis & Wilmot Horton publish their pro-slavery views.
1825	First ladies' anti-slavery society meets near Birmingham. Campaign to boycott West India sugar is revived.
1830	National anti-slavery society is renamed as 'The Society for the Abolition of Slavery throughout the British Dominions'.
1831	Death of Elizabeth Heyrick.
1833	The Abolition of Slavery Act is passed by the British Parliament abolishing the practice of slavery in all British territories. Slavery is replaced by apprenticeship. Death of William Wilberforce.
1838	Apprenticeships come to an end. Full legal emancipation in British colonies.

Key Characters

Reverend John Aikin (1713-1780), a distinguished scholar who established the Dissenting academy in Kibworth near Leicester, which was attended by Elizabeth's father, John Coltman.

Thomas Babington (1758-1837), politician and abolitionist, whose family owned Rothley Temple in Leicestershire and who was married to the sister of Zachary Macaulay. Like his friend William Wilberforce, he remained opposed to the involvement of women in the anti-slavery struggle.

Anna Letitia Barbauld (1743-1825), the daughter of John Aikin, Coltman's tutor and mentor at the Kibworth academy, who went on to become a successful poet.

Reverend Charles Berry (1783-1877), minister of the Unitarian congregation at Great Meeting in Leicester from 1803, and Elizabeth's loyal friend.

Mary Capper (1755-1845), an early member of Society of Friends in Birmingham, and one of Elizabeth's correspondents.

Thomas Clarkson (1760-1846), a major figure in the abolition movement and a relentless campaigner who was generally supportive of women's involvement. Elizabeth's mother once met him in Leicester and described him as the greatest man in the kingdom.

Mrs Elizabeth Coltman (née Cartwright) - (1737-1811) a published poet, wife of John Coltman (senior) and our Elizabeth's mother.

John Coltman (senior) (1727-1808) - Leicester hosier who lived in St Nicholas Street, the husband of Elizabeth (née Cartwright) and father of John (1768-1844), Elizabeth (1769-1831), Samuel (1772-1861) Rowland (1774-1789) and Mary Ann (1778-1871).

Elizabeth Coltman (1761-1838), a friend of our Elizabeth who lived in the Newarke in Leicester but was not a relative of the Coltman family in St Nicholas Street, despite having the same name.

Ottobah Cugoano (c1757-c1791) was a freed African slave, a little-known writer, and a member of the group called Sons of Africa.

Robert Dodsley (1704-1764), eminent publisher, bookseller and writer, cousin of Mrs Elizabeth Coltman (née Cartwright), whom he employed in London before her marriage to help him with reviewing and editing.

Charles Ellis (1771-1845) politician, planter and slave owner, born in Jamaica. He led the West India interest in the House of Commons, was elevated to a peerage in 1826, sought amelioration of slavery but was opposed to abolition.

Olaudah Equiano (1745-97) a black intellectual and former slave, a member of the group called the Sons of Africa, now considered Britain's first black political organisation. They gave first-hand accounts of enslavement and campaigned for abolition.

William Fox (birth and death dates unknown), radical bookseller, pamphleteer, anti-slavery campaigner and collaborator of Martha Gurney (1733-1816).

William Gardiner (1770-1853), English composer and writer who lived in Leicester and was friends with the Coltman family.

William Lloyd Garrison (1805-1879), a prominent American abolitionist who founded his own anti-slavery newspaper called *The Liberator.* He was a supporter of Elizabeth and praised her 1824 pamphlet *Immediate not Gradual Abolition*.

Priscilla Gurney (1757-1828), a Quaker minister, born at Norwich in Norfolk, who met Elizabeth in Hackney in London. Priscilla's young cousin was Elizabeth Gurney who (as Elizabeth Fry) later became known for her prison visiting.

Elizabeth Heyrick (née Coltman, 1769-1831) was a pamphleteer and radical abolitionist. This is our Elizabeth and she was the eldest daughter of Elizabeth and John Coltman of Leicester.

John Heyrick Junior (1762-1797), the son of Leicester's town clerk, descended from the lyric poet Robert Herrick. He married our Elizabeth in 1789 and died suddenly eight years later.

William Heyrick (c1765-c1855) was the brother of John Heyrick Junior and Elizabeth's brother-in-law. He succeeded his father John Heyrick Senior as town clerk in 1791.

Catherine Hutton (1756-1846) was a Birmingham novelist and letter writer. She was a relative and friend of the Coltman family of St Nicholas Street, Leicester.

Angelica Kauffman (1741-1807) a portrait painter who was admired by Elizabeth's father and whom he hoped she might emulate.

Mary Lloyd (née Farmer, d. c1821) was a Quaker friend of Elizabeth's who lived in Birmingham and was married to Charles Lloyd who was a partner in what would become Lloyd's Bank.

Mary Lloyd (née Honeychurch, 1795-1865). Another of Elizabeth's Quaker friends, who was the co-secretary of the first women's anti-slavery society in Britain. She was married to Samuel Lloyd and was related to the older Mary Lloyd (above).

Zachary Macaulay (1768-1838) was the brother-in-law of Thomas Babington who owned Rothley Temple in Leicestershire. After returning from Jamaica where he had become inured to slavery, Macaulay experienced a radical change of heart and became an abolitionist. He was a sympathetic adviser to Elizabeth.

Thomas Moody (1779-1849) taught at a conservative Anglican school in Barbados before becoming the government's leading expert on African labour. Back at the Colonial Office, he worked with Robert Wilmot-Horton and together they argued that slave emancipation was dangerous and impractical.

Lindley Murray (1745-1826) was an American by birth, a Quaker and prominent grammarian. Elizabeth met him on her visit to York in 1802 and later described him as a little intimidating.

Richard Phillips (1767-1840) was a bookseller and publisher in Leicester who was prosecuted in 1793 for selling Tom Paine's *Rights of Man.* The Coltman family supported him on his release from prison though according to Elizabeth's brother Samuel, they were not fond of the man.

Dr Joseph Priestley (1733-1804) was a major figure in the British Enlightenment and an advocate of Unitarianism. He visited Leicester in 1787 and he and Elizabeth's father were overheard discussing their religious views in the family parlour.

Mary Reid (1769-1839) was Elizabeth's Leicester friend, who accompanied her to the dance where Elizabeth met John Heyrick. She was also present at Elizabeth's marriage.

Granville Sharp (1735-1813) was a civil servant who became involved in the anti-slavery cause before Elizabeth was born. She was only a child when in 1772 Sharp successfully obtained a judgement that became known as the Somerset Ruling. He was instrumental in bringing to court the owners of the slave ship called the *Zong* and he was a founding member in 1787 of The Society for the Abolition of the Slave Trade. With Clarkson and Wilberforce, he helped sponsor the establishment of a colony for freed slaves at Sierra Leone, a project to which Elizabeth's father also contributed funds.

Lucy Townsend (1781-1847) was Elizabeth's friend. She and Mary Lloyd (née Honeychurch) became the first joint secretaries of the first ladies' anti-slavery society founded near Birmingham in 1825.

William Tuke (1732-1822) founded The Retreat in York, and here adopted a radical and compassionate approach to mental illness. Elizabeth held him in high regard and he became her close advisor.

Esther Tuke (1727-1794) was William's second wife, and at Trinity Lane she ran the only Protestant Nonconformist school for Quaker girls in York. Probably Elizabeth taught here for a time in 1802.

Susanna Watts (1768-1842) Elizabeth's close friend, was called 'Sister Sue' by the family. Her father had died when she was a baby and for many years, she cared for her mentally ill mother, earning a living with her writing. She wrote a guide book to Leicester that is now acknowledged to be one of the earliest competent guides to a major English town.

William Wilberforce (1759-1833) was a politician, philanthropist, slavery abolitionist, evangelist and leading voice in Parliament of the anti-slavery movement. He did not approve of women's anti-slavery activities and unlike Elizabeth, he argued for a gradual rather than an immediate end to slavery.

Robert Wilmot-Horton (1784-1841) was a politician who, like his close associate Thomas Moody at the Colonial Office, held pro-slavery views.

Reverend Hugh Worthington (1752-1813) was a Dissenting minister at Great Meeting in Leicester during the Coltman family's attendance there.

**'Look for me in the whirlwind or the storm,
look for me all around you, for, with God's grace,
I shall come and bring with me countless millions of black slaves
who have died in America and the West Indies and the millions in
Africa to aid you in the fight for Liberty, Freedom and Life.'**

**from *Philosophy and opinions of Marcus Garvey*
(first published in 1923 and 1925
by Universal Publishing House).**

Searching for Elizabeth Heyrick

Who was Elizabeth Heyrick? From the beginning, I was intrigued. Like most people, I had never heard of an anti-slavery campaigner named Elizabeth Heyrick and I came across her quite by chance. I was drawn to her forthright language, her passionate, direct style. She was born Elizabeth Coltman and it soon became clear to me that in the nineteenth century she played a significant role in the ending of the slave trade and slavery itself. Ahead of most of her contemporaries, she had demanded an *immediate* end to slavery, not the gradual end that the main anti-slavery society were contemplating at the time but a halt, then and there, to the cruel and inhuman practices involved.

She sounded like someone I would like to have known. Yet the more I delved into the historical records, the more frustrated I became. There is now a wealth of writing about the abolition of slavery and the experiences of enslaved people; the Black Lives Matter movement has recently brought the scandal into sharp focus. There are many names that we associate now with abolition (the best known are William Wilberforce, Thomas Clarkson, Granville Sharp), but the names of women are relatively few.[1] After several years spent wading through historical and contemporary sources, picking out Elizabeth's story wherever I could find it, there are still significant gaps. All lives present themselves with gaps of course but a particular frustration for Elizabeth's biographers is the lack of any portrait or full drawing of her.

If I couldn't look her in the eyes, how could I get to know her? I knew of only one surviving image of her and that is a black and white silhouette held by the Library of the Religious Society of Friends in London.[2] The Gibson family had donated their collection of manuscripts to the library in 1903; it runs to six volumes of Quaker memorabilia, and includes letters, newspaper articles, drawings, sketches, watercolours and architectural plans of landscapes and meeting houses, as well as silhouettes. The silhouette of Elizabeth Heyrick is an ink drawing and is not signed. In the seventeenth and eighteenth centuries, close friends and family often exchanged silhouettes to be kept as mementos and Elizabeth's has frequently been reproduced. Photography had yet to be invented and in the eighteenth and early nineteenth centuries, silhouettes were far less expensive to produce than portraits. They could be cut from black paper and pasted over a lithographed background or they could be painted on glass, paper, ivory and many other surfaces. They could be cut freehand from real life or from a shadow such as that projected by a camera obscura. They might then be embellished. Sometimes silhouettes made in these ways were called 'shadow pictures' or 'scissor art'.

Yet what if anything can a single silhouette tell us about the woman herself? I now began to hunt her down in earnest. Were there any surviving family members who might be able to help me? It is almost two hundred years since her death so this was certainly a long shot but with the advice and guidance of a genealogist, I eventually tracked down a descendant of the Coltman family who was living at that time in Southampton. Though he knew little about Elizabeth, he remembered being given some family records many years earlier and to my amazement, from his attic he retrieved some bound volumes, containing handwritten letters and family papers. Many of these now fragile documents had been carefully transcribed by Elizabeth's sister, Mary Ann Coltman, before her death, and left in the care of her great nephew Thomas Worthingon Clarke who had died in 1901.[3] I already knew of the memoirs completed by Elizabeth's younger brother Samuel[4] which are held in The Record Office for Leicestershire, Leicester and Rutland and much of the same material is there, as well as in the reminiscences of Catherine Hutton, a family friend and relative.[5] Both would prove invaluable sources. Yet nestling amongst these new papers were some I had not seen before, and some were clearly 'original' in every sense. Here, for the first time, I came across the mention of 'the family scandal'. And amongst Mary Ann's carefully transcribed letters were tucked some silhouettes, including one of Elizabeth.

At first, I assumed this silhouette was the same as the one held by the Society of Friends. It was certainly very similar. Yet closer examination revealed some subtle differences. The two profiles are undoubtedly of the same person, with their identical noses, lips and chins but the sitters' hair styles, postures and head shapes are not the same. Now I began to wonder which silhouette was the 'real' Elizabeth and which was a copy?[6] And why do we have two? We have no way of knowing for certain who made either of them but as I ran my fingers gently over the face of the 'new' silhouette, I could feel the edges of the cut-out, even the sitter's tiny eyelashes, and the added details in her bonnet and hair style. It is a very delicate artefact and it has been carefully preserved by the family and their descendants. Though we cannot look Elizabeth full in the face, and we cannot read her expression, these details do allow us to date the silhouette with a degree of confidence.

Silhouettes followed fashions, as the art historian Sue McKechnie explains, and the Apollo Knot (worn here by Elizabeth) was introduced in about 1824 to emphasise the bun or coil of hair on the back of a woman's head.[7] At the end of the decade, frills or chin stays were added and tied under the chin to form a white frill around the lower part of the face. These features indicate that the silhouette of her sister that Mary Ann had slipped into the family papers had been cut in the last decade of Elizabeth's life. By this time, she had become a Quaker and had adopted their core beliefs. From 1800, the cutting of silhouettes was a popular hobby amongst Quakers who preferred them to portraits since they did not attempt a detailed representation of a person's dress and bodily appearance. Personal portraiture was considered to be expressive of a person's vanity and an emphasis on the appearance and the physical body rather than the spirit or 'the light within' met with disapproval in Quaker circles.[8]

Here, we may have a possible explanation as to why there is no surviving portrait of Elizabeth. Certainly, the records contain various other amateur family portraits but after her conversion to Quakerism, Elizabeth is bound to have viewed the possession of such images with disfavour.[9] Accordingly a portrait if there was one is likely to have been destroyed, probably by Elizabeth herself or her sister. These silhouettes are now all we have and they are designed to conceal as much as they reveal. In my quest to 'find' my subject, I needed to look elsewhere.

Yet quickly I again ground to a halt, confused this time less by the absence of a portrait than by duplicated names. When Elizabeth was growing up, there were actually three Elizabeth Coltmans living in Leicester. One was my subject of course, the next was her mother, and the third was someone who was an unmarried friend and not related to them at all. She came from a different Coltman family who were by coincidence living in the next street known as the Newarke. Like my subject, this woman was a religious Nonconformist, a writer, and an advocate of slave emancipation. Unlike my subject, however, she never married. Plenty of scope for muddle then and it is only recently that the work of these two Elizabeth Coltmans has been successfully disentangled. Dr Timothy Whelan, an American academic with expertise in women's writing from the eighteenth century, must take the credit for some important clarifications.[10] His work has enabled me to distinguish anonymous pamphlets that were written by 'my' Elizabeth (later Elizabeth Heyrick) from those written by the other Elizabeth Coltman, and from that, to understand better their respective world views.

Delving into Elizabeth's family and childhood threw up still more names needing to be unscrambled. Another historian, David Wykes, this time based in Leicester, has published his research on the hosiery trade in which Elizabeth's father made his living. This 'John Coltman' had several namesakes and the researcher identifies no fewer than four who were active in the town at this time, all of whom were Nonconformists.[11]

And some names changed during the story. In 1789, my subject married John Heyrick and as 'Elizabeth Heyrick' she became easier to find. Catherine Hutton assures us that the Heyrick family can be traced back as far as Henry III when the name was spelt *Eyrick.*[12] Today there is still a 'Herrick Chapel' in what is now Leicester Cathedral. Notwithstanding variations in spelling, Elizabeth's husband claimed to be descended from the seventeenth-century lyric poet Robert Herrick (1591-1674) and had poetic aspirations himself. Elizabeth's family appeared to take these claims with a grain of salt. Social prestige was important but as Nonconformists, barred from university and from holding public office, the Coltmans were positioned in the middle ranks of Georgian society. Following Amanda Vickery in her book *The Gentleman's Daughter,*[13] I decided not to use the vocabulary of social class that is now so familiar to us (upper, middle and lower or working class) because the people in this story did not describe themselves in those ways. Polite, genteel, the families of manufacturers and merchants, doctors and clerics, they did not aspire to pomp and splendour, and did not own vast tracts of land. I investigated further and came soon to see that Elizabeth hated privilege and inequality of all kinds.

As I pursued my inquiries, a final frustration was to discover, courtesy of Catherine Hutton, that at her death Elizabeth had left behind a mass of unpublished material, including essays, sermons, prayers, and doubtless letters and diaries too[14] that I could not locate. In all likelihood, it now seems many of these documents had been destroyed by her sister. A handful of letters and diary entries survived the family's cull, however, and Elizabeth's brother Samuel obviously kept some for he copied selected extracts into his memoirs many years later. Some of her letters were kept by their recipients and made their way into other family archives. The work of a biographer of course involves piecing such items together from wherever they can be found, making a tapestry from the loose threads. Probably most biographers want more material than they can find, but in Elizabeth's case, the lack of first-hand sources seemed particularly marked.

Was my search for an understanding of the life of a little-known slavery abolitionist called Elizabeth Heyrick a viable project? Long after her death, she remains hidden in the shadows of the anti-slavery movement. Yet in her published pamphlets, about twenty in all,[15] we can hear her voice clearly. We cannot look her in the eyes, see her face or her expression but in her writing, her character and her beliefs emerge strongly; here she speaks in a remarkably clear and strident tone. Thanks to a fog of ambiguity, misattribution and anonymity, she has lagged behind others in the anti-slavery story - but her pamphlets reveal that she was a key player and one of its most radical participants. Perhaps it is fitting therefore, if disappointing, that the only image we now have of her is her silhouette. She would have wanted us to focus on her words and her uncompromising arguments, not her face, and though she has been hard to find, she has been worth searching for.

Backdrop

'They say he has rum and sugar enough belonging to him, to make all the water in the Thames into punch.'

The audience love it. On a winter's night in 1771, when the curtain comes down at London's Drury Lane Theatre, they respond with wild applause. They have just watched the first performance of *The West Indian*, written by Richard Cumberland (1732-1811), a comedy that would go on to be staged on numerous occasions over the next twenty-five years.[1] Audiences would flock to Drury Lane to see it and it would also meet with acclaim in cities across North America - New York, Philadelphia, Boston and Richmond - and in the West Indies, too.

When the play was first performed, it was just two years after the birth of Elizabeth Coltman (later Heyrick) in the Midlands town of Leicester. The play's central character is a young Mr Belcour and at the beginning of the story, he has just arrived in England on board a ship from Jamaica. He has recently inherited enormous wealth. The historian David Olusoga notes that in the 1760s and 1770s, thanks to the British slave trade and the plantation system, islands like Jamaica were among the most profitable territories in the world. The phrase 'as rich as a West Indian' had entered common usage and plantation owners returning to England were widely known for their ostentation and conspicuous consumption.[2] Belcour's reputation precedes him and the word is that he has 'rum and sugar enough belonging to him, to make all the water in the Thames into punch.'[3] The young man has grown up in the West Indies and soon admits that 'accustomed to a land of slaves' he has just behaved 'a little too roughly' with port officials in London. When a furious scuffle breaks out, he is obliged to make a hasty retreat. He observes: 'My happy stars have given me a good estate, and the conspiring winds have blown me hither to spend it.'[4] The scene is set for a cheerful, theatrical romp through a well-heeled world of family secrets and conspiracies, long lost relatives, amorous pursuits and fainting women, theft and deception, a threatened duel and enough humour and intrigue to make the play a favourite for years to come. The young Belcour's conduct is challenged but he comes readily to acknowledge his mistakes and his warm and generous nature endears him.

Although some contemporary critics noted a lack of originality, and some the play's inaccuracies, there was no doubting its popularity. In the opinion of *The Lady's Magazine* a month later, the play's faults were outweighed by its beauties and its general morality was 'just and striking'.[5] Richard Cumberland had tapped into contemporary values and his play raised no serious questions about Belcour's excessive wealth. How, for example, had the Belcour family acquired all that rum and sugar? The audience would have assumed that, like other British and European families in the West Indies at the time, the fictional Belcours had owned plantations - and most of the spectators would have been aware that in these large-scale agricultural operations, slaves were used systematically, to produce marketable crops like sugar.

Sugar production was labour intensive. The demand for it in Europe was escalating and although early plantations used a mix of labour (including some European settlers and local indigenous peoples) as the operations increased in size, the demand for imported slave labour grew exponentially. The plantation model was also used elsewhere in various ways to grow cotton, tobacco and rice, but in Jamaica, Belcour's homeland, sugar out stripped other crops and working conditions were especially harsh.

Sugar slaves had first to carry dripping, eighty-pound baskets of manure on their heads to fertilise the soil and then the canes had to be planted. During the intense harvest season, hour after hour in hot sun, they had to bend and slash the stalks with a heavy machete while clearing away cut canes with the other hand. Sugar canes are sharp and can tear, pierce and jab the flesh. Men did the skilled work, making sugar barrels, or repairing machinery so that it was largely women who were left to work in the fields. Slaves on sugar plantations lived shorter lives than slaves elsewhere and in mid eighteenth century British West Indies, half of all women sugar slaves never bore children.[6]

So the spread of the plantation system went hand in hand with the growth of the slave trade.[7] England's participation in what was called the Triangular Trade had begun in earnest in the sixteenth century[8] and by the time Cumberland's play was being performed in London, it was well-established. On the first leg of their journey, the traders took muskets, rum, tobacco and other goods to Africa to exchange for slaves. They then transported their captives to the West Indies and North America and sold them on at a profit, usually for use on plantations like the one owned by the Belcours. Winds and tides were favourable and for the last part of the journey, they brought cargos of rum and sugar back to England. The slave trade was making the country prosperous and all over Britain, families benefited. In the 1760s and 1770s, few voices were raised in protest.

Yet if Cumberland's play asked no questions about such a brutal system, and fashionable London theatre audiences were untroubled, it would nevertheless not be very long before such questions *were* being raised-in courts of law, Parliament and some churches. In 1772, a year after the play had opened at Drury Lane, a famous court case became a national sensation. Not all slaves were tucked safely out of sight, working on colonial plantations far away or shackled in the holds of ships. Some found their way to ports, towns and cities in England and some were afterwards able to tell their stories. Unlike the Belcours, most plantation owners lived in Britain and some brought their household slaves back with them from the Americas to perform domestic work. The captains of slave-trading ships were allowed to transport a few slaves in each cargo for their personal profit and any 'human left overs' might be auctioned.[9] There were also black sailors who were employed rather than enslaved and who might be discharged from their ships in ports like Liverpool or London. Yet the legal status of African slaves in England remained ambiguous. Were they to be regarded as property or people? In June 1772, news would have reached Elizabeth Coltman's family in Leicester of a court judgement that became known as the Somerset Ruling. Widely celebrated (and widely misunderstood), the ruling provided for the release of a slave named James Somerset, who had escaped his owner in England and been recaptured before he could be forced onto a ship bound for Jamaica.[10] With the assistance of the abolitionist Granville Sharp (1735-1813), the case eventually found its way to a public trial. Despite a common belief to the contrary, the resultant ruling strictly concerned the right of a slave owner to remove a slave forcibly from the country. It did not allow for the emancipation of all slaves in Britain, and in any event, many owners continued to re-capture and deport them.

Mr Earnshaw, in Emily Brontë's novel *Wuthering Heights*, appears to save the child Heathcliff from just such a fate. In the summer of 1771, having promised to bring his children gifts, Mr Earnshaw sets off to walk to Liverpool, a distance of 60 miles each way. Instead of the promised gifts, he returns with 'a dirty, ragged, black-haired child' bundled up in his arms. He tells a tale 'of seeing it starving, and houseless, and as good as dumb in the streets of Liverpool.'[11] Nobody knew who it belonged to, he said, and he was determined not to leave it as he found it. Brontë does not overtly refer to Heathcliff as a slave or as the child of one, but there are clues enough in the descriptions she does give.[12] At this time, the port of

Liverpool dominated the slave trade and Earnshaw's visit there takes place on the eve of the Somerset Ruling. More intriguingly, from school days spent at Cowan Bridge, where the daughters of clergy were educated, the Brontë sisters would have known about the local Sill family who owned Providence Estate in Jamaica[13] and had brought slaves back to work at their Yorkshire home.[14] Recent Brontë scholarship points out that William Wilberforce, the abolitionist, was a patron of the school at Cowan Bridge and had sponsored the Reverend Patrick Brontë, Emily's father, through Cambridge University.[15]

We can imagine that the injustices of slavery might have been much debated as the Brontë children were growing up. Yet Emily Brontë chooses to set the beginning of Heathcliff's story at a time when the anti-slavery movement had hardly begun to make itself heard. In the 1770s, there were just faint rumblings of discontent, mostly in small, religious Nonconformist groups.[16] The Church of England was complicit in the trade and turned two blind eyes to the African suffering involved. It had inherited plantations in Barbados from the colonial governor, Christopher Codrington, in 1710 and would eventually be richly compensated for the loss of the resident slaves. As the academic James Walvin observes, at this time there was no sense in which slave ownership was thought to conflict with religious principles or beliefs and Anglican clergy in the Caribbean were famously indifferent.[17] When a Christian voice was raised against the slave trade, it was led by the Quakers. One of the earliest protests was made by the French-born Quaker Anthony Benezet (1713-1784) in his pamphlet *A Caution and Warning to Great Britain and Her Colonies*.... that was first published in 1766.[18] In the piece he intends, he says, to make more widely known 'the aggravated iniquity attending the practice of the slave-trade'[19] which he believes is not consistent with Christian doctrine. He recounts some of the atrocities committed against enslaved Africans and ends with a quotation:

> 'How can you lift up your guilty eyes to Heaven? How can you pray for mercy to him that made you? Or hope for any favour from him that formed you, while you go about thus grossly and openly to dishonour him, in debasing and destroying the noblest workmanship of his hands in this lower world? He is the father of men; and do you think he will not resent such treatment of his off spring, whom he hath so loved, as to give his only begotten Son? (……) Think then, and tremble to think what will be your fate, who take your fellow servants by the throat, that owe you not a penny, and make them prisoners for life.'[20]

Such Christian outrage would find an echo several decades later in the writings of Elizabeth Heyrick by which time she would herself have become a Quaker. During the 1770s, however, as she was growing up in Leicester, she would have heard little about the abolition of slavery or about African slavery itself, which was now at its peak. Yet in 1769, the year she was born, ninety slave ships left Liverpool bound for the coast of Africa and by 1771, the year the fictional Heathcliff was adopted by the Earnshaw family, the number had risen to 105.[21] Slavery went on largely beneath the radar. Occasionally, an enslaved person rose to prominence, as happened in the summer of 1773, when Phillis Wheatley, who had been taken from the Gambia as a child and sold to a wealthy merchant in Boston, arrived in England. Aged about 19, she immediately published a volume of poems entitled *Poetry on Various Subjects.*

It was rare enough for someone who was both a slave and a woman to learn to read and write, let alone acquire the classical knowledge and sophisticated learning that underpin her work, and though little is known about how she acquired her learning, Wheatley had undoubtedly been fortunate. The support of the philanthropic Countess Selina Hastings was pivotal to the development of her career and in London, she met many notable people, including Granville Sharp who befriended her.[22] She seldom addresses the question of slavery overtly in her poetry but she does make claims for racial equality that would have been considered radical in her day.

In England, there were black Georgians everywhere, in all parts of the country, and though exact figures for the period are not available, their numbers were increasing.[23] People would have been aware of their presence, a few like Wheatley whose talents were celebrated and many who led quite different lives. Some were free and others unfree. Black servants of the eighteenth century are often regarded by historians as having been enslaved[24] but their treatment and living conditions varied and some black people made their way through the ranks of Georgian society with apparent ease. Edward Juba, for instance, was the son of a black servant who lived first with the Wentworth family in Kirkby Mallory in Leicestershire. He was baptised in 1734. He was apprenticed as a wool comber in Leicester and later moved with his family to Earl Shilton. Eventually he became Leicester's first black Freeman.[25] Black people were represented in paintings and portraits, most frequently as domestic servants, positioned at the margins. In his work, the English painter, William Hogarth (1697-1764), satirises fashionable society and black figures abound. Often they are serving tea which was of course drunk with sugar from plantations in the West Indies. In the painting from about 1742, *Taste in High Life*, the black child in his feathered turban is dressed in such long tails that he would certainly have been unable to walk. Like the ludicrously unwearable clothes of the central character, he is there for decoration, an object and a fashion accessory.

Eighteenth-century audiences were accustomed to seeing black people as they performed on stage and in fairgrounds, particularly in London and Bristol, and newspaper advertisements seeking the return of escaped African slaves or offering them for sale were commonplace. When a slave escaped from the Sill family estate near the Brontë home in Yorkshire in 1758, the following item appeared in a Liverpool newspaper:

> 'Run away from Dent in Yorkshire on Monday the 28 August last, Thomas Anson, a Negro man about 5'6" high, aged 20 years and upwards and broadest. Whoever will bring the said man back to Dent, or give any information that he may be had again, shall receive a handsome reward from Mr Edmund Sill of Dent or Mr David Kenyon, in Liverpool.'[26]

Though the wording of this advertisement, like many others of the time, indicates that the missing person was enslaved, sometimes boundaries were blurred and the word 'slave' was not often used.[27] Sometimes, however, it was used, as in this notice that appeared in Bristol in 1768:

> 'To be sold, a healthy Negro slave, named Prince, 17 years of age, 5 feet 10 inches high, and extremely well grown. Inquire of Joshua Springer, in St Stephen's Lane.'[28]

Effectively, African slavery had been introduced into Britain through the back door and, as the historian Kenneth Little observes, the presence of slaves on large estates in the home country sharpened criticism.[29] Yet a full challenge to the slave trade was some years away and to achieve it would take a massive shift in popular outlook as well as the combined efforts of many abolitionists, including the formidable Elizabeth Heyrick.

PART I

1760–1770

Chapter 1

'.....in hopeless disaccord'

It was winter, 1769. The county town of Leicester was cold, damp and dark. At night, though one or two streets were lit with oil lamps, most of the town lay in inky blackness and locals were obliged to take hand lanterns with them whenever they left their homes. It was the residents themselves who had clubbed together to pay for the new oil lamps and they were also called upon to clean the roadway outside their own homes. The unpaved surfaces could be treacherous even in daytime, and lack of sanitation resulted in foul puddles which had to be carefully skirted. Lying low in the valley of the River Soar, the town was prone to flooding and those who lived near the river inserted sliding boards in their doorways to try to keep the water at bay. Public authorities were not much in evidence either if you were unlucky enough to be burgled or violently attacked in an unlit street; typically, you would publish an advertisement offering a reward to a would-be informant.

The house where Elizabeth Coltman (later Heyrick) was born, on Monday, 4 December, was ancient. It had already been in existence for 700 years and in his memoirs, her younger brother Samuel recalls with pride its many historic associations. Sometime after his release from prison in the 1670s, John Bunyan (1628-1688), poet and peripatetic preacher, had addressed local Nonconformists there and about eighty years later, John Wesley (1703-1791), another Dissenter and a founder of Methodism, also preached in the house. Dressed all in black, with flowing white locks and an aquiline nose, Wesley had an earnest and intelligent countenance.[1] Though too young to have remembered the man or to have witnessed these encounters, as they grew up the Coltman children cannot have been unaware of them and Samuel, in particular, seems to have taken pleasure in recounting them. He would later recall overhearing his father deep in conversation in the family parlour with yet another religious leader, the theologian, Dr Joseph Priestley (1733-1804), who visited Leicester during 1787.[2] Priestley was a strong advocate of Unitarianism and would become a major figure of the British Enlightenment.[3] Unitarians believed in one God rather than a Trinity and at this time, they attracted a growing number of professionals, an 'articulate minority' who wanted to rid religion of all but 'liberal politics and middleclass morality'.[4]

The Coltman's house stood on St Nicholas Street, formerly known as Shambles Lane. In medieval times, all meat had to be sold in a public 'shambles', or butcher's slaughter house. Samuel again: 'I well remember the old Shambles.... a very long dark building which gave name to the street.'[5] He does not mention, though he might have done, hearing the animals being led to slaughter, the clip clop of their hooves on the cobbles or their gentle mooing.

Leicester was an agricultural centre and here, villagers from the surrounding countryside came to exchange their produce. They brought pigs, corn, sheep, cattle and cheeses. There were Saturday markets and regular pleasure fairs hosting sword swallowers, wrestlers and armless ladies as well as all manner of tricksters. The townsfolk sought diverse entertainments, and at this time of year particularly, singing and music were popular. Two days after Christmas, the choir of St Margaret's Church held their annual Singers' Feast at a local inn called the Three Cranes. About a hundred of the town's better-off citizens dined well and consumed vast quantities of ale. William Gardiner, who grew up with the Coltman children and was a fellow Nonconformist, wrote many years later of the numerous feasts enjoyed in the town every year. However, the chief amusement amongst the gentry was cockfighting. 'Even men of rank and fashion,' he wrote 'joined in this cruel sport, and, like our Saxon ancestors, hunted all day and drank all night.'[6]

Georgian women were largely absent from these gatherings. By the middle of the eighteenth century, amongst the more prosperous, mothering and domesticity were becoming fashionable.[7] Women like Mrs Coltman (1737-1811), our Elizabeth's mother, had begun to take an interest in nursing their babies and training their toddlers. In her study of the lives of genteel women in the Georgian era, Amanda Vickery observes that women typically bore six to seven live children but that regardless of their rank, the birth process was unpredictable and hazardous. In the absence of the efficient use of forceps, antiseptics, antibiotics or analgesics, the physical and emotional trauma could be acute and life threatening.[8] Mrs Coltman could not have escaped hearing about women who had died in labour and their infants, too, were at risk. Outbreaks of fever usually followed the floods in Leicester and contributed to the high rates of infant mortality for which the town was notorious.[9] At the time of Elizabeth's birth, the town's population was about 11,000 but residents had to wait nearly two more years for an infirmary which (like the oil lamps) was paid for by local subscriptions.

* * *

Elizabeth was Mrs Coltman's second child. John had been born a year earlier in 1768, then Samuel arrived in 1772, Rowland in 1774 and Anne (also known as Mary Ann or Nancy) in 1778. Elizabeth's mother left her eldest daughter to the care of others a short time after giving birth to her. She travelled first to her parents in Duffield in Derbyshire and then to Matlock Bath (already known for its warm spring waters). A letter written from there to her husband suggests the extent to which she drew on her personal resources as she made a determined return to full health:

> 'Yester-morn, while the beams of the day-break suffused a joy and serenity over the face of this delightful country, I set out alone for the well. The joyful prospect of returning health, with the pleasure which I thought it would give to a kind husband, and the advantage it might bring to my dear children, all conspired to raise in my mind the most pleasing ideas of grateful piety. I repeated aloud Milton's Morning and Thompson's Universal Hymns, with that emphasis which a feeling heart, unchecked by the fear of being overheard, naturally inspires.'[10]

Mrs Coltman's recitation of well-known religious texts in a time of difficulty reflects a Christian stoicism that was not uncommon amongst genteel women of her generation. Like many others, she believed God would determine her fortune. In submitting to childbirth, which she would have seen as her biological duty and her natural lot, she knew there were severe medical and cultural limits to her ability (or anyone else's) to affect the outcome. She had every reason to feel relieved now that her first daughter had been safely delivered and Matlock Bath was the ideal place to recuperate. Its mineral waters were believed to have healing properties and for Mrs Coltman, there were other happy associations, too, for it was here that she had first met her husband to be. In the next chapter, we back-track to follow the twists and turns of a particularly convoluted courtship but as they begin now to raise their family in late eighteenth-century Leicester, they draw on their own upbringings and beliefs and we learn more about the sort of people they were and what had brought them together.

Mr and Mrs Coltman were religious Nonconformists and in Leicester, they sought the company of some of the most liberal citizens in the town. They mixed with prominent and active people, many from the 'first families', educated and well-to-do but barred from holding public or professional office by dint of their religious views. The divide between the Nonconformists and the Anglicans in Leicester was social and political as well as religious. It was the key to local life; it was the single most important thing you needed to know about your fellow citizen. Families aligned themselves either with the Tory-led town Corporation (and their hatred of Nonconformity) or with the opposition which, as Elizabeth was growing up, was chiefly composed of successful Nonconformist industrialists, like her father. Thus, from her earliest years, she became accustomed to religious and political debate, to hearing views that were at odds with the prevailing orthodoxy.

Elizabeth's family worshipped regularly at Great Meeting which was a Presbyterian chapel in East Bond Street and the centre of nonconformity in Leicester. The building, erected in 1708, was one of the first in the town to be constructed of bricks[11] rather than wood and plaster, following the discovery of some good clay on the southern outskirts of the borough. It was a short walk from the Coltman's family home in St Nicholas Street. Turning their backs on the Anglican St Nicholas Church just opposite, the family walked along the High Street before turning left towards the chapel. The Reverend Hugh Worthington preached here in a hard, dry voice and held his congregation's attention with a bold tone, a pointed finger and a piercing eye. It was stirring stuff. By the time Elizabeth was born, Worthington had been at the Great Meeting for more than twenty years and the Coltman children would have become accustomed to his idiosyncratic delivery, his focus on moral rather than theological matters, and what one critic referred to as 'the entire nothingness' of what he had to say.[12]

Then, in the late 1790s, the chapel came under the influence of Dr Priestley and like many other Presbyterian congregations, they became Unitarians. It seems likely that Elizabeth's father, John Coltman (1727-1808), supported or perhaps even encouraged this change and at the time, protestant Nonconformists were tolerant towards a range of diverse religious opinions. There was scant regard for denominational boundaries and the 'rational Dissenters' (as they called themselves) formed a continuum. A family friend would remember many years later that John Coltman 'from his inner most soul abhorred an empty, noisy profession of religion'[13] and by the early nineteenth century, some of the family could be found worshipping at the Baptist chapel in Harvey Lane where they listened to the sermons of the eloquent Reverend Robert Hall (1764-1831) a man who would eventually become known as the greatest pulpit orator of his time.[14]

In Dissenting from the established church, in rejecting its doctrines and practices, Nonconformists set their faces against much that their fellow citizens took for granted. As a result of their beliefs, they were deprived of rights and excluded from universities, the military and public office. Dissenters were obliged to form their own educational institutions and in 1743, at the age of 16, Elizabeth's father had been sent to a Dissenting academy at Kibworth, an agricultural village near Leicester, where he studied with a distinguished scholar, the Reverend John Aikin (1713-1780). The Aikin family were Presbyterians and the village had by this time become established as a lively centre of dissidence.[15] According to his son, John Coltman's school uniform had consisted of a grey wig, purple velvet cap with gold tassel, and a plaid tunic or loose gown fastened with a leather belt. The whole, says Samuel, created 'a picturesque if not classical air'.[16] The curricula in the Dissenting academies included subjects far beyond the range of the universities and they became centres of liberal education.[17] Aikin influenced John Coltman profoundly, and here, the young man developed a taste for classical learning and a keen interest in antiquities that would never leave him.[18]

* * *

Just a few months before the young Coltman had arrived at Kibworth, Aikin's wife Jane had given birth to a daughter. By the age of 2, Anna Letitia had been taught to read by her mother. Later, she spent long hours in her father's library and persuaded him to teach her Latin and Greek. She eventually married the Reverend Rochemont Barbauld and, as Mrs Barbauld, she went on to achieve popular and critical success as a poet. She opposed slavery, became a pioneering writer of children's books, and enraged both Wordsworth and Coleridge with her anti-war stance.[19]

Perhaps Coltman followed the career of his mentor's daughter with interest but his own was destined to take a quite different turn. Even by his account, John Coltman was ill-suited for the world of business but since he was barred from entering university, this is where he found himself on leaving the academy three years later. He became a traveller for a wealthy uncle, Rowland Page, owner of a London distillery, and his travels took him around the country. In about 1757, he found himself in Matlock where, at the house of some mutual friends, he met the beautiful Elizabeth Cartwright.

Matlock lies north of the village of Duffield in Derbyshire where Elizabeth Cartwright was born in 1737. Today you can travel from Duffield to Matlock by train in under half an hour but in the eighteenth century, in a horse-drawn coach over uneven and unmade roads, it was likely to take three or four hours. Duffield was a small, agricultural village on the banks of the River Derwent and Cartwright had been brought up in modest circumstances. Her father was a yeoman farmer[20] and her mother, a 'Miss Grace', his former housekeeper.[21] She was their only child. In his memoirs, Samuel Coltman later recalled that his mother's mind 'was of that elevated sort that the mere drudgery of life could not suffice for its scope'. At a time when literary pursuits were little thought of for women, Samuel says, 'she cultivated a taste for reading, and fortunately for herself she wanted not friends capable of leading her to the study of the best authors.'[22]

In the spring of 1763, she visited her cousin Robert Dodsley (1704-1764), who was a bookseller, publisher and writer in London. Dodsley enjoyed considerable eminence in literary circles and was able to introduce Cartwright to some of his associates, including the literary scholar Joseph Spence (1699-1768) and the writer, William Shenstone (1714-1763) who was a friend of Alexander Pope. Cartwright helped her cousin with his reviewing and editing work and Dodsley's correspondence suggests that he came to admire her. A few years later, Spence bequeathed all his prints to Cartwright, some of which had been collected in Italy and were believed to be very valuable.[23]

Cartwright herself was a talented artist and before her marriage, a published poet too. Catherine Hutton believed Cartwright was 'qualified to shine either in a literary circle or an exhibition of painters'.[24] In a love song thought to have been written by Cartwright, the poet begs her imagined lover to avoid 'hyperboles', to address her openly and honestly, and 'to pay homage to my mind'. Such sentiments suggest that Elizabeth's mother had a radical and independent spirit. Most of her contemporaries expected little beyond marriage and domesticity but Cartwright continued to write. She also made landscapes, with a pair of scissors and writing paper, cutting the paper with such skill that the resultant images looked 'more like lace than paper'. Hutton claimed[25] that Dodsley thought one of her landscapes so extraordinary he arranged for it to be presented to Her Majesty.[26] When she met John Coltman, Cartwright knew she had found a soul mate, a kindred spirit who shared her literary and cultural interests, as their courtship letters would reveal. As young adults, both had intense and somewhat rarefied lives, pursuing intellectual and artistic passions in London and Kibworth respectively but marriage, especially for Cartwright, would eventually curtail these activities and domestic life brought compromises for them both.

Chapter 2

'I will not be trifled with'

When Elizabeth Cartwright met John Coltman in Matlock, she was staying with the Unwins, a wealthy and prominent family of hosiers from Nottinghamshire. In her home village, as an attractive twenty-year old, Cartwright was known as the 'Lily of Duffield' and Coltman (from Leicester) was ten years her senior. He was also part of the Unwin circle and sometime after their first meeting, he and Elizabeth Cartwright embarked on a lengthy and tortuous courtship. The eloquent letters that resulted tell a compelling tale and have been preserved almost in their entirety.[1] The extracts below suggest the nature of some contemporary marriage customs, as well as offering insight into the characters, lives and beliefs of both Elizabeth's parents.

The first letter from John Coltman, dated 1763, was written to accompany a gift. The enclosed book was Samuel Johnson's '*The Prince of Abissinia: A Tale*', published just a few years before.[2] A moral fable about happiness, it provoked a detailed and scholarly response from Elizabeth Cartwright. Largely self-educated, with advice from her learned London friends, Cartwright was very well-read indeed, and more than capable of marshalling an argument. Though she does not, she says, approve of correspondence between young people of different sexes, nevertheless three pages follow. Drawing on the poems of Alexander Pope, and finding Johnson's work altogether too dark and gloomy, she embarks on an optimistic defence of human nature which she is determined to view 'in its most amiable light'.[3] She will, she says, think people good till she finds them bad and happiness attainable till she finds herself miserable.

Over the next few years, her views are sorely tested and she does indeed find herself miserable on more than one occasion. It is a story that might have come from the pages of a romantic novel, littered as it is with twists and turns, misunderstandings, procrastination and perceived slights, rumoured betrayal and mixed messages. Letters were slow, but letters were all they had. In the 1760s, the post was taken from place to place by post-boys on horseback. Riders might be ambushed by highway robbers or delayed by the poor roads and a reliable mail coach would not be introduced for another twenty years. Most of the courtship letters we still have were written while John Coltman was living in London and Elizabeth Cartwright in Duffield, Derbyshire. They were dictated by their son Samuel to his wife when he was in his eighties. When he died in 1857, his journal came into the possession of his younger sister Mary Ann. She transcribed her brother's memoirs, including the letters, and left these records in the family's private possession.

After leaving the academy in Kibworth, it appears Coltman had returned briefly to Leicester but his father's second marriage, to a woman who brought several children of her own from previous marriages, led him to seek an escape from an uncomfortably crowded family home. Arrangements were made for him to live with an uncle in London. The uncle, Mr Page, ran a distillery business and so as well as shelter, he was able to offer employment to his young relative. The work involved travel to locations outside London and on these business trips, he and Cartwright were occasionally able to meet. We do not have a complete record of all their meetings but in March 1763, when they have known each other for about six years, a letter from John Coltman to Elizabeth Cartwright indicates that a few days before he has apparently made some kind of 'declaration'. This was nothing less, he says, than 'the genuine effusion of a sincere heart, overflowing with a tender affection'. He hopes she will pardon his 'freedom'.[4]

What exactly had taken place? And what was Elizabeth Cartwright's reaction to this apology? In her memoir, Catherine Hutton observes that Cartwright did not reply either in the affirmative or the negative. Yet Samuel believes that his father now thought himself rejected, or nearly so. Whatever the exact circumstances, the next four months passed in silence, and Hutton recalls how much the young Miss Cartwright suffered. She became despondent and withdrawn. She was, Samuel says, eventually persuaded to try a change of scene and went to stay with her friend, a Mrs Fieldhouse, at Halesowen near Birmingham.

It becomes difficult to track the chronology of their developing relationship in precise detail but in Samuel's account of his parents' courtship, at this point he includes a letter that Mrs Fieldhouse wrote to John Coltman. It is undated and unsigned. Clearly, she has decided to play Cupid:

> 'If those tears which my friend fancied she saw in your eyes at Sutton were real tears, and those professions of sincere affection and esteem which preceded them not quite forgotten, and you have no new attachment to a fairer female, I think

> I may venture from the knowledge I have of her sentiments to bid you not despair if you think her worth the trouble. A little delicate flattery, a little more of your pocket-book poetry, and a few letters or visits and if aright I deem, the victory is yours.'[5]

Elizabeth Cartwright has apparently told her friend the whole story. She has acknowledged that in refusing a man who loved her, she has caused him offence. But Mrs Fieldhouse's letter is a masterpiece of cajolery and persuasion. She accuses Coltman of acting like a whining schoolboy. 'Did you think to gain a wife like a plaything by crying for it?'[6] Coltman is the kind of man Elizabeth Cartwright desires since she is, her friend explains, 'a little prudish'. She does not want a husband who is heir to some 'dirty acres'. Mrs Fieldhouse ends her letter by urging Coltman to make his feelings plain immediately. 'She refused you but it by no means follows that she always will.'[7]

Coltman's next letter to Cartwright is dated 27 August 1763, and when it comes, it is by no means a grovelling capitulation. He asks her to consider how far her own conduct may have justified his silence. He had thought his attentions were becoming unwelcome, and feels now he had perhaps been too ready to believe what he wished was true. Perhaps this was his mistake 'for being ambitious to deserve your esteem, I once fondly thought myself honoured with a share of it.'[8]

Presumably emboldened by his anonymous informant, though he makes no mention of this, he ventures to suggest carefully they might renew their correspondence - and he ends his letter with a description of his recent travels. The reply comes promptly. Elizabeth assures her suitor she is in perfect health, and that his letter has calmed her mind. Then she asks: 'For how should I have borne the shocking news with which you partly threatened me the last time I saw you? News which would doubtless have frozen me to a statue…'[9]

What 'news' is she referring to? Is it possible that when they last met, Coltman had mentioned his uncle's wish that his nephew should marry someone else? For Mr Page had by now become fond of John Coltman and had begun to cherish the hope that as well as becoming his heir and succeeding him in business,[10] Coltman would marry his partner's relative, a young German woman by the name of Deborah Klockenbrink who also shared the London home. Such 'news' would indeed have been unwelcome to the young Elizabeth Cartwright. Yet much of the remaining content of her letter is playful and teasing, even flirtatious, and she concludes: 'I wish you a good journey and all possible pleasures, I mean as much as you can possibly enjoy in my absence…'[11]

Now, surely, John Coltman can begin to believe that his feelings are reciprocated. Yet still he does not reply and so late in September, Elizabeth writes to him again. Perhaps her last letter has not reached him? What else could explain his silence? A few days later, the reply comes. Her first letter had arrived just as he was setting out again on his travels and he had no time to write; he has been away from London for nearly a month. On his return he was 'alternately transported and alarmed'[12] to see a second letter had been delivered. This he did not dare open, he says, until he could find a 'shady retreat' for solitude and silence and be unobserved in case the news should prove unwelcome. He is more explicit now about his feelings: 'How often when travelling have I longed for your company and how little have I tasted without you of those pleasures felt by a contemplative mind from a survey of the beauties of the Creation.'[13]

His letters provide a fascinating portrait of a young Georgian man in love, nervous about how to conduct himself, fearful of being misunderstood and yet for some reason so tardy in his responses that he risks losing everything. About six months later, in February 1764, he is again apologising for a long gap in their correspondence. This time he has been very ill and not able to write or read. His physician advised him, he says, to avoid expressing his thoughts on any subject and to go away for a time, as soon as he was able. He again professes his admiration for her: 'I love you more for the freedom of your writing, and admire everything you say…'[14] Yet despite his protestations to the contrary, Cartwright has by now begun to suspect that his attachment to her has cooled and in a letter which crosses on the road with his, she expresses her hurt and anger. Has she been wrong to trust him? Has his attention been diverted elsewhere? '…when I am no longer <u>loved</u>, I would not be <u>pitied</u> and be assured I write not to alter your sentiments but only to be informed of them, if three months silence had not told me them already…'[15] And then: '(….) my better judgement disapproves and yet still I write, write to the man who has not thought proper to answer my last….' She quotes Shakespeare: 'Frailty thy name is woman'.[16] When his letter to her finally arrives, however, and she hears of his illness, she writes to him again, and her mood has lightened. She is sitting up alone at night to watch an eclipse of the moon, and her writing is again stylish, poetic and full of literary allusions. It sounds as if Coltman plans a visit to Derbyshire to see her but there is no confirmation in the records of what transpired on that occasion and at about this time, the couple's letters dry up. The courtship appears doomed.

* * *

Samuel writes in his memoirs of his mother's suffering at this time. Towards the end of 1764, she began to accept 'the mournful fact that she was either forgotten or that some rival had been allowed to usurp the heart she had so delighted to think her own.'[17] Elizabeth Cartwright was an only child. In the eighteenth century, parents expected to have a say over their children's futures[18] and hers were becoming restive. They were not pleased to think their daughter might live in London so far from their Derbyshire home and, even by contemporary standards, this courtship was dragging on too long. The wider society required obedience to superiors and seniors and Elizabeth Cartwright was increasingly obliged to heed their advice. Her father has told her it would be like 'burying his only child'[19] to have her settle so far away and she believes it is her duty to avoid doing anything that would distress her parents and 'cloud the evening of their days'.[20] Her continuing correspondence with Coltman can, she believes, 'answer no good end'; indeed, it has continued too long already. Coltman at first appears to misapprehend the situation, and still hopes that she will not abandon him. Cartwright becomes angry. 'I must take the liberty to tell you I will not be trifled with any longer and that this is the last letter which to you I ever mean to write'.[21]

The principled stand that Cartwright takes in her letters along with her hurt pride and anger will find echoes later in another better-known Georgian romance, between the young Elizabeth Bennet and her Darcy in Jane Austen's *Pride and Prejudice*. After Darcy has described her relatives as decidedly beneath his own, Bennet makes a speech which, like Cartwright's letter, is designed to put an emphatic end to his marriage hopes:

> 'From the very beginning - from the first moment, I may almost say - of my acquaintance with you, your manners, impressing me with the fullest belief of your arrogance, your conceit, and your selfish disdain of the feelings of others, were such as to form that groundwork of disapprobation on which succeeding events have built so immovable a dislike; and I had not known you a month before I felt that you were the last man in the world whom I could ever be prevailed upon to marry.'[22]

The courtship of Coltman and Cartwright, like that of the fictional Bennet and Darcy, will take some further twists before its resolution and there is now a gap of some seven weeks in their correspondence. Finally, Coltman again replies and desperately seeks to assure his lover of his great regard for her. She is 'the unrivalled mistress' of his heart, he says.[23] The letter contains some oblique references to his present situation (he is sure she would judge him less severely if she was more acquainted with it) and a postscript suggests he can write to her only in secret.

What is Coltman's 'present situation'? Why the secrecy and why has he not explained himself more fully? Early in 1765, he writes to a mutual friend in Chesterfield, one Mrs White, and her reply must have caused him anguish. Having met them both, she believes he and Miss Cartwright are entirely well suited and 'cut out for each other' but she now advises him that Cartwright is about to marry someone else, one Reverend Mr Sadler, a 'very sensible sober man', of 'very good character'.[24]

Samuel's memoir suggests that this had in fact all been decided a few months earlier, by the winter of 1764. The Reverend Mr Sadler had been waiting patiently in the wings and had earned Cartwright's gratitude and esteem through his efforts to soothe her broken spirits. A beautiful house was taken in the nearby village of Makeney and furnished in readiness for the couple. When he receives Mrs White's letter, Coltman is devastated. A few days' later, he writes again to Miss Cartwright. The news he has received, he says, has 'penetrated my very soul with grief and anxiety':

> 'Whatever appearances may have led you to think, my sentiments of you are not at all changed. As I profess a sacred regard for truth and sincerity, I own I love you incomparably beyond any other person. Nor will I ever give up my pretensions to you while I breathe if you can yet honour me with your esteem and reciprocal affection.'[25]

Yet it is too little and too late. Coltman has hesitated once too often. Samuel remembers his father's indecisiveness and recalls how different he was in that respect from his mother. Yet like Cartwright, Coltman is constrained by social circumstances beyond his control. His uncle in London took him in when he needed refuge and gave him employment. The older man treats him like a son. Coltman owes his uncle a huge debt of gratitude and feels unable to betray his trust, or to reject firmly the proposals being made by his uncle on his behalf. Respectable society expected familial obligations to be honoured and even in his mid-thirties, Coltman is not a completely free agent. Economic prudence strongly regulated decisions about marriage[26] and Coltman would not have felt able to jeopardise his own or his lover's financial security. Professional men often married late and there can be no doubting the strength of his attachment to Cartwright, but she has had enough.

In subsequent letters, Cartwright's tone has changed and on 13 February 1765, she lists her misgivings. She could not ever have proposed 'any scheme for separate happiness if I had not concluded as I thought from the most mature deliberation that it would be the most romantic madness ever to hope that felicity could attend our union.'[27] She has suffered, too, but she understands that Coltman's uncle is entirely opposed to their courtship. She knows that he intends his nephew should marry his partner's relative and also that he wishes to receive Coltman into a business partnership. Clearly, she is determined and proud and she cannot, she says, stand in the way of such good fortune. She will not be told by any man 'that he has refused better offers on my account'.[28] Further, she is aware that the uncle has several times put obstacles in the way of their meeting.

And as if all that were not enough, she recounts also a bizarre and unsettling episode involving a stranger in Chesterfield. On a visit to the town, Cartwright had received an anonymous summons to meet an unknown person at a local tavern. She does not go but she does eventually discover the source of the summons, and the stranger admits he has been sent by Coltman to plead his case with her. She is deeply insulted and very angry. Despite all, in the same letter she nevertheless assures Coltman of her lasting friendship and esteem which she says is all she has now the power to grant. She urges Coltman to keep his dignity:

> 'I cannot permit you to see me til you can do so without emotion - but I hope better things of you than that you should act the peevish infant and because you are deprived of a rattle throw away the substantial blessings always in your power.'[29]

She concludes by telling him that he does not know half the anguish his letter has given her and she bids him 'farewell forever'.

* * *

A few weeks later, Coltman begs yet one more visit before his 'fondest hopes of happiness' are destroyed. On 22 March 1765, he writes to her from Leicester. Certainly, says Samuel, his father had a tendency to procrastinate but he could also be tenacious and he asks now if despite everything, she could yet believe in their love for one another. 'Fly then to my arms thou delight of my soul and let me taste a joy beyond what is called happiness.'[30] All the objections she has raised in her last letter are now entirely removed. Presumably speaking about Miss Klockenbrink, the young woman his uncle wants him to marry, he writes: 'And that which you might perhaps look upon as the most difficult to overcome I declare it upon my honour never had a moment's residence in my heart. How should it when you occupied the whole?'[31] As for the 'friend' who contacted her in Chesterfield: 'I never sent him on such a fool's errand,' says Coltman.

The next letter we have was written only three days later and clearly the couple have again met, presumably in Duffield. Cartwright is distraught. Did Mr Coltman not notice how upset she was upon seeing him? Why after such a correspondence was he so cold and reserved? 'Was it possible for me to imagine that the person who had so often talked of seeing me, and had always found some excuse to delay it, who could hardly find time to write in four or five months, and then in so great a hurry that all his time was lost that was bestowed on the correspondence, who was either ashamed of or at least had not the courage to own such correspondence; I say was it possible for me to imagine that it was of any great consequence to this person how I disposed of myself?'[32] Some responsibility lies with her, she admits, for 'so hastily suffering a pique of female pride' and thus silencing his excuses. She would never have heeded his rival if Coltman had behaved differently:

> '…but it is now too late; honour, conscience, duty, gratitude, reputation, every sacred tie forbids my listening to you, and though I never more taste happiness (which I fear I shall not) yet he shall have my hand if he live to demand it.'[33]

For Fate has intervened and in fact, Coltman's rival is now very ill. On his way to see Cartwright one evening, he was caught in a storm. He sat in his wet clothes for a time and contracted a cold. As she writes, he is being attended by a physician and an apothecary. The mention of these two medical men would immediately have signalled to any eighteenth-century reader the seriousness of poor Mr Sadler's condition.[34] Physicians were expensive and knew very little by modern standards; apothecaries dispensed drugs, many of them dangerous. They were usually called only in the most desperate cases. Cartwright feels she cannot add to Sadler's sorrows by breaking the engagement with him, cannot bear to cause pain to such a kind and generous person and would not be able to suffer the reproaches of her 'justly offended parents'.[35] Coltman is not to answer her letter for six months so that when he writes, he can do so with more composure. She hopes they will remain friends:

'If ever I should again see London, I will call to see you if you will give me leave, and we will wander together through Westminster Abbey. And whenever you go into France, I hope you will favour me with an account of your travels.'[36]

A short time later, despite all efforts to save him, the Reverend Mr Sadler dies. On his death bed, he offers to marry Miss Cartwright so that as his widow she can inherit his estate. Principled as ever, she refuses.

* * *

And so to the last letters which their son, Samuel, has so painstakingly transcribed. We do not know how or when exactly Mr Coltman learned of his rival's death but a few months later, in a long letter written on 3 July 1765 from her parents' home in Duffield, Elizabeth Cartwright begins to signal her acceptance of her long-term lover. Now she permits him to hope.

Yet still she calls the shots. Though the courtship has now been going on for an extraordinary eight or nine years, they have had few opportunities for intimacy. Has he really thought about sharing her life in all its domestic detail? 'Pray good sir, did you ever consider this angelic creature as subject to ill health, ill humour, passion and prejudice?'[37] Will he still love and esteem her after he has discovered all her imperfections? And in spite of small pox and wrinkles? Further, she asks, how will they manage to keep their conversation alive for twenty or thirty years? 'Nay, I think it is presuming very much on one's own constancy to propose that two people shall continue so long together in the same mind when everything around them is in perpetual change: a powerful argument this against fetters.'[38]

It is a surprisingly modern one, too. Cartwright is prepared to put romantic feelings aside and be guided by practicalities. Yet her personal pride remains paramount and now she asks Coltman if his uncle has finally accepted her. There can be no marriage otherwise. Coltman also needs to understand that her fortune is small and that her father's consent is required. Her suitor must let reason not passion determine his actions and she will wait anxiously to hear. In the meantime, some subterfuge is required since others (presumably her parents) remain opposed to their union and will open her letters if she is absent. She is going to stay with her dear friend Mrs Fieldhouse, her 'preceptor, guide and guardian spirit' (and, unknown to her, Mr Coltman's anonymous informant of two years before). She may stay several months, she says, and Coltman may write to her there. We do not have Coltman's reply to this letter but Samuel assures us that soon afterwards, his future father was received by Mrs Fieldhouse 'and I need not say mutual oblivion of past unpleasant misapprehension took place.'[39]

The couple were eventually married in 1766 and their epic correspondence finally came to an end. The courtship had been a marathon, excessively drawn out even by polite standards of the time. Complete with interfering strangers and uncles, it had all the ingredients of a good romantic plot and in later years, as Catherine Hutton sought to build a literary career for herself,[40] she recalled her friends' courtship and recognised its dramatic potential. She published her third novel *Oakwood Hall* in 1812, originally in abbreviated form[41] and by this time, both John Coltman and his wife were dead. Hutton's novel was published in full in 1819[42] and Samuel believed that his mother was the inspiration for the heroine and his father for the hero. Though Hutton had taken some liberties, said Samuel, there was much truth in the story she told and in the portrayal of its key characters. As in her other two novels, Hutton used the epistolary style, and through letters written by one character to another, the academic Cheryl Wilson claims Hutton was able to 'create a space for women's voices'.[43] In her courtship letters, Cartwright's voice is strong and uncompromising. She will soon become a critical and demanding mother and her eldest daughter will not flinch either from the fierce expression in letters and pamphlets of her own beliefs and opinions.

Chapter 3

'…the prettiest and the ugliest of the litter should both be preserved'

There is a story from Elizabeth's childhood that surfaces again and again. It concerns kittens. Here's her brother Samuel:

> 'I well remember when a litter of kittens was condemned to the usual fate of such supernumeraries, all but one, the prettiest; when we were disputing which was the prettiest, my sister Bessy [a family nickname] insisted upon the ugliest being preserved. She felt for it, because it had no one to take its part and so earnest and so determined was she to save the poor little fright, that to put a stop to her crying it was agreed that the prettiest and the ugliest of the litter should both be preserved.'[1]

It is easy to see the appeal of this story and why her family and friends remembered it in the way they did as they looked back at her childhood. Another anecdote also recurs, in a similar vein, and this time as it is reported by Catherine Hutton:

> 'When a very little girl, she [Elizabeth] had two pence given her to buy gingerbread, and on her way, she met a beggar who asked her alms. Touched with pity she gave him half her treasure, but quickly relenting, she exclaimed aloud: 'Stomach! Thou shan't be gratified' and turning back, she instantly placed all she possessed in his hand.'[2]

This recollection, like the first, is forwarded as evidence of her 'self-denying temper' and her kind disposition, her sympathy for the oppressed and the down trodden. Knowing what we now know about how she chose to live her adult life, these childhood stories are irresistible. Yet they do not explain all her actions and decisions.

***

There was little formal schooling for girls like Elizabeth in the late eighteenth century. All education had to be paid for, none was compulsory and for the vast majority, there was no provision at all. The gentry could afford to pay for private schools and tutors, such as could be found, and the Coltman children were taught at different times in a variety of settings, some local and some further afield. Samuel remembers that in 1774, when he was about two years old, he was sent with his brother John (whom he calls Jack) and sister Bessie (Elizabeth) to a nearby dame school. Elizabeth was then about five years old and at home, her mother had just given birth to Rowland, a third son and a delicate child. Dame schools (the forerunners of nursery or infant schools) were small private enterprises run by women frequently in their own homes. Here, to variable standards, young children were taught the alphabet, some reading from the Bible and household chores.

William Gardiner, the son of a Leicester hosier who was John Coltman's business partner, recalls the local dame school he attended in the early 1770s. In a house in the High Street, soon to be converted into a fish shop, Mrs Loseby ruled the roost. She was 'a little sharp old woman, so crooked and lame that she could not move from her chair' and she was, says Gardiner, the horror of his waking and sleeping thoughts. 'How often have I dreamed that she hobbled after me, frightful figure as she was, and when upon the point of being caught, I have started from my sleep, miraculously escaping from her grasp.'[3]

Gardiner spent five years at this dame school. The other pupils were mainly girls though he did have one young male companion, the son of a town doctor. Later, after escaping Mrs Loseby, Gardiner had various tutors, including one Arthur Kershaw whose language classes he shared with Elizabeth's brothers, John and Samuel. Historians Zena Crook and Brian Simon comment that William Gardiner's education was 'not so much regularly acquired as picked up'[4] and the Coltman family's experiences were similarly diverse. John Coltman was ten and Samuel only six when, in 1778, they were both sent to the Nathaniel Newton Foundation School at Hartshill, near Atherstone, about 20 miles from Leicester. This was a large boarding school run by Quakers and it had been set up in 1742 with funds bequeathed by Newton initially to provide free education for just twenty-six children.[5] By the time Samuel and John arrived, however, it had expanded well beyond its early remit, and the Coltman brothers joined a large number of fee-paying boarders, most but not all of whom were Quakers. Samuel's recollection is that by the 1780s, there were ninety children at the school, and some would have been termly boarders like him and his brother, whilst others were daily or weekly boarders. He remembers learning orderly habits, punctuality and neatness, if little else. In a letter home to his parents, in large and careful copper-plate writing, he recounts his walks in nearby Hayes Wood to collect hazelnuts.[6] It is only in old age when he comes to write his journal that, intriguingly, he calls up a memory of being encouraged to fight by none other than the Master's wife. Odd behaviour for a Quaker, as Samuel suggests, yet it was her firm belief that fighting would strengthen the boys and do them good.[7] Indeed, life in the vast majority of eighteenth-century boarding schools was tough.[8] Physical abuse was the chief means of keeping discipline. Beatings were commonplace, and often inflicted by older pupils as well as teachers.

Six was young for a boy to be away from home and Samuel must have been glad of his older brother's company. Two years later, however, John is sent to a boarding school in London, and Samuel finds himself alone at Hartshill. As luck would have it, however, he then suffers an accident at home when a coffee pot falls on him and its scalding contents burn his leg so severely that he is not able to return to the school for six months. His sister Bessie [our Elizabeth], then aged about 11, is sent to Hartshill in his place. At the time, it was not unknown for brothers and sisters to attend the school together[9] though they were taught separately and in Samuel's account, Elizabeth was also to be a companion out of school hours for the Master's own daughters. She may even have resided with the family, as pupils sometimes did. Generally, girls were much more likely to be educated at home than sent to boarding school but wherever they were taught, the provision was invariably both decorative and superficial. We have no further records of Elizabeth's time at Hartshill. When she returned to Quakerism in adult life, it may have been, as Aucott suggests, this first and early experience that drew her back[10] but by then events in her life had taken a difficult turn. Catherine Hutton remarks, not altogether approvingly, that the Quaker's 'mode of worship' chimed with Elizabeth's much changed disposition in adulthood. In particular, Hutton believed the Quaker's focus on self-sacrifice was attractive to Elizabeth as she later struggled to make sense of the things that had happened to her.[11]

Meanwhile her older brother, John, after leaving Hartshill, found himself in a very different setting. The private boarding school in London that he was sent to was run by a Mr Smithers, and was highly reputable but in 1780, the journey to reach it from Leicester was challenging. The boy was entrusted to the care of a local market gardener and in an old horse drawn carriage, the pair made the journey together, leaving on Monday and arriving on Wednesday. In London, John lodged with Mr Page, his father's uncle. This was the same man his father had stayed with before his marriage some fifteen years earlier, the one who had consistently opposed the relationship with Elizabeth Cartwright and who had wished to see him marry his partner's relative instead. Presumably, if any hard feelings lingered, all parties now prioritised the boy's education and when Page died not long afterwards, John was sent to another London address to live with family friends.

London life was changing his outlook. He now wrote long letters to his younger brother, describing his sight-seeing trips and the fine things he had seen. He was four years Samuel's senior and, as any older brother might, he showed a degree of condescension. He even offered Samuel sixpence out of his pocket money to call him "Sir". Samuel recalls his brother's return from London in some detail. 'He came home a complete cockney beau,' writes Samuel, 'wearing a bright grass green coat with engraved mother of pearl buttons, a white waistcoat, black satin breeches, and blued silk stockings, a cocked hat and large shoe buckles.'[12] Though it may have seemed flamboyant to his young brother, John's dress was in line with the dictates of contemporary fashion. From the mid eighteenth century, gentlemen were increasingly likely to wear different colours and materials for each item of apparel, rather than a full suit of the same fabric. From the 1780s, buckles were gradually being replaced by shoe laces and though there were plenty of daring experiments in male costume, as Olsen notes, the overall trend was towards less ornamentation and greater simplicity.[13]

In fact, John Coltman was similar in nature to his reclusive father and his colourful appearance belied a serious disposition. He was thoughtful and grave; he was generous, held liberal views and was at one time deeply religious. He was fond of study and intellectual pursuits and had a strong interest in art. According to his younger brother, though he had fine features, John was lank and ungainly, absent- minded and in everybody's way. He was not a favourite either of his father's or grandfather's but he and Elizabeth were close. 'They were peculiarly and confidentially attached to each other,' wrote Samuel later in life, perhaps a little resentfully. Samuel, for his part, spent more time with his younger sister, Mary Ann, and Rowland, the fifth child and favourite of them all, died of consumption at the age of 15. Rowland was a talented if sickly boy, with a thirst for knowledge and an inventive mind. He learned to engrave on copper and he constructed a solar microscope, a camera obscura and a magic lantern. He was his father's favourite child and like him, he collected coins and antiquities, as well as fossils and plants. He studied Latin and Greek and bound his own books. All the Coltman children had a taste for drawing and Elizabeth had considerable artistic ability such that her father had at one time considered sending her to London 'to put her under the tuition of one of the best masters, and make an

Angelica Kauffman of her.'[14] Although nothing came of the plan, Elizabeth continued to draw and paint and there are several amateur family portraits still in existence, like the one of John, which may well have been completed by her. A poignant watercolour of the young Rowland can be definitely attributed to his sister because notes on the back tell us she completed it without tuition and whilst she herself was still a child.

Even more remarkable than her drawings was her needlework and Hutton describes a small oval medallion made by Elizabeth at the age of 15. It was only an inch and a half high and an inch wide. On it, using Hutton's hair, Elizabeth had embroidered the tiny figure of 'Maria' sitting on a bank under a tree, with her dog at her feet. Maria was a character in the novel by Laurence Sterne (1713-1768) '*A Sentimental Journey through France and Italy*' which was first published in 1768. Probably, Elizabeth had worked from a painting of Maria by the talented Angelica Kauffman, the artist her father so much admired.

* * *

If a young John Coltman sometimes gave himself airs, so too did his sister Elizabeth. The ever-watchful Mrs Coltman sought to check the 'early symptoms of pride' in her eldest daughter. Samuel remembers their holidays:

> '.....she made my sister Bessy as I remember, travel in a covered wagon or kilt as they then called such vehicles, to Freestone[15] for sea-bathing, under the charge of a distant relation - to the utter dismay of the young lady, who has sometimes imbibed notions of fashion and style that my mother greatly disapproved.'[16]

Mrs Coltman had a tendency towards puritanism that was not wholeheartedly shared by her husband[17] and for her, as for many of her contemporaries, modesty was a key female virtue. The way you dressed and spoke, the way you looked and danced were all important social (and sexual) indicators. A modest woman was a marriageable one and a virgin; she was pure in body and mind. Samuel Richardson's epistolary novel *Pamela* (published several decades earlier in 1740 and subtitled *Virtue Rewarded*) became a byword for virtuous modesty in Georgian times. As Mrs Coltman was growing up in the Derbyshire village of Duffield, the novel was creating a sensation. There were those who applauded it, even from the pulpit, and those who were its detractors. The young Elizabeth Cartwright cannot have escaped hearing about it since it was widely read and inspired numerous parodies.

Pamela Andrews, the book's heroine, is a servant girl. As the story opens, her mistress has just died and her master, Mr B., has begun making unwanted advances. She repeatedly rejects him and in letters home to her parents, she recounts these events in detail. When Mr B gives her the fine clothes that had once belonged to her late mistress, her parents become concerned and caution her:

> 'Be sure, don't let people's telling you you are pretty, puff you up: for you did not make yourself, and so can have no Praise due to you for it. It is Virtue and Goodness only that make the true Beauty. Remember that, Pamela.'[18]

Pamela will eventually be rewarded for her virtue and for heeding her parents' counsel. Despite numerous obstacles and obvious class tensions, she eventually comes to accept Mr B's proposal of an equitable marriage.

Mrs Coltman's letters to her eldest daughter a few decades later read to us now as if they, too, might have come straight from the pages of an eighteenth-century novel. Her parental admonitions and her attempts to constrain Elizabeth's conduct are very much of their time. And parents could not be ignored. All the Coltman children benefited from the assortment of private schools and tutors that were found for them but the parents also played an important part in their upbringing. Georgian mothers, in particular, took their role as educators seriously[19] and Mrs Coltman would have thought it her duty to criticise her daughter. When the girl was aged about 17, and staying with family friends in Duffield, her mother wrote, urging her to use her time virtuously:

> 'Nature, my dear girl, has been no niggard to thee; only thy garden is too much like the field of the slothful - two or three tall weeds (which only require a little vigorous exertion to pluck them up) choke the good seeds of virtue. Books of the sentimental cast or novels as they are called, I fear tend to encourage these weeds, namely Pride and Indolence; therefore, the precious hours of youth should be better employed.'

And, she concludes, 'you must also spell better.' She seeks to reassure her daughter that even when she is scolding her, she is her 'most affectionate mother.'[20]

Ironically, Mrs Coltman would in all likelihood have disapproved of Richardson's novel even as she expresses views that are barely distinguishable from those of Pamela's parents. Books of 'a sentimental cast' encouraged a focus on personality and the self at the expense of reason and restraint. The traditional outlook held that society only functioned properly if everyone kept their God-appointed place; fiction was controversial because it raised young women's expectations of marriage, encouraged pre-marital sex and wasted their time.[21] The 1760s and 1770s represented the heyday of sentimental writing[22] and even twenty years later in 1793, the *Evangelical Magazine* was taking issue with it in no uncertain terms:

> 'Novels generally speaking are instruments of abomination and ruin. A fond attachment to them is an irrefragable evidence of a mind contaminated, and totally unfitted for the serious pursuits of study, or the delightful exercises and enjoyments of religion.'[23]

Not all religious people scorned novels, however, and a few, like Laurence Sterne, even wrote them. As well as *A Sentimental Journey,* Sterne wrote *The Life and Opinions of Tristram Shandy, Gentleman* which remains his best-known work. Sterne was a highly eccentric Church of England clergyman and some readers struggled to square his penchant for sexual innuendo with his clerical career. The historian, Roy Porter, describes Sterne's fantasy novel as solipsistic and sentimental[24] but much less well-known are Sterne's published sermons. Here he is, under the pseudonym of Mr Yorick, writing earnestly on the impacts of slavery:

> 'Consider slavery-what it is, how bitter a draught, and how many millions have been made to drink of it - which if it can poison all earthly happiness when exercised barely upon our bodies, what must it be, when it comprehends both the slavery of the body and mind?'[25]

Sterne died the year before Elizabeth was born. His was one of the earliest voices to be raised in England against slavery and his correspondence with the African, Ignatius Sancho, begun in 1766, would become an important weapon in the abolitionists' fight. Sancho, a self-educated butler who had been born on board a slave ship in about 1729, wrote to Sterne asking him to use his talents to help publicise the plight of enslaved Africans. Sterne replied:

> 'There is a strange coincidence, Sancho, in the little events (as well as in the great ones) of this world: for I had been writing a tender tale of the sorrows of a friendless poor negro-girl, and my eyes had scarce done smarting with it, when your letter of recommendation in behalf of so many of her brethren and sisters came to me. But why her brethren? - or yours, Sancho! Any more than mine? It is by the finest tints and most insensible gradations that nature descends from the fairest face at St James to the sootiest complexion in Africa: at which tint of these is it that the ties of blood are to cease? And how many shades must we descend lower still in the scale, 'ere mercy is to vanish with them? But tis no uncommon thing, my good Sancho, for one half of the world to use the other half of it like brutes, and then endeavour to make 'em so.'[26]

Sterne promised he would not forget Sancho's letter but he died just two years later. Sancho continued to associate with prominent figures in London's cultural world and his life came to be celebrated by eighteenth century opponents of slavery as proof of the humanity of Africans and their inherent equality.[27] It was a view Elizabeth would come to share as she grew to adulthood.

PART II

1780–1790

Chapter 4

'No Presbyterians, no machines'

The attack lasted an hour. One of the factory workers raised the alarm soon after the family were in bed and Elizabeth's mother had just managed to collect some clothes from the back rooms when she heard a dreadful noise. Afterwards, she wrote to a friend that had she known two months earlier what was about to happen, it would have killed her with apprehension.[1] Now, on this cold December night in 1787, it sounded to her as if the whole house was coming down.

The trouble had begun elsewhere at the house of Mr Whetstone, who was Mr Coltman's business partner. It was eleven o'clock when a 'mob of drunken and infuriated people, some furnished with torches and others with missiles' gathered and 'amid hideous yellings and uproar' began to hurl large stones at Mr Whetstone's house, breaking all the windows.[2] Chillingly, Mr Whetstone and his companions retaliated by opening fire from an upstairs window, and several of their assailants were wounded. Others then took shelter under the house gables where they could not be fired upon and Mr Whetstone feared he might injure innocent bystanders if he continued to shoot. The historian, James Thompson, describes what happened next:

> 'The mob then obtained possession of the lower story, and destroyed all the furniture it contained. They attempted to ascend to the upper story but failed. Fearing though that they might succeed, Mr Whetstone was let down by a rope from a back window by one of his sons; and escaped, through the window of a summer house in his garden, to the ground behind his premises. After obtaining a horse from a friend, he left the town in the middle of the night.'[3]

The riot continued unabated. When the Mayor, Robert Dickenson, arrived with his town servants, he tapped some of the men on the back saying, 'Come on, my lads give over - you've done enough - quite enough.'[4] But the workers were not in a mood to be placated and began hustling him.

Violence was endemic in Georgian England and could erupt suddenly. There was no local police force and little formal structure for resolving workers' disputes.[5] Excluded from Westminster, and without other ways of making their case, crowds often took the law into their own hands. As the situation at the Whetstones' house worsened, the Mayor proceeded to read The Riot Act.[6] If those assembled numbered more than twelve and refused to disperse after the proclamation, they could be forced to do so, and even killed. On this occasion, however, it was the Mayor himself who came under attack. As he was ordering the rioters to leave, he received such a serious injury on the head from a stone that a few months later he died.

Meanwhile, the mob had moved on to the Coltman house. John Coltman ventured outside to try to reason with the men but they would hear nothing and he soon found himself in danger. A neighbour came to help and somehow lifted a half-dressed Mrs Coltman, her teenage daughter, Elizabeth, and son, Rowland, to safety over the high wall at the end of the garden. Later, Mrs Coltman recalled the turmoil: 'And yet I know not how it is, I have been surprisingly supported thro' it, and I know not that I have been in better health for years, and so have we all.'[7]

Mrs Coltman is personally resilient, as we have already seen, and in all likelihood, her words here refer to her strong religious faith. Her correspondent is one Miss Gifford, the daughter of a vicar and a lifelong family friend, and it would be entirely in keeping with Mrs Coltman's devout outlook, as well as contemporary belief, to ascribe her own and her family's survival to a higher authority.

Certainly, the family had been lucky. As the rampage continued, the window shutters and door were broken and almost every pane of glass in the house was shattered. Then the rioters returned to Mr Whetstone's place and plundered it, taking away everything they could carry. The unrest continued for another ten days to loud shouts of 'No Presbyterians, no machines'[8] - but the Coltmans had by now moved their belongings to safety and they spent the next fortnight out of town.

* * *

What had led to this unhappy state of affairs? What had the mild mannered and thoughtful John Coltman done to warrant such a violent attack? To find out, we need to turn the clock back to the earlier part of the eighteenth century when Leicester's hosiery trade was expanding. Joseph Coltman, John's father, came from a prosperous background. Though he had begun his working life as a baker's apprentice, by 1725 he was being described as a 'woolcomber', and as the worsted hosiery trade flourished in the town, he appears to have become a successful businessman.[9]

Worsted is a fine smooth yarn spun from long staple wool. As a woolcomber, Joseph Coltman would have learnt how to make all the fibres lie in the same direction, whilst removing the shorter ones to leave a loose sliver of long fibres ready for spinning. After spinning, the resultant thread could be knitted into items of hosiery and other garments, and knitting was mechanised. The first knitting frame was in use in Leicester in about 1670 and it could knit much faster than a single hand knitter. From the age of 12, children could be put to work on a frame but despite many modifications, it remained a demanding machine to use. Since it was complicated and expensive to make, many workers did not own their frames but rented them from their employers who made weekly deductions from their earnings.

By 1780, John Coltman's hosiery firm was well-established. He had purchased his father's house in St Nicholas Street in 1766, the year he and Elizabeth Cartwright married. He probably used his wife's jointure for this, and additional funds are likely to have been obtained through connections and introductions from fellow members of the Presbyterian Great Meeting.[10] Knitters like those employed by Coltman were struggling to better their working conditions since despite their best efforts they were not able to provide basic necessities for themselves and their families. Out of their meagre wages, as well as the frame rent, they were required to pay expenses to keep the machines in working order. Their masters owned everything and employed middle men to supply the yarn and collect the finished work. Knitters were at the mercy of a system which was open to abuse.[11]

In addition, framework knitting was arduous work. To operate the knitting frames efficiently, factory employees needed strong arms and legs as well as good coordination. Typically, nine operations were required to knit one row and a skilled worker (usually male) seated on a hard wooden bench (with a made-to-measure hole for his posterior) might complete two rows every second. As he flew along, using the natural light that fell from the high windows above him, his machine produced a deafening clatter. Six or eight frames might be housed together under one roof, in a workshop or factory, and apart from the physical impact of working long hours in such conditions, the framework knitters were also at the mercy of economic forces.

The key problem was that not enough yarn was available for them to use. Unlike knitting, spinning was not yet mechanised and the only source of yarn remained the domestic hand spinner. Preparing wool for spinning took some considerable time and as the worsted hosiery trade grew, and

Leicester found itself at the centre of it, there were considerable incentives for manufacturers to shorten their production processes. When the 1780s brought a revival in trade, following the end of the American Revolution, John Coltman and Joseph Whetstone decided to act. In 1787, together with Joseph Brookhouse (1758-1831) who was also a member of the Presbyterian Great Meeting in Leicester, they proposed the introduction of a new, labour-saving machine. Coltman already had experience of using technology in the manufacture of textiles. He was the first in Leicester to use James Hargreaves' spinning jenny and Richard Arkwright's machine for spinning cotton by rollers.[12] The new machine was based on Arkwright's principles but was for spinning worsted yarn and its introduction was intended to reduce shortages of the thread. As word spread, however, domestic hand spinners began to fear for their jobs.

The earnings of eighteenth-century cottagers were already under pressure from the established practice of 'enclosure' (in which fences or hedges were put around open land). Such initiatives usually came from large land owners and although enclosed fields were generally more productive and the stock healthier, those who had previously scratched a living from common land by, for example, grazing a pig or keeping a few hens, or those who had supplemented their farm wages in those ways were now badly hit.[13] The second half of the eighteenth century saw a dramatic increase in enclosure with large numbers of people being forced to leave rural areas to find work in towns and cities and many villages were left in a state of rural collapse. The Leicestershire village of Wigston Magna for example, which was a few miles from the Coltman family home, had been enclosed some twenty years earlier and the villagers were now reduced to rural labouring - or to framework knitting.[14] Many became factory workers as the Industrial Revolution gathered pace, and soon there were more framework knitters than could easily find work. By 1791, the borough of Leicester contained over seventy hosiery manufacturers, about 6000 people were employed in different branches of the industry[15] and some 3000 knitting frames were in use.[16]

Coltman and his associates would have known that the mechanisation of knitting, although more advanced than that of spinning, had not proceeded without controversy. Previously, in 1773, riots had broken out in Leicester over a new knitting frame that was rumoured to do the work of sixty people and produce a dozen stockings at once.[17] These and other extravagant claims, combined with harvest failure, an over-supply of workers and rising food prices, had led to popular unrest and violence. When Coltman and his colleagues proposed a new machine for spinning, it must have re-awakened familiar fears. The domestic hand spinners were themselves often the wives and families of the framework knitters and despite Coltman's efforts to allay his workers' concerns, the uprising of 1787 can have come as no real surprise.

* * *

Strikes against technical innovations and attacks on the machines themselves were commonplace in Georgian times. Jobs were in short supply and living standards were poor. John Coltman reportedly met with some of the hand spinners a few days before the 1787 riots and he also placed an advertisement in a local newspaper explaining his reasons and offering to limit the number of machines in use.[18] All appeals failed, however, and following the riot, the partners were obliged by the town corporation to sign an undertaking not to carry out any worsted spinning by machinery within 50 miles of Leicester. The industry continued to prosper in several other East Midlands towns but in Leicester, mechanisation was halted for more than twenty years when Brookhouse and his invention were driven out of the county.

The historian, Roy Porter, writes that rioters saw themselves as 'avenging angels'[19] who were usually intent on achieving specific and limited change. Riots were also often vehicles for the expression of religious hatred, particularly towards Dissenters, as the workers' cries in Leicester make clear. The town corporation was largely made up of High Anglicans and Tories whilst the middle-class opposition was mostly composed of Dissenting manufacturers. Since Nonconformists like John Coltman were prevented from entering universities and from holding civic office, they were obliged to make their living in other ways and in Leicester, they comprised some of the town's most successful manufacturers and tradesmen. This deep religious division between the Anglicans and Dissenting groups in Leicester was growing during the 1780s so that what began as a workers' protest against the impact of technical innovation escalated quickly into an attack on Nonconformists in general. A marked reluctance on the part of the authorities to intervene was interpreted by some (including members of the Coltman family) as evidence of official support for the rioters and an underlying sympathy for their cause.[20]

* * *

Another man might have persevered against such odds and tried again to introduce the worsted spinning machines, especially once they had started to appear in factories in some neighbouring towns. Yet John Coltman was not a natural entrepreneur and his heart was not in it. He had put his family at risk on that December night and in any case, he was now legally prevented from proceeding with his plans. He would face other hurdles in his professional life and his education had done little to fit him for business.

A classical education, such as the one he had received at Kibworth, was intended to prepare the sons of gentlemen for a life in the professions, including the ministry. It was not intended for those seeking to enter the commercial world. Most Leicester manufacturers would in preference have sent their sons to the grammar school or to one of the local commercial academies and then, like William Gardiner, the son of Coltman's business associate, into an apprenticeship or other training.[21] Instead, stimulated and encouraged by Aikin at Kibworth, John Coltman had developed scholarly and bookish interests that set him apart from his peers. His fellow townsfolk saw him as eccentric and unworldly, 'destitute of the knowledge of common life'[22] and it is easy to imagine that such a man might have struggled to communicate with his workforce. Still, those who knew him better found inspiration in his company and valued his conversation. 'What charmed me the most', says William Gardiner 'was his happy mode of talking (…) Everything he said was illustrated by the most apt similes, drawn from common life; and with the more learned he would adorn his conversation by citations from classical authors.'[23]

* * *

In 1791, just four years after the Leicester riot, Thomas Paine (1737-1809), philosopher and political activist, published *'Rights of Man'*. In this analysis of contemporary European discontent, which began as a defence of the French Revolution, he claimed that whatever the apparent causes of riots, the real one was always a want of happiness. Governments were at fault for dividing society instead of consolidating it, allowing a great mass of people to be thrown into poverty and discontent. Well ahead of his time, he proposed an interventionist programme of welfare redistribution to include old age pensions, marriage allowances and maternity benefits. The book created a sensation. It was widely read by reformers, including Protestant Nonconformists, before it was banned and Paine himself indicted and imprisoned for seditious libel.

John Coltman, in common with many of his fellow Presbyterians at the Great Meeting, held radical political views and when the local bookseller, Richard Phillips (1767-1840), was imprisoned in 1793 for selling Paine's book,[24] Coltman supported him. The young and ambitious Richard Phillips had arrived in Leicester in 1788. Initially, he invested what little money he had in a small commercial academy but by 1790, he was running a bookshop and stationery business in the town and two years later, he founded the *Leicester Herald.* Other enterprises included a 'Pamphlet Room' and a music and pianoforte department. Since the town lacked a Literary Society, he founded one in 1790, doubtless mindful, the historian Temple Patterson suggests, of the benefits this might bring to a bookseller. The gathering attracted respectable and cultured liberals from the town, and probably included John Coltman.[25] Phillips also instigated the Adelphi Society which met for co-operative study but was, according to William Gardiner, closed down by the town's authorities soon after the French Revolution began in 1789 since its meetings had a 'dangerous tendency' to discuss politics.[26] Despite this, however, Coltman continued to organise meetings and when an itinerant lecturer named John Waltire came to Leicester at about this time, Coltman invited him to his house in St Nicholas Street. Here an audience for Waltire's talk on mechanics included Mrs Coltman and her friend Mrs Reid.[27]

In these ways, the late eighteenth century saw the emergence of many debating and political societies like these in Leicester. They were relatively independent from the political order and from the private interests of members. Here, in what some commentators now call the 'civil society'[28], individuals came together, formed networks and engaged in debate on a range of social and scientific topics. Opinions were freely expressed and Phillips' radical and republican views would have chimed with those held by John Coltman. Yet in matters of literature and science, Phillips' opinions were regarded as absurd, even ridiculous. Further, he had an irascible temper. 'He was never a favourite of ours', remarks Samuel in his memoir,[29] but Samuel's father was willing to set personal feelings aside to help a fellow radical. The family provided Phillips with some financial support and offered him asylum upon his release from prison. In the nineteenth century came the development of 'advocacy approaches'[30], which also brought people together and included public campaigns for social reform, mass meetings and the formation of committed interest groups, like the Birmingham Ladies Society for the Relief of Negro Slaves in which Elizabeth would eventually become prominent.[31]

* * *

In his article about Elizabeth's father, the Leicester historian David Wykes argues that although innovative, the hosier lacked the ambition and drive usually associated with tradesmen and manufacturers of that period.[32] He was a shy and reclusive person and had little time for the town's 'more fashionable circles'.[33] His wife called him 'my philosopher' and he himself wrote to a close friend (just before the riot in 1787) that he was weary even of life itself:

> 'Life seems to have been thrown away upon me - I have very little satisfaction in the retrospect. How others can think themselves well employed in amassing wealth or plumming themselves with gaudy appearances I know not, but these are things which never enchanted my mind and which I now can look on almost with total indifference.'[34]

He read avidly and was known for his scholarship. He held a large and valuable collection of Roman coins, all found locally, and drew on his classical studies to catalogue and date the coins according to their Latin inscriptions and the names of the different emperors. He could more frequently be found in his study than his warehouse 'raised above this world by a contemplation of the works of Nature and of Providence, or by a Perusal of the Writings of the Poets and Orators of Greece and Rome.'[35]

By his own admission, he neglected his business interests and he took his eye off the ball most notably after his colleague Brookhouse had fled the riot in Leicester to settle in Bromsgrove, a town to the south west of Birmingham. Here, Coltman provided funds for the conversion of an existing cotton mill to spin worsted with the intention of supplying the Leicester hosiers who were still reliant on local hand spinners. He installed John Adams, a step nephew, to manage the enterprise and in spite of the distance from its main market, it was a success. In 1795, it was said to have earned Coltman £3000[36] but a year later, Coltman discovered Adams had defrauded him. In the absence of a formal partnership agreement, his young relative refused to acknowledge Coltman's interest and the older man was left with heavy debts. At this point, his wife stepped in and by selling her father's estate, of which she was the sole inheritor, was able to raise £2000.[37] In one account of the betrayal, Coltman acknowledges his shortcomings. In response to admiring comments about his coin collection, he exclaims: 'Take any! I can't bear to look at them. I collected them when I ought to have been watching a knave!'[38]

Then, several decades after she had been lifted over the family's back garden wall, to escape rampaging workers, John Coltman's eldest daughter took up her pen. Did she remember that night? Elizabeth was only 18 at the time but in her late forties, after her own life has taken many painful twists and turns, she begins to write about the lives of the people who attacked her family in 1787. Between 1817 and 1825, she would go on to produce four anonymous texts[39] about industry and labour and in each one she took the workers' part.

Chapter 5

'Never daring even to think of it'

During the 1780s, as the Leicester hosiery workers struggled for improvements in their living conditions and fought to protect meagre incomes, voices were being raised elsewhere on behalf of other oppressed groups, both domestically and abroad. News was filtering through to families like the Coltmans of events that they found hard to stomach and which eventually, in all conscience, they could not ignore.

Catherine Hutton, the Coltman family friend and relative, was like many of her peers, an assiduous reader and diligent correspondent. In 1783, the war of independence that created the United States of America was over and she had just finished reading extracts from a book that had been published a year earlier. She wrote to Mrs Coltman that although she admired much of the material in *Letters from an American Farmer*[1] she was so shocked by one particular episode that afterwards she could never dare even to think of it.[2] The book's fictional narrator had, he says, accepted an invitation to dine at the residence of a planter who lived 3 miles away:

> 'I was leisurely travelling along, attentively examining some peculiar plants which I had collected, when all at once I felt the air strongly agitated; though the day was perfectly calm and sultry. I immediately cast my eyes toward the cleared ground, from which I was but a small distance, in order to see whether it was not occasioned by a sudden shower; when at that instance a sound resembling a deep rough voice, uttered, as I thought, a few inarticulate monosyllables. Alarmed and surprised, I precipitately looked all around, when I perceived at about six rods distance something resembling a cage, suspended to the limbs of a tree; all the branches of which appeared covered with large birds of prey, fluttering about, and anxiously endeavouring to perch on the cage. Actuated by an involuntary motion of my hands, more than by any design of my mind, I fired at them; they all flew to a short distance, with a most hideous noise: when horrid to think and painful

> to repeat, I perceived a Negro suspended in the cage, and left there to expire!'[3]

The narrator goes on to describe, in appalling detail, the injuries that the birds have already inflicted on the unfortunate slave. Incredibly, he is still alive, if only just, and the narrator, finding he has no bullets to put him out of his misery, instead seeks to help the man by encouraging him to sip a little water. Since the *Letters* are now thought to be partly fact and partly fiction, we do not know if the narrator actually found a man in a cage in the situation he describes but upon its publication in Europe, the book had an immediate impact. Hutton omits the most chilling details of the episode in her letter to Mrs Coltman but she conveys her own horror clearly enough. Elizabeth was still a young girl, aged about 13, and it would be several decades before she became publicly involved in anti-slavery campaigns but Hutton's letter to Elizabeth's mother effectively underlines the family's sensibilities.

* * *

It was easier of course, to think of slavery as happening in foreign places. Occasionally, through the 1770s and 80s, stories like those from the *Letters* surfaced but it was news from closer to home that eventually prompted an intensification of the anti-slavery campaign. In 1783, word began to spread of an event that had occurred two years earlier on board the *Zong,* a slave ship registered in Liverpool. During the ship's transatlantic crossing, the captain had ordered his crew to throw 133 slaves overboard. The ship was dangerously over-crowded and sickness had broken out. Navigational errors had taken it off course and Captain Luke Collingwood now made a cold calculation. If the slaves were alive when they were thrown overboard, he reasoned, the ship's owners would be able to recover the loss from their insurers because live slaves were in effect 'cargo'. If, however, the slaves died a 'natural' death on board the ship, the owners themselves would be liable. Unfortunately for Collingwood, the insurers refused to pay and so the claim went to court where the horrifying details of the massacre were disclosed.[4]

The action brought against the underwriters by the ship's owners was intended to recover the value of the lost slaves (about £30 each, or nearly £3,500 in terms of today's purchasing power[5]). In legal terms, it was an insurance dispute, and initially it attracted little attention. It was the black intellectual and former slave Olaudah Equiano (1745-97) who first alerted the establishment after seeing a short, unsigned letter in a London newspaper on 18 March. The writer of the letter had been present at the trial and could barely believe what he heard:

> 'That there should be bad men to do bad things in all large communities must be expected; but a community makes the crime general, and provokes divine wrath, when it suffers any member to commit flagrant acts of villainy with impunity.'[6]

He imagines that those brave, unbound slaves who had voluntarily jumped overboard after their countrymen, to be drowned with them, had decided they would rather share death with their compatriots than life 'with such unheard of English barbarians.'

On reading the newspaper item, Equiano went at once to Granville Sharp, the writer and campaigner who had helped bring the Somerset case to court a decade before. Sharp now attended the *Zong* trial and ensured that all proceedings were recorded and transcriptions published. The Chief Justice, Lord Mansfield (1705-1793) who had presided over the Somerset case, led the court again and found against the ship owners. No one was ever prosecuted for the murders but the case was by now attracting huge publicity and as the dark details emerged, millions were shocked. Sick and disruptive slaves were routinely killed on ships but reports of events on board the *Zong* appalled many and even the conservative Mansfield himself admitted privately that the case 'shocks one very much'.[7]

* * *

If the Somerset case had prompted outrage in 1772 and caused some in the country to think about slaves and former slaves who might be in their midst, then news of the *Zong* massacre threw the spotlight on the transatlantic trade itself, on the infamous 'middle passage' across the Atlantic from Africa to the Americas and the cruelty and hardships suffered by those who were forced to undergo it. More than fifty years afterwards, the Coltman's family friend, William Gardiner, wrote in his memoirs[8] of the horror that he and others in Leicester felt at the revelations. He appears to confuse dates and timelines in his account and he misremembers some of the details but the essential truth of what had occurred on board the *Zong* had clearly stayed with him even though, like Elizabeth, he was a child at the time.

Nonconformist families like the Coltmans and the Gardiners brought their children up to believe they should live by God's commands. No man could make another man his property because all owed their creation to God and all lives belonged to Him. Obedience to God's law required self-interest to be put aside, subordinated to the needs of the community. Granville Sharp and John Wesley both argued that retribution would follow any failure to do this; God would judge without mercy, and punish those who showed no compassion for their fellow men.[9] To put your own interests ahead of others was to be guilty of self-love and pride, and as Elizabeth grew to womanhood in 1780s Leicester, she would be reminded of this, time and again. Religious ideology underpinned her life, and from her earliest days, she was taught that proud individuals would feel God's wrath. Slave traders and slave holders oppressed others in pursuit of their own interests and so were guilty of sacrilege. The case involving the *Zong* had sparked public outrage, and at about the same time anti-slavery campaigners began circulating a diagram of another slave ship operating out of Liverpool that, on a close viewing, brought people up short. Between 1783 and 1793, 878 slave ships left Liverpool[10] and the diagram was a careful drawing to scale of the spaces below decks on a ship called the *Brookes*. As you move in to examine it, gradually you realise that the tiny black stick shapes, wedged together around the sides of the hull like so many dead insects, represent people. These are the top, side and end views of a fully loaded slave ship.

The image was created in 1787. The slaves lay on their backs, or on their sides, with barely room to turn, and most were chained. Before the days of photography, this iconic image found its way across the world and became a powerful weapon in the campaign. It began appearing in newspapers, magazines, pamphlets and books; sympathisers hung posters of the image on the walls of their homes and in local pubs. The writer, Adam Hochschild, describes its impact: 'Precise, understated and eloquent in its starkness, it remains one of the most widely reproduced political graphics of all time.'[11]

Some years later, Catherine Hutton boarded a slave ship that was tied up at Liverpool docks. It was 110 feet long, carried sixteen guns and was licensed to take 365 slaves. 'The man who showed us the vessel seemed not inclined to unfold the mysteries of his calling,' says Hutton wryly, but she quizzed him and he eventually acknowledged that the slaves were naked and chained together. A certain number at a time were permitted to go up on deck for air but at night, the hatches were shut down. When they were opened in the morning, the stench was intolerable. Hutton asked if they ever made a voyage without losing one of the slaves but did not receive a direct answer. Her guide, she says, seemed to think this was not to be expected.[12]

An estimated two million Africans died on the Middle Passage, between 10 and 15 percent of those forced to undertake it.[13] A further 15 to 30 percent are thought to have died during the march to the African coast or in their confinement once there. Few first-hand accounts of the experience of enslavement exist but Equiano's autobiography, *The Interesting Narrative of the Life of Olaudah Equiano or Gustavus Vassa the African*, first published in 1789, describes vividly the hardships that he and others endured on board a slave ship, the galling chains, the filthy tubs full of excrement, and the desperation.[14] The book was a best-seller, ran to nine editions and was translated into Dutch, German and Russian. By this time, Equiano himself was a free man in London and although some historians now dispute certain features of his account, its publication was timely and it was keenly promoted by the author and others. The abolitionist movement was building, slave ship diagrams were appearing everywhere, and Westminster politicians were at last beginning to debate the matter in earnest.

* * *

In May 1787, four years after Catherine Hutton had read *Letters from an American Farmer* and just a few months before Elizabeth would be lifted over a wall to escape rampaging hosiery workers in Leicester, twelve men came together in a London printing shop. Today, if you step away from the busy thoroughfares around Bank Station, and elbow your way free of the crowd, within minutes you will find yourself in a maze of alleys, lanes and courtyards. The printing shop was at number two, George Yard, and though it no longer exists, and there is no memorial plaque to mark the spot, the meeting that took place there is now widely regarded as constituting the formal beginning of the anti-slavery movement in England.[15] There were no women present and nine of those assembled were Quakers. All were opposed to the institution of slavery and the trade itself, finding it both religiously and morally repugnant. They resolved to organise in opposition to it, both inside Parliament and beyond, and so a committee was formed which established the 'Society for the Purpose of Effecting the Abolition of the Slave Trade'.

Those who attended this early meeting included Granville Sharp and a young Thomas Clarkson (1760-1846), red-haired, tall and clad all in black, who would become the movement's central figure. In the years to come, he would spend long days on horseback, riding the length and breadth of the country, organising petitions and meetings, setting up hundreds of local committees, and gathering witnesses who might testify to the abuses of slavery. On his travels, he engaged with local supporters and on one occasion in Leicester, he met Mrs Coltman. By this time, her health was failing. She had only two years to live but the encounter lifted her spirits. She wrote to a friend about it:

> 'And now I must tell you that I have lately had the honour or impertinence, I don't know which you will call it, to introduce myself into the company of the greatest man in the kingdom, at least in my opinion.'[16]

During the anti-slavery campaign, Thomas Clarkson covered thousands and thousands of miles. The petitions that he and others initiated, and left for signing in town halls, pubs, printing shops and coffee houses throughout the country, became hugely important political tools. In 1788 alone, an estimated 103 petitions seeking the reform or abolition of the slave trade were presented to the Parliament at Westminster, signed by between 60,000 and 100,000 people.[17] There were far more signatures on abolition petitions than had ever been received on any other subject. In a country where so few could vote, petitions were a time-honoured means of exerting pressure, and the nearest thing, as Hochschild comments, to a referendum.[18] And having witnessed the impact that the diagram of the *Brookes* had, Clarkson now commissioned two small wooden models of the ship, one of which was used in Parliament by William Wilberforce (1759-1833) (who had been elected to the House in 1780) to illustrate the cruelty and the horrors of slavery to his fellow MPs.

* * *

Outside Parliament, in towns everywhere, people began gathering. Some events hosting anti-slavery speakers drew crowds in the tens of thousands and there was always the opportunity to sign petitions afterwards, or buy abolitionist pamphlets and books. In Leicester, in February 1788, a general meeting gave its unanimous support to the cause and a petition started in the town had soon attracted 500 signatures.[19] One of those initiating the meeting here was Thomas Babington (1758-1837). A year earlier, Thomas had married Jean (1764-1845), the sister of Zachary Macaulay (1768-1838). Several members of the Babington family, including Thomas's mother, Lydia (1726/7-1791), donated funds to the 1787 anti-slavery society[20], and Rothley Temple, the family's home in Leicestershire, became a meeting place for leading abolitionists during the late eighteenth century as they drafted legislation or worked on strategy. William Wilberforce and Zachary Macaulay (1768-1838) both visited the Babingtons at Rothley, using the house as a sort of retreat, and for Macaulay especially, it was a place to recuperate. In 1789, he had returned to England from working on a Jamaican sugar plantation as an administrator and was much the worse for this experience. The young man had been repulsed at first by the brutality of the slave system he witnessed but says he soon became indifferent. Visits to his sister in Leicestershire and conversations with his brother-in-law brought about what his biographer calls 'a conversion experience'. He became intimate with those in the Babington circle and 'his better nature began to assert itself.'[21]

These are some of the people who will come to populate Elizabeth's later story as she reaches adulthood and embraces the anti-slavery cause. Macaulay eventually became Elizabeth's sympathetic advisor though Thomas Babington, who became a Leicester MP in 1800, remained opposed to the involvement of all women in the anti-slavery movement. He was in agreement with his friend, William Wilberforce, who later wrote that 'for ladies to meet, to publish, to go from house to house stirring up petitions - these appear to me proceedings unsuited to the female character as delineated in Scripture. And though we should limit the interference of our ladies to the cause of justice and humanity, I fear its tendency would be to mix them in all the multiform warfare of political life.'[22] Women, in other words, belonged at home. In citing the authority of the Bible, Wilberforce was in tune with evangelical Christians of his time. He grounded his case, he said, in the writings of St Paul, who believed, for example, that women should be silent in church and take direction from their husbands.[23]

Yet many of the women in the anti-slavery movement also held passionate religious convictions and they, too, appealed to the scriptures. Elizabeth was devout throughout her life and saw no contradiction between her Christian faith and her activism. Rather, she drew on her beliefs to underline the importance and necessity of her work. The criticisms she directed at slavery and those who continued to practise it even after the trade itself had been legally abolished in 1807[24] were based on religious argument. After explaining to readers of her 1824 pamphlet what a slave is and how he is treated, she cites 'divine law' which commands us to 'love our neighbour as ourselves' and to 'do unto others whatsoever we would that they should do unto us'. The reader should act towards the enslaved African like the good Samaritan: 'pour "oil and wine" into his bleeding wounds; break the cruel yoke of slavery off his neck; raise him from the condition of a brute to that of a man and a Christian.'[25] Nothing could be more contrary to Christian precepts, she believed, than the practice and institution of slavery.

Members of Dissenting sects were particularly likely to understand the oppression faced by the slave. Nonconformists, like those who attended the Presbyterian Great Meeting that the Coltman family belonged to in Leicester, were discriminated against both socially and politically and were powerless to address the inequalities they faced in their daily lives. So it was that both women and Dissenters, writes the academic Edith Hurwitz, 'could find in the slave society the perfect image of tyranny and despotism greater, powerful and more enormous for them perhaps than the tyranny of the established church.'[26] Despite the opposition of men like Thomas Babington and William Wilberforce, women all over the country were already working for the cause. Both married and single women made financial contributions to the first abolition society and in 1788, females made up about 10 per cent of the total number of subscribers.[27] Only about a quarter of these women seem to have been related to male subscribers, suggesting that many of them were acting as independent individuals.[28] The names of Thomas Babington and some of his family appear in the first society list but Elizabeth's family is not listed, and neither is Catherine Hutton, though all were sympathisers by this time. Some people found other ways to contribute to the cause and Elizabeth's father, always a humanitarian and by now a successful businessman, contributed financial support for the founding of Sierra Leone.[29]

* * *

Plans for a colony in West Africa, initially called the Province of Freedom, had their origin in the American War of Independence that had ended in 1783. Large numbers of black slaves had fled American plantations to join the British side on the promise of freedom and land after the war. Now, at the end of the conflict, many of these Black Loyalists had come to England to look for employment. Most failed to obtain it and in increasing numbers, they found themselves destitute on city streets. Granville Sharp, already known as an anti-slavery champion, now gave radical form to a plan for a settlement in Sierra Leone. Fellow members of the evangelical Clapham Sect[30] supported him and the venture soon became a symbol in the fight for abolition. Funding was provided by the British Government; in this new colony, it was hoped freed slaves and the black poor[31] could be re-settled and begin new lives.

Slavery was to be prohibited in this new province and the community was to be entirely self-governing. Sharp had even provided them with a constitution. In total, about 400 sailed for Africa in February 1787 but they had received poor advice about the conditions that awaited them and though the settlers made a valiant attempt to give form to Sharp's dream, the experiment failed as the inhospitable climate, sickness, death and local disputes overcame them.[32]

Eventually, again under the stewardship of Granville Sharp, another scheme to establish the colony began and in 1791, after many setbacks, The Sierra Leone Company[33] received its charter. It was promoted as a charitable venture and those willing to support the initiative numbered about 100. Shares were taken up by many in the provinces as well as in London[34] and Samuel Coltman recalls his father's decision to invest in the scheme.[35] Undoubtedly John Coltman was drawn like many others to the project's philanthropic aims and it is easy to see why he was persuaded. There was mention in the company's Prospectus of the 'well-watered' land with 'salubrious springs' on a 'fruitful peninsular', of plentiful timber and 'perhaps the finest harbour in the World'[36] but no mention of the high summer temperatures, life-threatening diseases, the poor soil and cold rainy seasons. From their settlement beside the river, the newcomers would have been able to see the slave ships still in operation, and probably they could hear and smell them, too.

The Company sought subscribers who were not concerned with private profit but who were willing to promote this charitable venture. The colony might be important, they suggested, to Britain's manufacturing and trading interests in the future but its main role, says the historian John Peterson, was in terms of suppressing the slave trade by introducing Christianity and civilisation along the coast.[37] Company shares cost £50 each (the equivalent of nearly £6000 in terms of today's purchasing power[38]) but shareholders would not be personally liable for Company debts. They might not have expected great returns on their investment but equally they probably did not expect to lose it altogether. By 1794, however, the French Revolutionary Wars were under way and this small, idealistic British colony became a target. The colonists had been joined in 1792 by about 1200 freed slaves from Nova Scotia[39] led by John Clarkson, the younger brother of Thomas, and Granville Town, as it had been known, was now renamed Freetown. Unfortunately, the settlers were no match for their French assailants who soon came ashore:

> 'The people fled, leaving their homes to be ransacked. Every house was broken into and plundered. Not content with taking

what they wanted, killing livestock, shooting pigs, dogs or cats as they went, they smashed everything of use or value. Furniture, books and papers, the printing press, the library, telescopes and barometers were deliberately destroyed. They broke every bottle in the apothecary's shop. The church, a special object of their revolutionary fury, was gutted, Bibles and prayer books torn up, even the clock broken.'[40]

For a modern reader, there are intriguing insights here into the lives, values and aspirations of the new colonists. They were doing their noble best to build a sustainable community, to promote knowledge and religious understanding but now for the second time, everything had been destroyed. Zachary Macaulay was by now the colony's Governor and the attackers set fire to his house. A few days later, they burned down all the Company buildings. Rebuilding was arduous and the Company was by now under severe financial strain. It had turned its back on the riches of the slave trade but found no substitute in Sierra Leone. The Anglo-French wars led to high insurance charges and the costs of supplying the colony were now exorbitant. During 1798 and 1799, several British ships were captured before they could reach Freetown and by 1802, it was clear that the Company had no future as a financial venture. In 1807, it ceased trading and Sierra Leone became a Crown Colony. With the French attack in 1794, John Coltman's investment had been destroyed and the loss was significant enough for Samuel to recall it years later, as he reflected on the many circumstances of the time that had caused anxiety to his parents.[41]

* * *

A year after the first freed slaves had landed in Sierra Leone, hoping to make a home for themselves, the writer Hannah More published *Slavery, a poem*.[42] More was a traditional and conservative thinker and, like Wilberforce and Sharp, a member of the evangelical Clapham Sect, which campaigned for the abolition of slavery.[43] She had a large readership amongst both the educated and the poor, and she wrote the poem early in 1788, in support of the launch in Parliament of the first anti-slavery campaign. In her poem, she challenges the nation's hypocrisy:

Shall Britain, where the soul of Freedom reigns
Forge chains for others she herself disdains?

More recognised slavery's racist underpinnings and believed that participation in the trade shamed her country:

> Perish the proud philosophy, which sought
> To rob them of the powers of equal thought!
> What! Does the immortal principle within
> Change with the casual colour of a skin?[44]

A year later, a counter-attack was launched in the form of a musical play called *The Benevolent Planters* that opened at the Theatre Royal in Haymarket. In the narrative, two black lovers are separated in Africa, then reunited in the West Indies, Christianised and 'saved' by their kindly owners. Hochschild comments that although the play had less of an impact than More's poetry, the pro-slavery lobby was now awake to the danger it faced.[45] It would be a long struggle.

The writer, David Olusoga, names Hannah More and Elizabeth Heyrick amongst the many whose contributions to the anti-slavery cause have been largely forgotten.[46] It would be more than thirty years before Elizabeth came to echo More's charges in her own writing but when she did, she was forthright. In her pamphlet *An Appeal Not to the Government But to the People of England on the subject of West Indian Slavery*, she accuses the country's statesmen of 'high sounding but empty declamation against oppression and cruelty', and of 'lofty pretensions'.[47] Like More, she identifies the cruelty, hypocrisy and the racism of slavery as she explains rather deliberately 'to those who may not know' that the slave can be distinguished from his master by his black skin, 'and is considered and treated by him, not as a human being, but as a beast of burden, whom he buys and sells like cattle in a market.'[48] Both writers also identify the breaking of familial bonds that enslaved people suffer as a particular cruelty. In *No British Slavery or an Invitation to the People to Put A Speedy End to it,* Elizabeth writes about the emotional impact of being separated from wives and children, a loss that is often taken deeply to heart, and sometimes causes madness and even death.[49] In her poem, Hannah More also recognises the pain of families forced apart:

> By felon hands, by one relentless stroke,
> See the fond links of Nature broke!
> The fibres twisting round a parent's heart,
> Torn from their grasp, and bleeding as they part.[50]

A number of contemporary male writers also attacked slavery[51] but the popular understanding was that women were more sympathetic and kinder than their male counterparts. As well, slavery represented an attack on the women's self-image and their religious positioning. When individuals were enslaved and deprived of family life, women lost their influence over the rearing of off-spring; they were commercially and sexually exploited. As Hurwitz explains in her book, the intense involvement of women like Elizabeth Heyrick and Hannah More in the anti-slavery cause is rooted in the attack on their identity that slavery represents.[52] They understood what it meant to their African sisters to be denied a maternal role. When Hannah More first published her poem on slavery, Elizabeth was still a teenager and her family's records suggest that as the 1780s came to a close, she had other things on her mind for she was about to make a fateful decision, one that would have a bearing on all her future decisions and a hold over her for the rest of her life.

Chapter 6

'All the work of a moment'

The young Elizabeth came forward shyly, cheeks pink, eyes down. The concert was now at an end and the seats were being hurriedly removed to make a space for dancing. In the late 1780s, the gentry of Leicester did not dance waltzes (which had yet to be introduced in England) or 'galopades' (named after the way horses run); William Gardiner remembers that instead he and his friends took to the floor in an elegant couple dance known as the court minuet. Based on the French minuet but with smaller steps and some spectacular etiquette, the dance was popular in the court of Louis XIV and in eighteenth-century Leicester.

Gardiner's father had persuaded Elizabeth's parents to allow their daughter to attend and she was accompanied by her friend, Mary Reid. Serious Dissenting families in the town did not usually take part in these entertainments and the Coltmans could not have known what the evening would bring for their eldest daughter. Now in her late teens, Elizabeth had no experience of fashionable life and in St Nicholas Street, the family lived in quiet seclusion. Yet her mother had ensured her daughter's manners were refined and the dancing school that Elizabeth attended with William Gardiner had taught her ballroom etiquette. According to his account, despite her religious education and grave demeanour, Elizabeth had a 'native grace' and now her excitement grew:

> 'Our recluse, like a nun released from the cloister, was elated with the novelty of the scene, in which she found herself. A hundred whispers ran round the room. 'Who is she? How very beautiful!'[1]

At this moment, an elegant young man made his entrance. He was dressed to the nines:

> 'I remember well,' says Gardiner, 'the coat of the gay Lionel was a light grey mixture, approaching to white, with a black silk collar and silver cord buttons.' He wore 'sky-blue ribbed silk stockings' that 'showed a handsome leg' and diamond

> buckles adorned his shoes. 'Rich lace ruffles set off the hand, and a cocked hat surmounted a head of hair dressed in the height of French fashion.'[2]

'Lionel' was in fact John Heyrick and he now took Elizabeth's hand and led her to the top of the dance. This was their first meeting. In Gardiner's memoir, she is called 'Louisa' and the use of pseudonyms so many years after the event is intriguing. Gardiner's recollections, published in 1838, hint at the secrecy and shame that will envelope Elizabeth's story until well after her death. The plain-speaking family friend, Catherine Hutton, also felt constrained to scramble the identities of the two young protagonists when she was writing about them in 1844, long after both were dead. In her piece, they masquerade as 'Elizabeth Adeling' and 'James Shirley'.[3] The Coltman family themselves also later took pains to guard against breaches of their privacy and Mary Ann, Elizabeth's younger sister, is believed to have removed some pages from Samuel's writings at a point in his narrative where he seems about to disclose some telling details. Mary Ann is thought to have intervened again after Elizabeth's death and to have destroyed her sister's letters and diaries, though she later denied this.

What was it they were all worried about? As the young couple began their courtship that evening, there were few who doubted the intensity of their attraction for one another. Convention dictated that an unmarried woman should remain circumspect. 'Demure reticence was obligatory', writes Vickery. By contrast 'all peacock display was expected of the male'[4] and John Heyrick was not the only young man dressed extravagantly on the night in question. Etiquette further demanded that he now make the acquaintance of Elizabeth's parents and when he visited the Coltman family the next day, he was received as a suitor.

We know little else about the courtship but for a story that has emerged involving a late-night escapade, a brace of birds, and a gun. On hearing that the object of his affections was staying with family friends in Duffield, Heyrick set out to walk there from Leicester, a distance of about 30 miles. Desperate for a sight of Elizabeth, he arrived at the house unannounced, with a gun on his shoulder and the dead birds in his hand.[5] 'Courtship was an invigorating challenge to manhood', writes Vickery.[6] A Georgian woman needed to be convinced of her suitor's intentions before confessing her sentiments. The story of Heyrick's late night trek may have gained something in the telling but these young people were both ready to follow their hearts and neither was made in the conventional mould. John Heyrick was passionate and impetuous. He was 'a high-born gentleman of engaging manners'[7] and she, by her brother's account, was high-spirited, self-willed and proud. It was, says Hutton, 'all the work of a moment'.[8]

The romantic (but sometimes unreliable) William Gardiner suggests that the two were married a few weeks later and were deliriously happy: 'For a season, music, love and every earthly delight, reigned uncontrolled in the temple of pleasure.'[9] Hutton also remembers how happy the two young people were initially and how absorbed in each other. In her account, they did not marry immediately, in fact not for another two years, and Samuel suggests that Mrs Coltman may have tried to dissuade her daughter. She disapproved of Elizabeth's conduct, her 'notions of fashion and style' but, says Samuel 'she could not afterwards prevent her from forming an attachment the very reverse of prudent.'[10] It cannot have been the way she pictured her daughter's future: the mother's courtship so lengthy and ponderous, the daughter's so wild and ill judged. Was Elizabeth trying to escape that cloistered upbringing, her mother's hold over her and the constant criticism? Was she aggrieved or frustrated at not being able to pursue an artistic career, as the academic Claire Midgely suggests?[11] Eighteenth century families had many considerations, and amongst the gentry, economic prudence and stability were also important.[12] John Heyrick was the son of Leicester's town clerk and a practising solicitor; on the face of it, he offered good prospects and social stability.

The couple were married on 10 March 1789 when Elizabeth was aged just 19. Teenage marriages were uncommon and since she was a minor, her father's consent was required. Further, this was a marriage across the religious divide in Leicester because John Heyrick was from a Church of England family - and a prominent one at that. Since tensions between Conformists and Nonconformists were a fundamental part of town life, the Coltmans would probably have preferred their eldest daughter to marry within her own community. Yet whatever their misgivings about the union, they did not stand in her way and the couple were married in the Anglican church of St Nicholas,[13] opposite the Coltman family home.

Despite growing up so nearby, this might well have been Elizabeth's first visit to St Nicholas's Church. Although Nonconformist families had their own places of worship, unless they were Quakers or Jews, the law required them to be married by the Church of England.[14] They could be married by the reading of banns or by licence - which Nonconformists often preferred even though it was more costly because matters could be less publicly and more swiftly concluded. The record indicates that Elizabeth and John Heyrick took this route. Those present at the ceremony included Elizabeth's friend, Mary Reid (1769-1839) who had accompanied her to the Leicester dance two years before. She, too, was from a local Nonconformist family and her father, like Elizabeth's, was a hosiery manufacturer. Like the Coltmans, the Reids worshipped at the Great Meeting, but unlike Elizabeth, Mary Reid did not marry. Instead, she rejected her many suitors and with the help of inherited wealth, built an independent life around her political and literary interests.[15]

Elizabeth shared these literary interests. Her parents were both well-read, even erudite, as their courtship letters had revealed and John Heyrick also had eminent forebears, notably the seventeenth-century lyric poet Robert Herrick (1591-1674). He was 'not a little proud of his poetic ancestor', writes Samuel and believed that he had inherited some of the man's genius. Herrick is best remembered now for his line 'Gather ye rosebuds while ye may' which opened one of the poems in his major work *Hesperides.*[16]

In his spare time, and from his earliest days, the young John Heyrick tried his hand at poetry, too. His initial collection entitled *First Flights*[17] would not appear in print until after his death but it was accompanied by a claim that the author would be remembered by all who knew him 'as a man of superior talents, a soldier of 'undaunted courage and a gentleman of unbounded liberality'. It was a generous assessment of Elizabeth's husband, and it would turn out to be quite at variance with her family's view.

For the marriage had descended quickly into acrimony. As Catherine Hutton observed of the couple: 'Mr J Heyrick was as fond, as romantic and improvident as herself. How they lived together I know not. I believe they knew no medium: it was always my plague, or my darling.'[18] Later William Gardiner marks 'the disastrous result' of the union by composing a song:

'With humble vows men first begin,
Stealing, unseen, into the heart;
But by possession settled in,
They quickly act another part.'[19]

How much did Gardiner or the Coltmans' other friends at the time know of the couple's distress? How much did they know of what took place within the marriage? First-hand sources are scant and despite its missing pages, Samuel's memoir provides the fullest account. He believes the marriage began happily and that at first his sister was 'intoxicated….by the homage paid to her as a bride and a beauty.' She felt flattered and elated, says Samuel. 'She was greatly admired in the superior circle of the society of Leicester to which her marriage with the Heyrick family had introduced her.'[20] The 'superior circle' that Samuel alludes to was composed mainly of members of the Tory-led Corporation where Heyrick's father (John Heyrick

Senior) was the town clerk. Nonconformists like the Coltmans were not permitted to hold public office and the two families were worlds apart-socially, religiously and politically. Catherine Hutton also suggests, in typically ambivalent terms, that marriage changed Elizabeth:

> 'Her style of dress before marriage had been elegant, yet somewhat independent of fashion; one of her costumes was a black silk cloak that covered her from head to foot, and a black beaver hat of extraordinary dimensions; her figure was extremely good, and her carriage and manner of walking had been taken great pains with by her husband.'[21]

The image here of a beautiful young woman, impressionable and eager for acceptance, is a far cry from the person who would emerge at the end of this turbulent relationship. After the marriage, the couple went to live in Bow Bridge House which they had built near the River Soar.[22] At the time, Samuel writes, it was almost in the country 'watered by the river, shaded by groves and overlooking fields,' 'a sweetly rural residence' where the singing of birds, the waving of trees and the murmur of water below 'made it a delightful spot.' The house was spacious and convenient and in 'so fair a dwelling,' remarks Samuel, it should have been possible for the couple to enjoy 'all the romantic happiness they had pictured to themselves.'[23]

Yet it was not to be. It was just a few months after the wedding that Elizabeth's young brother Rowland died. His grieving mother wrote to her friend the Reverend Gifford that the boy's 'passage was calm and easy, not a sigh, or a groan, or a discontented expression ever escaped him when awake; indeed, the transition was momentary, he had walked out of the room himself not two minutes before he expired.' Mrs Coltman admits to 'the partiality of a parent' in seeing Rowland 'as near to perfection as human frailty allows.' As she writes her letter, on the lid of the boy's coffin, she sees a countenance which is so sweet in death that she imagines he would speak to her.[24]

* * *

Again, Mrs Coltman's religion is her solace. Both Rowland's parents continued to grieve for him and may well have been too preoccupied at that time to notice that their eldest daughter's marriage was failing. Peace eluded Elizabeth and John Heyrick, says Samuel, and though his sister behaved with 'the utmost discretion' she could not calm her husband's 'ill regulated mind'.[25] His resentful fears and suspicions, his instability and financial profligacy created tension; he would leave his wife at times uncertain of his whereabouts or when he would return. Samuel recalls Elizabeth's maid, Kitty, coming to the Coltman family home frequently to see if Heyrick was there and having to return to her mistress without news of him. It is here that sections of Samuel's writings have been scored out in the original manuscript but even though we cannot be sure of every detail, the essence is clear enough.

Then, in 1795, Heyrick left the legal profession and turned to soldiering. He first took a commission in a Volunteer Corps but soon gave that up to enter the King's Own Regiment of Light Dragoons. A man designated by some as 'the Apollo of the town'[26] might certainly have found the regimental attire appealing but he might also have had genuinely patriotic motives. The outbreak of the French Revolution in May 1789 had initially been met with enthusiasm by reformers in the town but by September, following the murder of some 1200 people in the streets of Paris, most English reformers had become alienated from the Revolution[27] and in the early 1790s, a backlash was underway. It was dangerous now for anyone to show sympathy with the French Revolutionists and there was a rising expectation, here as elsewhere, that the country would soon be invaded. In Leicester, young men were urged to volunteer for military duties and in this way to demonstrate their patriotism. Heyrick had responded to the call and records show that in March 1795, now a Captain, he was summoned by the Mayor to quell a local disturbance. A troop of volunteer cavalry arrived in the market place just ten minutes after the bugle had sounded.[28]

The King's Own regiment was chiefly engaged in reconnaissance and patrolling and the troops, mounted on horseback, were lightly armed. It was a peripatetic life that entailed long absences from home. In both England and Ireland, the Heyricks lived in army barracks, a far cry from the comforts of Bow Bridge House. The Mitcham Road Barracks in Croydon where the couple stayed at one point had been built in 1794 as part of the British response to the French Revolution and they remain in use today as an Army Reserve Centre. Heyrick's military activities cannot have endeared him to the reform-minded Coltman family but Elizabeth joined her husband and Catherine Hutton describes how she rode with him to the field wearing a ceremonial uniform of 'a blue, richly braided habit, silver epaulettes, and a helmet covered with bear skin.'[29] Yet beyond appearances, we know little. Still in her twenties, how did the young Elizabeth find army life? Did she enter into the spirit of parades and skirmishes or was she starting to feel uncomfortable with her husband's soldierly ambitions? Was this a full and satisfying marriage for either of them?

For some months, says Samuel, while Heyrick was in army barracks, his sister returned to live in the family home. With her marriage now under severe strain, she accepted help from her brother who wrote later of how he had sought to relieve his sister of the 'pressing embarrassments which the disposition or extravagance of her husband occasioned.' Clearly, to add to her concerns about her husband's temperament and their constant rows, there were now worries about the couple's debts.

How had these debts accumulated? Was Heyrick a gambler? Roy Porter remarks that England was gripped by gambling fever and you could bet on almost any future event. Rich and poor alike placed wagers on boxing matches and horse races, even on how long it might take to drink pints of gin or eat live cats.[30] John Heyrick was certainly impetuous and impassioned. That much is beyond doubt but he was lucky, too. Once your expenditure exceeded your income, you were left with few options and the most usual consequence of falling into debt was imprisonment. In 1770, almost half the entire prison population were debtors.[31] On the other hand, you might seek help from a charity or from your friends and relatives, as Heyrick was able to do, to his wife's evident shame.

Samuel believed that the military life Heyrick chose was intended to take his sister away from her family but Elizabeth did not always accompany her husband. In 1795, with Heyrick confined to barracks in Croydon, Elizabeth returned to the family in Leicester. A warm letter from Mary Reid who was away in Cheshunt indicates that Elizabeth has confided in her friend. 'I as well as you,' writes Mary, 'have lost somewhat of my romantic feelings but I am still alive to friendship and happy in the idea of renewing my intimacy with you.'[32]

While the two women were sharing feelings of sadness and personal loss in their letters, in the military camp John Heyrick was writing romantic poetry. Of course, no poet can be wholly trusted when he or she says 'I' and many of Heyrick's poems were dedicated to unknown women. Yet some were clearly addressed to Elizabeth (called 'Eliza' or 'Betsy') as in this extract:

> 'But Betsy the unreal scene disdains
> Mocks the romantic fervours of my soul;
> Ah! Cease to trifle with my tears and pains
> Cease to insult them as they silent roll.'[33]

Despite discord and difference in the relationship, some of his poems suggest the couple shared certain values and beliefs. In this extract from *To The Sympathetic: An African Picture*, Heyrick describes the cruelty and distress caused by enslavement:

> 'View, if your aching eyes can view, yon pair,
> The piercing groans of real anguish hear,

Behold the swarthy Chieftain's fixed despair,
Behold her eye distil the rapid tear.

"Take then my freedom, take my worthless life,
From Europe's Sons to cherish hope were vain,
But spare my children, spare my frantic wife"
Ah no! behold they clinch the double chain.

That manly heart must learn no more to heave
For her who kindly sooth'd in every care;
Her sympathising heart must cease to grieve
When the keen lash his quiv'ring flesh shall tear.'[34]

The poem is undated. In the 1790s, the anti-slavery cause to which Elizabeth would soon devote so much of her energy was still in its infancy but the man she had fallen in love with was clearly sympathetic. Though his marriage was collapsing and his relationship with his wife under serious strain, Heyrick now wrote compellingly about the cruelty and hardship that others were experiencing.

It may be that Elizabeth's family saw little of this side of the man their eldest daughter had chosen to marry or that they were simply more focused on her personal welfare. The marriage produced no children - and it is impossible to know why. There are slim archival pickings for those wishing to know about the sex lives of Georgian women since few were willing to commit such experiences to paper[35] but the family clearly had their worries and it was Heyrick's behaviour that gave them cause for disquiet. It was not just the endless quarrelling. In his memoirs, Samuel seeks to excuse his sister from 'errors' of conduct that might simply be explained by her youthfulness (a lack of foresight and prudence, a degree of impatience). Far more serious, he claims, were the failings of her gifted but impetuous husband. Heyrick emerges now as a jealous and controlling man, obsessive and prone to angry outbursts. Elizabeth returned to take refuge in the family home more than once and there spent her time in 'melancholy seclusion'. Sometimes, according to Samuel, she would begin to hope and always she found excuses for a man she still loved ardently.

* * *

In the spring of 1789, in the earliest days of her daughter's marriage, Mrs Coltman had written to Elizabeth about how she should behave.

The older woman said she had seen many other instances of unhappiness between people 'who have come together with strong attachments.' To avoid friction, she advises her daughter to guard against slovenly dress. 'A wife's ambition ought to be to shine in the eyes of her husband.' She recommends early rising and setting the house in order while Heyrick is busy. Elizabeth should always 'have a bit of work ready whenever he is at leisure to sit down and chat with you.' She urges her daughter above all to read the Bible 'seriously, attentively, with fervent prayer' for 'religion is the only anchor sure and steadfast.'[36]

As well as the Bible, women from genteel families studied 'conduct manuals' like those of Hester Chapone. *Letters on the Improvement of Mind,* originally written to her young niece and first published in 1773, was Chapone's most celebrated work and Mrs Coltman echoes its sentiments. Any 'scheme of life' that does not please God or end in 'the attainment of real excellence,' says Chapone, is vain and absurd. 'It is with the rules of the Gospel we must compare ourselves and not with the world around us.'[37] Elizabeth herself would come to advocate a life based on these principles when events overtook her, leaving her downcast and distressed. For now, however, she had to endure a rancorous marriage. On one occasion, her eldest brother, John, reached the end of his tether. A great deal of animosity already existed between him and his brother-in-law and on first hearing of what he considered to be the ill-treatment of his sister, he challenged the man to a duel. Seconds were chosen, and all preliminaries completed. Although too young to recall all the details, Samuel remembers that the affair was quashed somehow and the duel did not take place.

In the late eighteenth century, it was still common for genteel men to seek the resolution of a grievance by issuing such a challenge and honour would normally require that it should be met. Reputation, wounded pride and unpaid debts might all lead to a challenge and it could not be lightly dismissed. In Parliament in 1792, William Wilberforce, already a committed abolitionist, spoke of the cruelty to slaves shown by one Captain John Kimber who had allegedly flogged a pregnant slave girl to death.[38] The naval captain was later acquitted of a murder charge and then pursued Wilberforce with threats of violence. Another discontented naval captain challenged Wilberforce directly to a duel but rather than take him up, the MP opted instead to give the slave trader a full explanation of his reasons for opposing duelling as a means of resolving disputes. The practice did not come to an end in England until the middle of the nineteenth century by which time a growing distaste for violence and new ideas of manhood and honour had helped to reduce its popularity.[39] John Coltman (Junior) was close to Elizabeth and presumably when he issued the challenge to his brother-in-law, he acted out of loyalty to his sister. It suggests that he may have believed Heyrick to be abusive, neglectful or even violent. The duel was a genteel means of settling a private grievance. Still, it sits oddly with what we know of Coltman family life - with the studious, unworldly father and the learned, devout mother. Elizabeth was fortunate to have the support of her family but her desertion of her husband, even for limited periods of time, put her at odds with social convention. It is likely that the family 'scandal' referred to years later by Hutton and others stems from the shame of Elizabeth's toxic marriage. Yet as a victim of domestic violence, if indeed that is what she was, she had few options. Divorce was prohibitively expensive and extremely rare. In strict legal terms, a wife could not even leave the house without her husband's permission. Further, there were powerful social prohibitions against any kind of informal separation and the writer, Amanda Vickery, observes that only the most desperate or the most protected women could countenance leaving a marriage in that way.[40]

* * *

Elizabeth may well have been desperate but she was left reeling by what happened next. She and her husband were away from Leicester visiting his parents. Heyrick had not appeared well for some time and did not accompany his family to church one evening in June, 1797. Elizabeth had offered to stay with him since he seemed a little dejected but he had insisted that she should do what she felt was right. On her return, she found her husband stretched lifeless on the floor. The man had suffered a heart attack and Heyrick's poor father was dreadfully overcome, recalls Samuel. It was a blow from which Elizabeth herself never recovered. Many years later, Samuel reflects cheerfully on the 'short and restless career' of his unhappy brother-in-law 'who gifted by nature with no mean talents, and a fine person, debased himself by reckless self-indulgence while he destroyed the peace of mind of an adoring wife by his capricious violence and suspicion.'[41]

Elizabeth was certainly devastated. She moved back to live with her family and they watched helplessly as she now withdrew from them and the wider world into what Samuel called a 'gloomy ascetic solitude'. Her diaries (now lost) later made painful and depressing reading for her brother as each day she listed resolution after resolution, to refuse all indulgences, all social enjoyment: 'This day I solemnly engage with myself to eat no cheese after dinner, no butter to my tea, and no supper but bread - to drink nothing but water, and retire unto my room when supper is announced.'[42]

Heyrick women were accustomed to taking snuff, a common practice in the eighteenth century, but Elizabeth now resolved to abstain from it. 'To like anything,' says Hutton 'was an immediate reason for its being sacrificed'[43] in case self-indulgence should gain ground.

Most widows of Elizabeth's generation needed to find employment and some took up their husband's trade.[44] Re-marriage was another obvious path to a secure future and widowers often sought new wives who might care for their children and keep house. Indeed, men were more likely to re-marry than women. As an attractive young woman, Elizabeth might have been expected to take a second husband but there was no financial necessity. Her father gave her an allowance and cushioned by circumstance, she also refused to take the army pension to which she was entitled, opting instead to donate it to charity. The period of mourning could vary but Elizabeth carried her penitential and pious observances to extremes, said Samuel. Each time she broke any of her self-denying resolutions, she immediately renewed them. On each anniversary of her husband's death, she would withdraw into the strictest seclusion, determined says her brother to obtain 'a victory over nature' and to adhere rigidly to her self-imposed rituals, whatever the cost. Just as her courtship had been 'a grand passion', so too her bereavement exceeded social norms.

For Elizabeth blamed herself for her husband's death. She believed that she was the principal cause of his 'errors,' says Samuel, and she became deeply despondent. In her isolation, her damaged mind was 'apt to prey upon itself' and she suffered acutely. From her surviving diary entries, it is clear she considered taking her own life. Should she return without delay 'to my Father's house' or waste 'a little more of this life and health and talents.'[45] Does God have a plan for her? or is He punishing her? Should she live in the service of God and the world a little longer? If she does, she fears she will become completely abandoned to the fears and deceitful pleasures of the world and that the pain of her loss will never leave her.

Why did she believe she was responsible for Heyrick's demise? Should she have realised how ill he was? In the late eighteenth century, the symptoms of heart disease were only poorly understood and effective diagnosis and treatment were many decades away. Did she feel guilty about their tempestuous marriage, their ceaseless quarrelling and the lack of trust between them? Did she believe she had made Heyrick unhappy or had failed him? Worse still, did she feel she had somehow deserved to be mistreated in the way she was?

* * *

Contemporary views about marriage and the proper role of women within it had been challenged by Mary Wollstonecraft in *A Vindication of the Rights of Woman*, first published in 1792. She argued that although the education of women was receiving more attention than previously, they were still considered to be a frivolous sex. Women's physical and intellectual strengths were being neglected, 'sacrificed to libertine notions of beauty'[46] so that the only way women could rise in the world was by marriage - and in order to find a husband, young women had to learn how to behave. Hester Chapone, who became one of Elizabeth's favourite authors, had written some years earlier that in choosing a husband, young women, knowing so little of the world, were unqualified to judge for themselves. So much depended on the choice of a life companion that they would do well to take the advice of their parents and make the decision on rational grounds, on the basis of character, mutual esteem 'and the prospect of a real and permanent friendship.'[47] In failing to pay heed to her parents' concerns about her proposed marriage to Heyrick, perhaps Elizabeth had now come to believe that she was at fault for embarking on a union like those Chapone had advised against, one that could 'be productive of nothing but misery and shame.' 'The passion, to which every consideration of duty and prudence is sacrificed', warns Chapone, 'instead of supplying the loss of all other advantages, will soon itself be changed into mutual distrust, repentance, reproaches, and finally perhaps into hatred; the distresses it brings will be void of every consolation; you will have disgusted the friends who should be your support; debased yourself in the eyes of the world; and, what is much worse, in your own eyes, and even in those of your husband; above all you will have offended that God, who alone can shield you from calamity.'[48]

Cautions to young women about their marriage choices were also contained in some fiction of the time. In 1798, a year after John Heyrick's death, Mary Wollstonecraft's unfinished novel *Maria: or, the Wrongs of Woman* was published posthumously by her husband William Godwin. In this story, the central character of Maria has made an ill-judged marriage to escape an unhappy home life. Initially, her husband presents himself as a respectable and honourable young man but she quickly discovers his true character and comes to regret her early marriage. Through his gambling and whoring, the couple are soon bankrupt; Maria is trapped in a neglectful and abusive relationship and eventually her husband seizes their child and imprisons his wife in an insane asylum. Wollstonecraft identifies the double standard:

> 'Women who have lost their husband's affection are justly reproved for neglecting their persons, and not taking the same

> pains to keep as to gain a heart; but who thinks of giving the same advice to men (…) Yet why a woman should be expected to endure a sloven, with more patience than a man and magnanimously to govern herself, I cannot conceive; unless it be supposed arrogant in her to look for respect as well as a maintenance.'[49]

It is unlikely that the grief-stricken Elizabeth was mindful of the hypocrisy that Wollstonecraft is describing. From the scant sources available, it seems more probable that for a time at least her spirit was completely broken, that she was overwhelmed by loss and her own sense of failure. Heyrick's army career had lasted just two years when, in the cemetery at St Martin's Church[50] on 20 June 1797, Elizabeth buried her ill-tempered and violent husband.

Throughout her married life, convention had required Elizabeth to conduct herself modestly, without pride or vanity, to keep a tidy home and please her husband. Her mother's letters are evidence of the pressure she was under from her family to conform to social expectations. Yet like the fictional Maria, she appears caught in a bind. Early in 1796, she notes in her diary, as if addressing herself, that 'every unpleasant and painful occurrence particularly the neglect and unkindness of your dearest friend' should be considered as a trial of your principles. Your own misconduct might be to blame and if you suffer provocation and show ill humour or resentment then you may be sure your principles have not had 'a proper influence on your heart and dispositions.'[51]

So it follows that it is always your own fault and there is no way out. In the year before Heyrick's death, Elizabeth appears to be taking full responsibility for the collapse of the marriage. Later, in the same entry, she acknowledges that she has always struggled to find equanimity. 'And thus have passed six and twenty years of my life, in not one day of which could I call myself happy.'[52] Family sources suggest that like her brother John and their father, Elizabeth suffered from what they might have called melancholia, and that like them she had a dark and serious disposition. Long before her disastrous marriage to John Heyrick and his subsequent death, in other words, she had battled with what today would be termed depression. If many women were trapped in unfulfilling marriages by the strictures of society, as Wollstonecraft argued, then it was also true that Elizabeth had her own personal frustrations. She would eventually make her own way out of this impasse but at some cost.

PART III

1790–1800

Chapter 7

'...an emblem of the Wise'

Soon after John Heyrick's death, a group of women met in Leicester to form a book society. When the Reverend Robert Throsby heard of the gathering, he asked to join them - but was given short shrift. More than a little peeved, he accused them of being a 'set of Dragons'. They responded:

> 'We own, good sir, your simile is keen -
> Perchance you think to rouse our female spleen -
> Not so! Your judgement we politely trust
> And, with a curtsey, own th' allusion just.
> A Dragon is by naturalists defined
> A wondrous creature of the serpent kind;
> And serpents - Holy Writ this truth supplies
> Are ever deem'd an Emblem of the Wise.'[1]

The writer of the poem is Susanna Watts (1768-1842) and she goes on to challenge Throsby by turning his intended insult about mythical monsters into a barbed joke:

> 'Vast wings they spread - and these you'll not deny
> Are fancy's pinions, form'd to soar on high;
> Their tongues are forky - here the truth you hit;
> For sure, a pointed tongue denotes a Wit;
> They vomit flames - your simile is here
> By ev'ry rule of rhetoric, strong and clear; -
> For see you not - how from our mouths transpire
> High blazing volumes of poetic fire?'[2]

It was not unheard of for men like Throsby to participate in gatherings of 'bluestockings'[3] but these Leicester women were in no mood to make concessions. They were themselves routinely excluded from intellectual gatherings in the town and the single women amongst them might be especially marginalised. Through marriage, women gained strength, protection and status.[4] They were supported financially by their husbands and many contemporaries believed marriage was the only way for most women to establish themselves in genteel society. If she was not a homemaker and wife, a woman would expect to live on the periphery, deprived of more meaningful public roles.

* * *

So now that she was a childless widow, Elizabeth was at a crossroads. If John Heyrick had lived, she might have escaped her dysfunctional marriage as some women did or she might have endured it, and with the help of her family have found a way to manage her distress. Either way, it's hard to avoid the conclusion that she would have had little chance of happiness or contentment. 'Learn to be happy wherever you are', urged her mother in the first few months of her daughter's marriage. Elizabeth must be at pains to correct her habit 'of seeing things in the most disagreeable light.' She must accept her situation, insisted her mother, because the only lasting 'source of comfort in this fluctuating world is a disposition resigned to the will of God.'[5]

Religion, says the writer Roy Porter, was 'the idiom of the people' and in its many variants, it indoctrinated them for life.[6] Parents commonly appealed to the Divinity when advising their offspring, spelling out duties and responsibilities, and Elizabeth herself would soon be casting her criticisms of others (slave owners, bull baiters, employers) in religious terms. Her own faith would deepen as she struggled with her loss and Heyrick's abrupt and untimely demise now obliged her parents to accept a profound change in their eldest daughter's status. She was taken back to the family home where she was received with tenderness and loving sympathy.

Catherine Hutton believed that from that moment all Elizabeth's prospects were 'blighted'[7] but there were other contemporary voices too, like that of Hester Chapone who believed that any woman who was unlucky enough to find herself single, should not be afraid. Better that than be forced to endure 'the calamities of an unhappy marriage'[8] because a virtuous woman will have no shortage of valuable friends. The calamity that had befallen Elizabeth would prove a turning point in her life and her friends would indeed be her mainstay.

* * *

One of her most intimate friends was Susanna Watts, the proud and witty spokeswoman for the Dragon set. Samuel remembers how the

Coltman family drew her into their circle, how his mother and both his sisters came to admire and appreciate the woman they called 'Sister Sue' whose circumstances were so different from their own. Watts' father had died in 1769 when she was only fifteen months old and the family was left in financial difficulty. Her two older sisters died of tuberculosis and by the time Watts was in her teens, the family was impoverished and she found herself having to support both herself and her mother. Having taught herself Italian and French, she now took on translation work in an effort to make ends meet, and her first publication appeared in 1784 when she was barely 16.[9] By the early 1800s, her tall, black-eyed and prim mother had become insane. By one account, the poor woman could not keep still. Her wrists, elbows and neck twisted constantly, her eyes and all her features moved in all directions so that she appeared 'electrified'.[10] No mother could have been more different from the stern Mrs Coltman; this was a powerless mother to be pitied and cared for and Watts struggled with her filial responsibilities. She was in her late 30s when her mother finally died at the age of 75. She was profoundly affected by her mother's illness and feared ever afterwards that she would inherit the disorder and end her days in a similar fashion.[11] She was luckier, however, and is remembered now for her writing, translations, philanthropy and tireless activism.[12] Her guide book *A Walk Through Leicester,* published in 1804, remained anonymous until her death and is now acknowledged to be one of the earliest competent guidebooks ever written about any of the major towns of England.[13] It takes the reader on a tour of historical sites, detailing contemporary changes and developments. Watts may well have drawn on the older John Coltman's knowledge of local history and archaeology and his love of antiquities, as suggested by writers Felicity James and Rebecca Shuttleworth.[14] And a poem written by John Heyrick, and published in his posthumous collection in 1797, is entitled *To Miss Susanna Watts, the elegant translator of Tasso*, providing further evidence of the friendships that centred around the Coltman family and their intellectual interests.

As well as her published work, Watts left behind a scrapbook, containing a diverse collection of letters, notes, invitations, portraits, drawings and poems - the assorted memorabilia of a life, or as James and Shuttleworth describe it, an artefact that illustrates the 'female connection, creativity and activism in Leicester in the early nineteenth century.'[15] Here, in Watts' scrapbook, we find her angry poem to the Reverend Throsby - and several others including one about friendship:

'A Friend
Say, which is the chiefest of blessings below
Which charms us in joy and supports us in woe,
On which our best comforts must ever depend?

Our hearts answer truly - That blessings a Friend.
Say, which is the chiefest of blessings above,
The source of our Faith, be our Hope and our Love?
Tis a friend - yes, that Friend who is 'Mighty to save'
And who will be by our side thro the gloom of the grave.'[16]

As well as Watts, other women in Elizabeth's Leicester circle included her friend and fellow Nonconformist Mary Reid (1769-1839) who had witnessed her marriage in 1789, Elizabeth's sister Mary Ann Coltman (1778-1871), and another Elizabeth Coltman (1761-1838) who was no relation of the family in St Nicholas Street despite having the same name.[17] This woman had grown up in a section of the town known as the Newarke which dated back to the fourteenth century and was not far from St Nicholas Street. The Leicester friends met to share their reading experiences, to discuss, recommend and exchange books. The academic, Amanda Vickery, observes that at this time genteel women, though they had few opportunities for formal education, had unprecedented access to the world of print.[18] Very few were illiterate and they also had leisure time of course, unlike their less well-off sisters most of whom were obliged to take up employment. Yet literacy was not confined to the wealthy and the better-off; magazines, biographies, political tracts, newspapers, journals, pornography, sermons, collections of poetry, folklore and ballads circulated widely and were avidly consumed[19] and the Leicester group would doubtless have read Wollstonecraft's *The Rights of Woman* published in 1792.

* * *

Mary Hays' controversial novel *Memoirs of Emma Courtney* was published a few years later in 1796, just a year before John Heyrick's death. This intensely autobiographical story is told partly through letters which the heroine writes to her unattainable friend, Augustus Harley. Obsessively and passionately, and ultimately without success, Emma actively pursues the man she loves. Her parents who had married for vanity and material gain have a short and unhappy marriage, and in seeking a union that is by contrast based on nature, reason and virtue, Emma believes she will find happiness. Through Emma's story, Hays explores the status of women, the philosophical nature of romantic love, and contemporary marriage.

In a non-divorcing society, comments Vickery, Georgians favoured the prudent romance[20] and within marriage, most sought to balance male authority with practical and emotional need. Yet as Elizabeth had discovered, the impact of love on marital power relations was 'wildly unpredictable'.[21] As she grieved, she might have recognised the fictional Emma's fierce passion, her struggle for independence and her determination to overcome all protests. She might also have recognised Emma's frustration and resentment at finding that after her father's death, there were few avenues open to her. 'Why was I not educated for commerce, for a profession, for labour? Why have I been rendered feeble and delicate by artificial refinement?'[22] As she faced life without the husband she had chosen, Elizabeth might have sympathised with Emma - and with Emma's creator Mary Hays, whose friend and mentor was Mary Wollstonecraft. Both Hays and Wollstonecraft argued that women needed to be better educated so that they could be independent; the customs of society, says Emma, 'have enslaved, enervated and degraded woman.'[23]

Women were excluded from Parliament and university and the legal and medical professions. Hobbies, like music, drawing and needlework, offered some scope for self-expression but the most significant field open to them was the arts. Women became actresses, playwrights, poets and novelists and with an expanding culture of literariness in Georgian England came a huge intensification of female correspondence. In their private letters, women like Catherine Hutton and Mrs Coltman were able to sustain family and friendship networks in many different parts of the country and they also participated in contemporary debates. Vickery notes: 'It was in their tireless writing no less than in their ravenous reading that genteel women embraced a world far beyond the boundaries of their parish.'[24] The Leicester book society left no formal records of their proceedings but much of the women's writing survives. They produced numerous poems (often as gifts for friends or to mark significant events); they wrote pamphlets and magazine articles. Their writing was by turns learned, combative, speculative, witty and angry. Yet if it was intended for public consumption, it was likely to be anonymous, since writing was still not considered an entirely respectable activity for women. Watts was unusual in needing to generate an income from her published work and her success as an author speaks of her ability and tenacity in a male dominated world. After her husband's death, Elizabeth became a prolific pamphleteer but it is only thanks to the scholarly detective work of academic Timothy Whelan that we can now be sure which anonymous pamphlets she herself actually wrote and which were probably written by the other Elizabeth Coltman.[25]

* * *

It was 1809 when Elizabeth first picked up her pen and, in two published pamphlets, she challenged the contemporary practice of bull-baiting that she had witnessed in Derbyshire that summer. Since the French Revolution, pamphlets had become powerful polemical weapons in England, as in France. They were amongst the first printed materials and were initially used to publicise religious controversies, but during the nineteenth century, they played a part in political movements too, including Chartism, which was a working-class movement for political reform, Irish Home Rule which sought political autonomy for Ireland, and the Oxford movement which wanted a revival of Roman Catholicism within the Church of England. Pamphlets were short, unbound, typically brief and spontaneous and were usually intended to advance a particular line of argument. Over the coming decades, Elizabeth would develop her writing techniques. Like a modern-day blogger, she sought to interest and engage with her readers and in all she wrote about twenty pamphlets.[26]

That summer, she had gone to the tiny, isolated village of Bonsall to see her sister who was taking the waters at nearby Matlock. Mineral waters were believed to have health benefits and Mary Ann was recovering from illness. The women would have known that Bonsall, like Leicester, was an important centre for framework knitting. They would have recognised the distinctive workshops by the many windows they had at upper levels which, in the absence of electricity, were designed to let as much light in as possible. Oil lamps were used when daylight faded so that the stockingers could continue to work long hours in their efforts to make ends meet. Some of the original workshops can still be found in the village.[27]

It was the day before the annual village 'wake' in Bonsall and local people were preparing to witness a brutal contest, the highlight of their celebrations. Having heard what was planned and fearing what was in store, Elizabeth rose at three that morning and walked over the fields to Matlock, a distance of about 3 miles. Her sister was not well enough to accompany her and so she walked alone, lifting her long skirts clear of the uneven ground. Bonsall is located on the southern edge of a high limestone plateau and numerous footpaths criss-cross the fields. Once in Matlock, she spent some hours trying to rouse local dignitaries, begging them to help her stop the grisly proceedings. There was little time to act and Elizabeth could find no one willing to render assistance. So she returned hurriedly to Bonsall where preparations were already underway.

The early morning mist still gathers in pockets around the steep little village and behind it, Elizabeth would have seen the high spire of St James Church built in the thirteenth century. In the centre of the village, at a place still known as The Cross, a bull was tethered to a ring fixed in a large stone in the ground. The animal was distressed; probably its nose had already been blown full of pepper. As the dogs were being readied, Elizabeth remonstrated with the crowd, appealing, it was afterwards said, to their 'better feeling and humanity'.[28]

Bonsall was not on a through route to other places nor was it a market town but it boasted numerous inns and good grazing for horses. The Cross provided a central meeting place for traders and a welcome overnight stop. Many in the assembled crowd had been drinking for several hours and they were not in an obliging mood. They would have placed bets too, on particular dogs or on the bull itself. Excitement was mounting. Would the dogs succeed in immobilising the bull? Would they manage to get their teeth into its snout? Would they be gored to death or just tossed into the air? (Less injurious for the dog but disappointing for the crowd.)

It must have taken considerable courage for Elizabeth to do what she did next. Women did not customarily involve themselves in public events but here, in a village market place in Derbyshire, at some risk to herself, Elizabeth now made a decisive intervention. Quickly she located the bull's owner and for an undisclosed sum, she purchased the animal. It was led away to a local cottage to be held in safety while the crowd's rage and frustration subsided.

The origins of bull-baiting may have been innocent enough since it was genuinely thought that the activity would tenderise the animal's meat and make it fit for human consumption. And it was not the only blood sport still practised in England at the time. Cockfighting, for example, was also popular and though some Georgians were starting to disapprove of these activities, it was at least partly because of the social mixing that resulted. Women from more prosperous families were particularly likely to object to the contact their menfolk had on such occasions with 'social inferiors'. Voices were beginning to be raised, too, on behalf of the beasts themselves, in growing opposition to the ill-treatment they suffered. Yet in many places these cruel diversions persisted.

* * *

How do you change people's minds? How do you persuade them to abandon age-old beliefs and pastimes? When two years later, Elizabeth returned to Bonsall, again with her sister, she came armed with the two pamphlets she had written. In *Bull-baiting: a Village Dialogue between Tom Brown and John Simms (*1809), she creates a fictional conversation between two invented characters and using this narrative device, she explores opposing points of view. Since the pamphlet was published anonymously, and her characters were not real, she could express her opinions freely. 'John Simms' is clearly her mouthpiece, and his companion, 'Tom Brown', a frequenter of bull-baitings, is John's foil. We learn that the men began life in similar situations but that their interests and pleasures have now diverged and John counters in turn each of the arguments put forward by his friend. Elizabeth would have heard such arguments before. Through the fictional John Simms, she challenges Tom:

> 'You dragged out these poor, unoffending animals, day after day, to be torn and mangled by dogs, whose natural ferocity you had tried every art to increase: and, that they might not escape their cruel tormentors, you chained them to the ground, and (with worse than savage barbarity) have made sport of their sufferings.'[29]

And then:

> 'To make suffering of any kind, either in man or beast, the subject of pleasure, is not only very inhuman, but very sinful; and whatever may be the examples of the rich, we must believe, when we think seriously upon the subject, that a holy and just God will hereafter punish every kind of cruelty.....'[30]

Fear of a retributive God was real for Georgians and Elizabeth would use the argument again when she came to articulate her anti-slavery views. Now, as she seeks to persuade her audience to abandon blood sports, she also identifies the contradictions between a religion based on love and the cruelty inherent in their favourite pastimes. The second pamphlet she distributed on her return to Bonsall that year was entitled *Bull-baiting: A Christmas Box for the Advocates of Bull-baiting* and again Elizabeth insists that there are sound religious reasons for opposing such an inhuman activity:

> 'I need not tell you that the religion which you profess is a religion of universal love - that its tendency is to root out of

> the heart every malignant and cruel passion, and to implant in their room every tender and amiable virtue - that it calls upon us to remember our high original, that we are the children of a holy and merciful God who delights in the happiness of all his creatures....'[31]

Here once more she ponders the best way to change other people's behaviour. Some have told her she is wasting her time, that because Parliament has just failed to make bull-baiting illegal, she 'might as well reason with the winds and the waves', that she 'might as soon expect to excite tenderness and humanity in blocks of marble' as the hearts of her countrymen.[32] Yet she insists her audience is just as capable of wisdom and goodness as anyone else, despite their disadvantages, and she reminds them that Christ himself did not chose 'the rich and the great' to be his disciples. If, instead of acting as 'the tyrants and tormentors of the inferior animals' the villagers were to become their 'guardians and protectors'[33] then everyone would benefit:

> 'By exercising justice and humanity towards the inferior animals, your dispositions towards each other will become more kind and generous; your hearts will be softened, and better disposed to receive the yoke of Christ......'[34]

Their treatment of animals reflects the values of their society as a whole for, as Elizabeth explains:

> 'He who can delight in tormenting brutes, would equally delight in tormenting his fellow creatures, could he do it with equal impunity....'[35]

Elizabeth has yet to turn her energies to the fight against slavery but already in her writing, she is cajoling, chastising, and shaming those she seeks to influence. In direct, muscular language, she appeals to their human decency, their Christian beliefs and their fear of punishment. She had some allies in Bonsall and Catherine Hutton recalls how the local rector at the time, the Reverend Henry Maddock, harangued his parishioners and elicited a promise from them that they would give up their cruel amusement.[36] Yet he was ready for their likely change of heart and he too, rescued a bull from its gruesome fate. Bull-baiting was not made illegal in England until 1835 and records suggest that right up until that date, despite the interventions of Elizabeth and others, it was still being practised in Bonsall.[37] Evidence can still be found in the village and controversy surrounds a massive limestone boulder that is tucked underneath a front pew in St James' Church. Clearly a bull-stone, with an iron shackle fixed to its top, one story suggests that it may have been used to tether a parish bull whose stud services were used to supplement the rector's income. Other sources suggest, however, that the enormous stone may have been dragged or hauled in a cart to the church from the market place as early as 1815 by a former rector who like Elizabeth opposed bull-baiting and wished to put a stop to it.[38]

* * *

Over the next few decades, Elizabeth continued to write and distribute her tracts. Following a visit to Smithfield Market in London in 1823, where she was again appalled by the sight of animals suffering at the hands of their masters, she wrote a fierce attack on those involved. She invited her readers to visit Smithfield on a Monday, known as the great cattle day, between the hours of ten in the morning and three in the afternoon. Here, they could watch from an upper window as she had done and 'acquire a deeper insight into human nature - into the extremes of depravity into which it may be sunk, than they could easily obtain from any other quarter.'[39]

Gone now is the coaxing voice of 'John Sims' and Elizabeth is soon in full flight, describing in uncompromising terms what she has witnessed at the market. On Sunday evening, about 35,000 sheep and lambs are driven in to the central area. Later, the horned cattle are brought in but the space is insufficient so many are left loose in the road. A short, sharp goad is used and the point is driven with such severity into the most tender and sensitive parts of the animals that blood often flows. Elizabeth tells of the animals' suffering as they are forced to do the drovers' bidding. 'I have heard them bellow, and have seen their eyeballs roll, as in intense anguish from violent blows upon their horns (which I am told are exquisitely sensitive.)'[40] Eventually the animals rush in search of some secure shelter 'sometimes plunging their heads under carriages, and sometimes forcing their way through the close ranks of their confined companions.'[41] Once, she passed close by one of these wretched animals:

> 'Its perfect stillness under the infuriated passion of its tormentor, who had been battering its head with the most violent blows, in every direction, till it was evidently stunned and knew not which way to move, arrested my attention.'[42]

In that chilling moment, she was aware that any verbal remonstrance would have been extremely foolish.

> 'But the remonstrance conveyed in the pleading of my countenance caught the eye of a drover, who stood idly by, and who instantly lifted his weapon against me with such a savage, vindictive menace, as if he would, had he dared, have felled me to the ground.'[43]

Just as in her earlier writing about bull-baiting, Elizabeth makes the comparisons that are for her inescapable. If you do not show compassion to animals in your care, how will you treat other human beings? For it is not just the victims of cruelty that we should be concerned about but also the agents and perpetrators of the abuse. Whatever his rank, she writes, however 'cultivated his mind or polished his manners' the man who torments the animals in his care he must be a 'selfish, sordid, unfeeling character'.[44] She then combines her truly modern concern for animal welfare with religious arguments, insisting that Christian kindness and universal love can eradicate such selfishness.

It was the following year when she turned her fire directly onto slavery and the slave trade but as with her fight against cruelty to animals, she did not rely on her pen alone. And as she negotiated widowhood and turned her back on re-marriage, Elizabeth continued to mourn her husband. Every year, on the anniversary of Heyrick's death, she adopted her widow's garb and withdrew, effectively signalling her unavailability to potential suitors. Yet quiet acquiescence was not her style either and widowhood gave her a kind of freedom. Just as her original love affair had been passionate and unconstrained, so protest and rage came to mark her later years.

Chapter 8

'If we purchase the commodity, we participate in the crime'

'I own I am shocked at the purchase of slaves,
And fear those who buy them and sell them are knaves;
What I hear of their hardships, their tortures, and groans
Is almost enough to draw pity from stone
I pity them greatly, but I must be mum,
For how could we do without sugar and rum?
Especially sugar, so needful we see;
What, give up our desserts, our coffee, and tea?'

The verses are from a poem *Pity for Poor Africans* that was written by William Cowper in 1788,[1] one year after the twelve abolitionists had met in the London print shop to set up what some historians now regard as the first pressure group of the modern age.[2] Elizabeth and her Leicester writing friends would surely have been familiar with Cowper's poem as he was one of the most popular poets of his time. Sugar was Britain's largest import and was used in making pastries, puddings, cakes, and sweets as well as in various liquors. It sweetened the bitter taste of tea, coffee and chocolate and was a preservative in candied fruit, jam and marmalade. A recipe for apple pie in *The Art of Cookery Made Plain and Simple* by Hannah Glasse, first published in 1747,[3] reveals the type of ingredients that were available to households like the Coltmans and others who could afford them. Glasse advises the cook to 'make a good puff paste crust, lay some round the sides of the dish, pare and quarter the apples, and take out the cores, lay a row of apples thick, throw in half the sugar you design for your pie, mince a little lemon peel fine, throw over, and squeeze a little lemon over them, then a few cloves, here and there one, then the rest of your apples and the rest of your sugar. You must sweeten to your palate', she tells her reader.[4]

Apples were freely available during the harvest season and a walled garden might shelter a variety of fruit trees but sugar, like other luxury foodstuffs, had to be bought in local shops or direct from the importer. It was not the only slave-grown product available in the eighteenth century (tobacco, coffee and cotton could also be purchased) but since the country consumed so much of it, a boycott of sugar had the potential to become a powerful weapon in the struggle against slavery.[5] In the homes of the Leicester gentry, by the late 1780s, there was no shortage of sugar and controversy about its origins was growing.

* * *

Refined sugar had been all but unknown in England before the seventeenth century. Yet by the beginning of the eighteenth century, supporters of the trade in slave-grown sugar were ready to declare that it was a physical necessity and not simply a luxury.[6] It had health-giving properties, they claimed, and abstaining from it might damage a person's constitution. In 1714, one Dr Frederick Slare claimed sugar had cured his gums and whitened his teeth. Further experiments had shown him that it cured ailments of the hand, mouth and nostrils; it also healed the stomach and bowels. Infants were especially in need of it and Slare argued that since breast milk had a fine, delicate, and sweet taste, sugar could be used as a substitute. In the dedication to his treatise entitled *A Vindication of Sugars*[7] he boasts that the West Indian merchant 'who loads his ships with this sweet treasure' will be pleased with his defence of sugar. 'By this commodity have numbers of persons, of inconsiderable estates, raised plantations, and from thence have gained such wealth, as to return to their native country very rich, and have purchased and do daily purchase great estates.'[8] Slare lists a multitude of unlikely benefits to be gained from the consumption of sugar, with only one caution - 'to those that are inclining to be too fat.' These are members of the 'fair sex' who 'are afraid of their fine shapes'[9] but in the author's view, sugar's rich nutritional qualities more than compensated for any downside.

Dr Slare was not alone in his enthusiasm for sugar and consumption doubled in Britain between 1690 and 1740. By the mid-1770s, Britain was importing 100,000 casks of sugar a year, with each cask holding 63 gallons. British imports from tiny Grenada were worth eight times those from all of Canada[10] and by the 1780s, the French colony of Saint Domingue[11] on the Caribbean Island of Hispaniola was producing 30 per cent of the world's sugar.[12] On the other side of the Atlantic, however, there was now increasing opposition to the trade that was generating such extraordinary wealth at the expense of enslaved African people. The 1780s saw a surge in abolitionist sentiment and activity and in 1788, 102 petitions arrived at Westminster from places across the country.[13] Although women were rarely given the chance to sign them,[14] they may well have persuaded their menfolk to do so[15] and there were far more signatories now calling for an end to slavery than had ever been received on any other subject.[16] The British people were becoming better informed and some compelling first-hand accounts now found their way into the hands of sympathisers.

In 1787, a freed African slave named Ottobah Cugoano, who was by then living in London, published his autobiography.[17] In it, he wrote in bitter and forceful prose about his experiences in captivity. On a sugar plantation in Grenada, he had witnessed first-hand the cruel punishments inflicted on his fellow slaves merely for eating a piece of the sugar cane. Some had their teeth pulled out to discourage any repetition of the offence.[18] With his friend Olaudah Equiano, Cugoano would go on to become a radical abolitionist. Both were prominent members of the London-based pressure group that called themselves 'The Sons of Africa' and Cugoano's grim autobiography is believed to have found its way into the hands of King George III.[19]

Other campaigners were also now circulating their anti-slavery tracts. William Cowper wrote several more anti-slavery poems and the late 1780s also saw the publication of Hannah More's *Slavery, a poem* and *The Guinea Voyage* by James Stanfield. In its first year of operation, the newly formed 'Society for the Purpose of Effecting the Abolition of the Slave Trade' distributed more than 80,000 pamphlets and books.[20] Anti-slavery paintings and caricatures appeared and, most famously, a porcelain medallion was produced by Josiah Wedgwood (potter and friend of Thomas Clarkson) bearing an image that would become an icon. Wedgwood copied the original design from the Society's seal and in it, a kneeling slave lifts his shackled hands; an inscription reads 'Am I not a Man and a Brother?'

Like the diagram of the slave ship the *Brookes*, also produced in 1787,[21] the slave medallion found its way into sympathetic homes all over the country, reproduced on domestic objects such as milk jugs and sugar bowls. It also appeared on fashion accessories, including bracelets and hair pins. At abolition tea parties, where slave-grown sugar was banned, abolitionists sought support for their cause by distributing pamphlets, petitions and poems and during the winter of 1787-88, a step change occurred in the campaign. It was, comments Wilberforce's biographer, William Hague, 'a decisive moment of advance'.[22] If, in the early 1770s when Richard Cumberland's play *The West Indian* was being performed in London, there was little unease about England's dependence on slave-produced sugar, almost twenty years later the public mood had changed.

* * *

For radicals everywhere, the 1790s were a new dawn.[23] The American War of Independence had ended in 1783 with the signing of the Treaty of Paris and the recognition of the United States of America as an independent country. In France, the revolution was under way. Closer to home, the Coltman family could not have escaped hearing the furore that followed the publication in 1791 of Thomas Paine's *Rights of Man* which was soon on sale in their local bookshop.[24] The author was personally known to them and according to Catherine Hutton, he had travelled to America on the same ship as a relative of theirs named Robert Coltman. Hutton reports that Robert Coltman and Thomas Paine became close friends on board ship and since both favoured the American cause, agreed that in the American War of Independence (1775-1783) one of them should write and one should fight. Robert Coltman fought until the war ended in 1783 and Thomas Paine eventually produced his classic book.[25] In it, he strongly supported the French Revolution and the book sold as many as a million copies. It was popular with Protestant Dissenters amongst others and we can be sure the Coltman family would have read it.

Then, in the summer of 1791, a few months after Paine's book had been published, when the newly-married Elizabeth was setting up home and adjusting to her life at Bow Bridge, an anonymous pamphlet appeared which was soon so widely distributed that it eclipsed *Rights of Man*.[26] It was written by a radical named William Fox[27] and produced in collaboration with his fellow Dissenter Martha Gurney (1733-1816). Before becoming a pamphleteer, Fox had operated a London bookshop where he sold a number of unusual works, including Glasse's classic cookbook. Now, the bookseller himself took up his pen and in less than a year, Fox's anonymous pamphlet, entitled *An Address to the People of Great Britain, on the Propriety of Abstaining from West Indian Sugar and Rum* had gone through twenty-six editions in London and elsewhere. With some variations in its title, it eventually became the most widely distributed pamphlet of the eighteenth century.[28]

In it, Fox argues that if the people of Britain were to stop using sugar produced by slaves in the West Indies, if they were to refuse to buy it, this would bring about an end to the trade itself. For the crime of slavery does not rest solely with those who sell, hold and drive the slaves. We are virtually the agents of the consumer, he tells his readers; we are the first movers in the horrid process and by holding out the temptation, we are the original cause: 'If we purchase the commodity, we participate in the crime.'[29] Fox marshals a range of arguments against the continuance of slavery in a hard hitting and graphic portrayal of its abuses. What would be our reaction, he asks, if roles were reversed? What if some Africans wanted to establish sugar plantations and sailed up the Thames looking for people to enslave? 'Suppose our wives, our husbands, our children, our parents, our brethren swept away, and the fruit of their labour, produced with agonising hearts and trembling limbs, landed at the port of London. What would be our conduct? Should we say sugar is a necessary of life? I cannot do without it. Besides, the quantity I use is but a small proportion (.....) and paying for the sugar, I have a right to consume it however it may have been obtained.'[30] The pamphleteer hammers home his point. The only difference between his hypothetical case and what is actually happening, he argues, is that in one instance 'our relation to the enslaved is rather more remote' but 'in both cases they are our brethren.'[31]

In the opening lines of his pamphlet, Fox alludes to the defeat in Parliament in 1790 of legislation that would have put an end to the slave trade. Just a few months before, William Wilberforce, leader of the Parliamentary wing of the abolitionist movement, had failed to persuade the House of Commons to approve the bill which was defeated by 163 votes to 88. Parliament had been made more cautious and conservative by the recent outbreak of the French Revolution[32] (1789-1794) but Fox expresses a hope that discussions in the House of Commons and the way public attention has been excited by the debate would not have been in vain.

Shortly after the Parliamentary defeat, Thomas Clarkson left London, intending to gather additional evidence against the slave trade, and he discovered that the impact of Fox's pamphlet had indeed been widespread. He estimated that some 300,000 people in the country had abandoned the use of West Indian sugar and claimed that the boycott was proving a successful, practical strategy.[33] The 'anti-saccharite' campaign, as it was popularly known, was taking the abolition movement beyond Westminster, out into the towns, market places and the homes of ordinary citizens.

* * *

It was not the first consumer boycott in history although the word itself did not come into the language for nearly another century.[34] Inspiration may have come from events leading up to the Boston Tea Party in Massachusetts where famously, in 1773, (angered by the imposition of taxes by a Parliament in which they were not represented and by the competitive advantages enjoyed by the East India Company[35]), protestors boarded ships and threw 342 chests of tea into the harbour. In her book *Liberty's Daughters*,[36] Mary Beth Norton explores the way American women now found themselves on the frontline of a struggle against imperial Britain. Female cooperation was needed to implement a boycott of tea and, in the years preceding the revolution, abstention was widely seen as patriotic. Norton cites many recorded instances of female activism, occasions when women, their families and friends, believing their participation was important to America's future, refused to purchase or consume tea. Much as the women of England later understood their boycott of slave-produced sugar to be a vital and moral decision, their colonial sisters had political motivations, too. Never before, says Norton, had American women 'formally shouldered the responsibility of a public role, never before had they claimed a voice - even a compliant one - in public policy.'[37]

In both countries, women were ideally placed to lead the abstention movements. Typically, it was they who bought provisions for the family and knew which foodstuffs were available locally. They held significant power in domestic settings[38] and anti-slavery campaigners were keen to harness it. In England, the genteel Georgian home could be a place for informal discussions, salons and political meetings as much as for family life and here, women like Elizabeth and her mother were free to express their convictions. The case for sugar abstinence was given practical meaning.

Out in the community, too, women took the initiative. Excluded from Westminster and without a public voice, in the 1790s Leicester women began a door-to-door campaign. Led by Elizabeth's friend, Susanna Watts, they set out to persuade townsfolk to boycott slave-grown sugar.[39] Elizabeth herself visited all the grocers of Leicester to urge them to take part in the campaign. The women did not stand on platforms to address meetings but face to face, there were many opportunities on the doorstep to explain the cost in human terms of purchasing West Indian sugar. Though footsore, Elizabeth remained energetic and passionate, and unafraid of confrontation. Later, when she began to publish her pamphlets, Hutton remembers that Elizabeth's 'efforts with the pen were followed up by very vigorous and varied personal exertion.'[40]

* * *

The ideas that were circulating in the 1790s must have left some families bemused. It was a year after Thomas Paine's controversial book was published that *A Vindication of the Rights of Woman* appeared. Mary Wollstonecraft (1759-1797) was an acquaintance of Paine's and a fellow radical. Like him, she had greeted the fall of the Bastille in 1789 with joy and had even travelled to France to witness events there. Her book was an immediate best-seller and by the mid-1790s, Wollstonecraft had become the best-known female political writer in Europe.[41]

She was ten years Elizabeth's senior and like her, from a moderately prosperous background. Like her, she had little formal schooling and was largely self-educated. Her brother Ned on the other hand, received the kind of education reserved for the sons of gentlemen to prepare him for the bar. No doubt, comments her biographer, Barbara Taylor, the passionate indignation with which she later attacked the disparity between men and women's educational opportunities was 'anger acquired at first hand'.[42] A proper and systematic education could free women from their oppression. 'Strengthen the female mind by enlarging it, and there will be an end to blind obedience.'[43]

Several times in her *Vindication,* Wollstonecraft compares women to slaves, most memorably when she draws on the contemporary controversy about the sugar they produce and appeals to her readers to be guided by principles rather than prejudice:

> 'Is sugar always to be produced by vital blood? Is one half of the human species, like the poor African slaves, to be subject to prejudices that brutalise them, when principles would be a surer guard, only to sweeten the cup of man? Is not this indirectly to deny woman reason?'[44]

Now regarded as one of the founders of modern feminism, 'the mothership' as Zoe Williams calls her,[45] Wollstonecraft draws a complex analogy. Both women and colonial slaves are oppressed and brutalised by the actions of men. Abstaining from sugar will deny men the sweetness they crave, lessen the power they have over others, and give the boycott both radical and feminist potential, as the writer Claire Midgely explains.[46] Several decades later, when she comes to make her own case for sugar abstinence[47] Elizabeth focuses on its practical potential to undermine the slave economy, to inflict damage on slave holders and hurt them financially so that using slaves will not be in their best interests. If only people would stop buying West Indian sugar, she argues, those who grow and sell it would soon find themselves out of pocket.

No records suggest that Elizabeth ever met or corresponded with Wollstonecraft but hers was another book that the younger woman would certainly have read. They shared a passionate insistence on the need for greater equality in society, yet Elizabeth makes little specific mention of the position of women, in particular.[48] If she was influenced, for example, by Wollstonecraft's views on an ideal relationship,[49] if she tried to put such ideas into practice in her own marriage, there is no way for us to know this.[50]

* * *

As the 1790s progressed, Elizabeth struggled. A toxic marriage and a deepening depression absorbed most of her energies during this time and after her husband's sudden death, her distress was compounded. Many families in the town gave up using sugar in response to the campaign but interest in the cause fell away after 1792.[51] Further, such collective non-parliamentary action did not sit well with William Wilberforce, and by the summer of 1793, he feared that unruly popular movements would alienate the moderate MPs whose support was needed to abolish the slave trade.[52] The declaration of war with France had brought a clampdown on public meetings and extra-Parliamentary activity. Abolitionists were now linked with those promoting social and political upheaval and the war became a rallying cry against political reform in general. Following the success of revolution in France and America, there was now the explosive prospect of English civil unrest. Over time, build-up of stress points led to the expression of political radicalism but in the event, 'the talk about liberty, natural rights and a new order did not engender a new order of things.'[53] No-one stormed stately homes or cathedrals, no heads rolled. And many magistrates were fearful. The sugar abstinence campaign would eventually return but not until the 1820s and in the meantime, Elizabeth had to confront her demons.

Chapter 9

'Peace – when there is no peace'

Following her husband's death in 1797, Elizabeth slowly began to take stock. 'I am living at random - days, weeks, and months are passing over me unimproved - I will wait no longer in indolent expectation of these lively and strong impressions, but try to improve such as I have, lest the feeble and almost smothered voice of conscience should become quite extinct.'[1]

With a steely resolve, and no small amount of courage, Elizabeth now began to emerge from what her contemporaries described as a spiritual crisis. Gradually, she reached out, and now found herself increasingly drawn to Quaker friends. In 1798, a year after her husband's death, on a visit to see family friends in Hackney in London, she met Priscilla Gurney (1757-1828) who had become a Quaker minister a few years before.[2] Gurney was living at this time in the small Shropshire village of Coalbrookdale but she travelled widely. Her troubled young cousin Elizabeth Gurney (1780-1845, later Fry) was inspired by her calm and sympathetic relative[3] and formally adopted Quaker speech and dress soon after meeting her in 1799. Fry is now best remembered for her work in women's prisons, but although Elizabeth may well have been similarly inspired by her meeting with Priscilla Gurney, one anonymous biographer suggests that Elizabeth herself had begun prison visiting in Leicester some years earlier.[4]

Prison visiting was part of a Quaker tradition. In English prisons, women were often held with their children, packed into a few crowded and unsupervised rooms, in appalling conditions. Charity offered an outlet for the energies and talents of those who were barred from professional life and many genteel women seized these opportunities.[5] In Leicester, however, Elizabeth found her prison work hindered by bureaucracy. Some prisoners had been incarcerated for minor offences, such as poaching, but had not been released at the end of their sentences because they were unable to pay the 'gaol fees'. With the assistance of William Heyrick, her Tory brother-in-law, Elizabeth approached local magistrates and paid the fees herself, eventually securing the release of a number of inmates.[6]

Much later, she attacked the penal system in her writing[7] and she was not alone in her criticism. The system was known to be ineffectual; there was no proper police force, no public prosecutor for the Crown and many punishments were unnecessarily severe. Others, too, were insisting that laws prescribing execution for both murder and 'lifting handkerchiefs' could not be taken seriously and were not likely to reduce serious crime. Punishments must be proportionate; excessive chastisement would turn youthful offenders into incorrigible criminals.[8]

* * *

In the early 1800s, Elizabeth, like the two Gurney women, continued to battle with her religious and spiritual dilemmas. Often at this time Quakers recorded their private religious experiences in journals and 'spiritual autobiographies' and although she had not yet formally joined the Quakers, Elizabeth did this too.[9] In a study of the reading habits of a small group of Quakers living in Hackney in the late eighteenth and early nineteenth centuries, the writer, Jane Desforges, finds evidence in their diaries of their shared reading, their discussion of religious texts and their spiritual battles, often after a family death.[10] They were both consumers and creators of texts and it is easy to imagine how Elizabeth might come to feel comfortable in the presence of these serious-minded people. What emerges most clearly from the study by Desforges is, she says, the confidence of individuals about their own place in the world, as readers and writers.[11] They were not at all in awe of print culture and were always ready, as Elizabeth would soon be too, to compose and circulate their own writings.

Yet not everyone approved. In 1802 Catherine Hutton was ready with her candid opinion about what was drawing Elizabeth towards this group of Dissenting Protestants:

> 'A mind like hers, having renounced mankind, could only find refuge in religion. Methodism might have done but Quakerism presented itself, which was preferable in two respects: first, in enjoining a more savage renunciation of all her taste and elegant accomplishments. Secondly (for if we shut vanity in at one door, it will out at another) it presented a distant prospect of displaying her fine sense and elocution, for, if she continues a Quaker, she will certainly one day be a distinguished speaker.'[12]

It was rare for women to speak in public and although Quakers had a tradition of female ministry (as shown by Priscilla Gurney, for instance) and although they were comfortable with women expressing their views on spiritual, intellectual and political matters, within the group female institutional authority was very limited.[13] By now, after several years of contemplating her next move, Elizabeth was on the verge of formally joining the Quakers but it was not a decision she would take lightly. Her links with the Society of Friends were strengthening. An anonymous friend, writing decades later, explains how grief had awakened Elizabeth to a sense of what could be achieved if she were to dedicate her life to serving God. The loss of her husband was a turning point and a crisis in her spiritual history: 'Those who have sounded the "divine depths of sorrow" know best how to "weep with them that weep" and to comfort the broken hearted'.[14]

Elizabeth's decision to join the Quakers might then have been less about vanity, as claimed by Hutton, and more about compassion, more about finding ways to heal her own wounds as well as those of others. Elizabeth left few of her personal thoughts and feelings behind and without her missing diaries, her motivations cannot be known for sure. At the time of her marriage, there was a small Quaker meeting house in Soar Lane, near the River Soar, whose members retained the 'simplicity of dress and manners' that was traditionally associated with the group.[15] Yet there are no records that link Elizabeth with the Quakers at this time.

She may have retained happy memories from her childhood experiences at Hartshill, the Quaker school outside Atherstone in Warwickshire, as historian Shirley Aucott suggests[16] but family connections with other Nonconformist groups, including the Presbyterians, Unitarians and Baptists and since her marriage, with the Church of England itself, suggest that denominational boundaries were unimportant to her. And it was not until long after Elizabeth's death, that her sister Mary Ann, though she had not previously belonged to any church or religious society, began to show interest in the Quakers, declaring that when the time came, she wished to be considered as 'dying in union with Friends'. She was, Catherine Hutton recalls, well-read in their literature and by now, like 'her beloved and honoured sister' she counted many Friends amongst her most intimate associates.[17]

* * *

Between 1700 and 1800, Quaker numbers had declined in England. The historian Roy Porter describes them as a tight, stable group. They segregated themselves 'by their distinctive, aggressively humble manners, antiquated sombre dress and plain speech'[18] and they did not proselytize. In their seclusion, members practised 'quietism', a doctrine of Christian spirituality that emphasises contemplation and calm acceptance. Elizabeth had suffered a great deal and even before John Heyrick's death, had succumbed to regular and severe bouts of depression. In the immediate aftermath of her bereavement, she had removed herself from her family and friends almost completely.[19] Then, five years later, she took a decisive step; it was one that would lead her away from Leicester and her family and set her on an independent path.

It was 1802 when she travelled to York which, unlike Leicester, was not feeling the benefits of growing industrialisation and had little in the way of manufacturing. At this time, it was primarily a market centre, a place where goods and services were sold, where those from the surrounding districts could buy and sell their produce.[20] The Industrial Revolution had made little impact on the lives of the inhabitants and although the population was slowly increasing, economically York was lagging behind other local towns. Partly this was due to the corporation's structure, apathy and failure to encourage industry but as the historian Sheila Wright points out, it was also a consequence of York's geographical position. The town was on a plain, surrounded by estates owned by large land owners and it had none of the water power that had facilitated industrial expansion in places like Leeds, Halifax and Bradford.[21]

At the time of Elizabeth's visit, religious and civic life was dominated by the Anglican Church but York also had a small Nonconformist community. There were Unitarians, Presbyterians and Methodists, amongst others, and in 1780, about a hundred Quakers.[22] As Quaker ministry declined, increasingly members became obsessed with outward form and discipline rather than with inner spirituality. Wright notes that the doctrine of quietism was being challenged and that members were becoming more and more affluent. With their upward mobility, they began to integrate more and Quakerism was soon infiltrated by Evangelicals from the Established Church.[23] The York Meeting experienced a revival. At the heart of this revitalisation was a group of powerful and influential women led by Esther Tuke whose husband, William, was soon to become Elizabeth's close advisor.

* * *

William Tuke (1732-1822) was born in York to a Quaker family and from the mid-1760s, he was a committed activist. He was amongst those in the Society of Friends who wanted to see stricter discipline but his historical reputation rests now on his radical and compassionate approach to mental illness.[24] Local Quakers had become concerned at the death in 1790 of a widow from Leeds. Hannah Mills had died in the York asylum and fellow Quakers, her family and friends had been refused permission to visit and offer her religious consolation.[25] Doubts about her treatment and anxieties about conditions in the asylum more generally circulated in the city and with characteristic energy and focus, Tuke took up the baton. Against strong practical and ideological opposition, he eventually succeeded in launching The Retreat, a mental establishment run by Friends for Friends.

William Tuke's grandson, Samuel, later describes the location that was chosen for the institution. Set in the countryside outside York, about half a mile from the walls of the city, on elevated ground, the site 'afforded excellent air and water, as well as a very extensive and diversified prospect.'[26] Surrounded by beautiful gardens, it opened in 1796 and here Tuke and his colleagues pioneered a humane regime for the treatment of the insane. Echoing the words on the iconic anti-slavery medallion from 1787,[27] the insane, says the author Anne Digby, were to be understood as 'the brothers of the sane'[28] and were to be spoken to and treated as rational beings. In contrast to traditional asylums, where methods were typically brutal and constraining, The Retreat offered a mild regime, with minimal use of restraint and a pervasive religiosity. Humanity and discipline were cornerstones of an approach that became known as 'moral treatment'.[29] The comfort of patients outweighed the convenience of their lay keepers, who were seen simply as mere instruments of God's will. Recovery if it occurred would be as a result of Divine rather than human intervention.[30]

Some patients entered The Retreat with 'melancholia', or clinical depression. In 1800, one Dr Gilbert Thompson requested admittance for his patient, aged 22, who had 'repeatedly attempted to destroy her life'.[31] As she grieved after the death of her husband, Elizabeth, too, had contemplated suicide.[32] No records suggest that she actually ever attempted it but she had certainly sounded the 'depths of sorrow' and would have recognised the suffering of the melancholic. When she visited York, perhaps she imagined herself in The Retreat, being taken care of and finding peace in a therapeutic setting.

The York methods were not unique, and at the time, there were psychiatric reforms underway elsewhere in Europe too.[33] Yet therapists at The Retreat were apparently unaware of approaches being adopted in other places and they continued pragmatically to emphasise the restorative potential of kindness and good order within an attractive environment.[34] Tuke himself was becoming known in Quaker circles. It seems Elizabeth knew of him before she came to York, presumably from her Quaker contacts in London or Leicester, and in one of very few surviving letters to her mother, written from York in 1802, she describes him as 'a man of acknowledged experience' and 'sound judgement'.[35]

The Tukes became her friends. Long after her death, a pencil sketch that she had made of William Tuke one day, while he was taking his afternoon nap, surfaced in the Tuke family papers.[36] In 1877, Tuke's granddaughter photographed the sketch and sent it to her cousin - and though sadly neither the sketch nor the photograph have survived, it is evident that Elizabeth held a fond regard for the founder of The Retreat.

In York, she worked in a school for about three months, clearly in some sort of assistant teaching position. At this time, the only Protestant Nonconformist school in York was Trinity Lane school for Quaker girls, established in 1785 and run by Esther Tuke.[37] Though Elizabeth is not listed in the historical staff records, it is likely that she had obtained a training position here with the help of the Tukes. Ann Tuke (1767-1849), the couple's daughter and a contemporary of Elizabeth's, also helped at the school in York but she had begun her travelling ministry before Elizabeth's arrival[38] and it is probable that the two women never met. Ann Tuke (like Elizabeth) eventually also became involved in prison visiting and wrote about this work in 1819.[39] Here, she argued that it would be much better for all if a man who had been imprisoned for stealing was instead kept in work until he had made full restitution to his victim and paid all their expenses. Elizabeth had adopted the same approach in her dealings with a Leicester beggar. She found the man a job so he could repay his debt and avoid prison.[40]

By the time of her visit to York, Elizabeth was already planning to set up her own girls' school back in Leicester. She had returned to live in her marital home at Bow Bridge House and she would have seen her experience at Trinity Lane as an important stepping stone. After initially offering their support, her parents then appeared to oppose her plans and their criticisms must have stung. As the situation developed, back in Leicester friends were gossiping and expressing their disapproval. Some believed she was acting out of sentiment without sufficient regard for the shortcomings of the house at Bow Bridge. There is doubt over some funding that Elizabeth had believed would be forthcoming and her entire project was in jeopardy. The core of the disagreement appears to be the suitability and location of the property. In flinty and impassioned language, Elizabeth fights her corner. How could those who have never lived in the house know more about its suitability than she does? Just because her family and friends disagree with her, as her mother claims, this doesn't mean her 'own judgement is to be discarded as a useless thing'. She has already been offered pupils for her school and now, after three months teaching in York, she is confirmed in her belief that such employment would be congenial and satisfying for her. She mentions William Tuke, who supports her Bow Bridge proposal, in an effort, she says, to add some weight to her argument.[41]

Angrily, Elizabeth now accuses her mother of closing up her way 'on every side'. Her mother's opposition to the proposed school is forcing her to abandon the idea and has left her feeling mortified, the more so since it was apparently unexpected. She acknowledges her mother's concern for her welfare but remains 'very doubtful whether she will always think that on this occasion she has taken the most likely means of securing it.'[42] Her combative tone readily calls to mind the letters her own mother had written to the man she would eventually marry during their prolonged courtship. When her pride was wounded, like her daughter now, she had stood up angrily to confront her critics.

Teaching was one of the few occupations open to women from the middle ranks of Georgian society and the number of schools for girls was increasing. In the 1780s, Mary Wollstonecraft had set one up at Newington Green in London, though it taught little more than reading, sewing and drawing.[43] A woman might also take up her pen, as Wollstonecraft later did, and Elizabeth would have known too that, before her marriage, her own mother was a published author.[44] Elizabeth herself had no need of a salary since she received an allowance from her father but she is now determined to make her own way. She is bitter at the prospect of having to abandon all thoughts of an independent future. She will, she says, be able to compose her mind when the time comes to return home 'but I shall not so easily lose the conviction that I have both inclination and capacity for more active employment….,' work she insists that would be of benefit both to her and to those in her care. Nevertheless, she is impatient to return. In a terse acknowledgement of the family tensions, at the end of her letter she remarks 'I am more anxious to return home than any of you can be to have me…'.[45]

We know that somehow, in the end, her parents were obliged to give way. Documents show that a school ran successfully at Bow Bridge for several years until an outbreak of typhus led to its relocation to Welford Road.[46] It is also evident from surviving records that Elizabeth had the support of her friend Susanna Watts who taught French at her school.[47]

* * *

Back in York that year, as she continued to plan her future, Elizabeth had met another prominent Quaker, an American lawyer and grammarian named Lindley Murray (1745-1826). Born in Philadelphia, Murray had settled in England in 1784 and lived in Holgate, near York.[48] At the behest in 1795 of a couple of teachers at Trinity Lane school, Murray had written and published an English grammar book containing rules, exercises, and readings. It became hugely popular and eventually was published in many languages. He came to be known as the 'father of English grammar'[49] and Elizabeth was one of many teachers who valued his textbooks.

He and Elizabeth stayed in touch after her visit to York and in 1807 she described him as 'one of those *perfect* characters from whose intimate inspection I cannot help shrinking'.[50] Murray sent Elizabeth the introduction to his 'French Reader', in the evident hope that it might help her with learning the language[51] but for her, he seemed 'too much raised above the common level to be able to sympathise with such wanderers as myself'.[52]

Plainly, though she found Murray a little intimidating, she was a serious and conscientious teacher and though sources are now scant, she also appears to have been close to at least one of her pupils. Isabella Perry's father was an army friend of John Heyrick's, and an officer in the same regiment, who had lost his wife while the men were together in barracks in Ireland.[53] On her death bed, Mrs Perry commended her children, especially Isabella, to the care of Elizabeth. Isabella was taken to Malta by her father with his regiment but when he died there of consumption, his daughter, aged about 14, returned to England. Elizabeth, now widowed and living with her parents in Leicester, took the girl in.

Eventually, as Isabella sought employment, various teaching positions were found for her with families in Nottingham, Germany, and then Sussex where she stayed with the Reverend Lewis Way. Way was a religious activist who had been influenced by evangelical clergymen of the period, including William Wilberforce.[54] From Way's palatial residence at Stansted Park in 1819, Isabella wrote to Elizabeth, addressing her as 'my dearest Mother' and describing in detail her grand new surroundings.

Yet the young Isabella's life was already nearing its close. After a few years of toil, 'sinking and weary,' she returned to be with Elizabeth, and on the 6 May 1824, at the age of only 29, she died. She had passed we are told 'as a pilgrim from station to station, having no abiding city'[55] and it was Elizabeth and her sister Mary Ann who cared for her at the end. To Elizabeth, despite the girl's 'rustic and coarse' appearance, Isabella was 'a diamond still' with a sweet temper and a grateful disposition. The Coltman family home was the only one Isabella ever knew and here the arms of her adopted mother had 'been ever stretched out towards her'.[56]

* * *

It was September 1806 when Elizabeth eventually replied to a letter she had received from her friend Mary Lloyd (née Farmer, d. c1821). She began in characteristically forthright if troubled terms:

> '...whenever I have attempted to reply to thy letter, the conviction has painfully revived that all my religious friends are permitted to be under a delusion respecting my real character and state of mind and consequently are induced to say peace - when there is no peace.'[57]

Elizabeth's correspondent lived in Bingley House in Birmingham and was married to Charles Lloyd (1748-1828), who was a partner in the forerunner of Lloyd's Bank.[58] The family were Quakers and although his religion prevented him from holding public office, Charles was active in community life and supported the campaign to abolish the slave trade.[59] Mary Capper was another Quaker contact and after one of Elizabeth's visits to Birmingham in 1806, Capper wrote to her. The two had apparently missed the chance to meet in person but Capper writes warmly, in the hope that a 'word of encouragement from a fellow traveller' will be acceptable. She understands that even 'in the midst of society' anyone can feel lonely:

> 'I feel for thee, dear Elizabeth, in all thy difficulties; in all thy doubts seek the power of 'within', silently, patiently wait, resign thyself as thou art to the disposal of a gracious Creator.'[60]

Increasingly, as she continued to suffer, Elizabeth sought the company of individual Friends until on 23 March 1807, the Leicester Quakers received notice from her that she wished to join them - and only two days later, the Slave Trade Act was passed in the British Parliament. This legislation abolished the trade that had taken more than three million enslaved Africans onto British ships for the infamous middle passage.[61] Its prohibition was greeted triumphantly by abolitionists everywhere and as his Parliamentary colleagues paid tribute to him, William Wilberforce wept.[62] Yet it was not so much Parliamentary leadership as public pressure and twenty years of community campaigning that had led to this moment. Elizabeth's decision to join the Quakers at this time may well have been influenced by political events and her determination to work for the complete elimination of slavery itself but she was also drawing comfort from the support of her Quaker contacts. A couple of months after her initial approach to the Leicester group, she was visited by two of them; they reported back to their colleagues 'that they felt sympathy with her' and believed she understood their religious principles as well as the need to conform to them.[63] By now, Elizabeth had shared her personal feelings of loneliness and depression with several Quaker friends and when, in June 1807 she converted to the religion 'by convincement,' she formally accepted their core beliefs.

This did not entail a dramatic shift in her outlook. The Quakers' belief in a need for 'forgetfulness of self,' simplicity and withdrawal from the world chimed with the tenets of her existing life. Ever since John Heyrick's death, she had regularly withdrawn into solitude and before her conversion, she had already begun dressing in dark sombre colours. Already she looked 'Quakerish' as Jane Eyre would later describe herself in Charlotte Brontë's novel.[64] Quaker dress was a by-word for plainness but the style seemed to suit Elizabeth. The outspoken Catherine Hutton had remarked to Mary Ann after Elizabeth's visit to see her in 1806 that she rejoiced to see her sister looking so well. 'It requires no strength of imagination to fancy her Bess Coltman still.'[65] A few years later, after another of Elizabeth's visits to Birmingham, Hutton tells Mary Ann that she would never forget the two hours she had spent with her sister. 'Such an open, unreserved communication of each other's thoughts was new and most delightful to me. She laid aside the Quaker, and while I admired Mrs Heyrick, I saw and loved Bess Coltman.'[66]

Elizabeth's marriage had taken her away from her Nonconformist childhood but now in joining the Quakers, and again rejecting the established church, she embraced some distinctive beliefs. The Quaker understanding that everyone had a direct relationship with God meant that all were equal before Him, that there was no need for intermediaries, for churches, priests and sacraments. The inner or inward light, the direct awareness of God, allowed a person to know God's will for them and as she struggled with her depression, and listened to her friends' counsel, Elizabeth would have understood that women might assume a role and an importance not available to them in other religious denominations. The Quakers are still celebrated as leaders in the campaign against slavery in the eighteenth century but they came to that position at least partly because for generations many of them were themselves slave holders.[67] Elizabeth's own experiences of suffering and her observations of the way others were oppressed (in prisons, workhouses and factories) had brought her to the Quakers and their values would now underpin her activism.

Then, one year after her conversion, her father died. To a Quaker, 'a good death' was one borne with patience and resignation, in which the dying person felt supported by the hand of God.[68] Those at the death bed would pray for death to come easily. According to Samuel, it was Elizabeth who first noticed a change in her father's features 'which indicated the near approach of dissolution.' She 'gently asked if he felt himself supported by the arms of the Almighty and equal to meet the approaching conflict? His reply was by a most expressive smile of joy and affectionate grasp of her hand, adding 'Fear not, fear not, fear not.'[69]

John Coltman was a solitary and unassuming man, known for his candour and his love of truth. He held a firm belief in the principles of civil and religious freedom[70] but beyond his Nonconformity, we know little of his personal faith. Did he believe (as his family and most of his contemporaries did) in a life beyond the grave? Samuel seems to suggest he may not have done but as John Coltman lay dying, his children were left with 'a most grateful impression on all our minds; and an assurance of the happy change which took place in our father's views respecting futurity'. This 'afforded consolation and support to our beloved mother which appeared supernatural.'[71] Elizabeth, too, would have been heartened by her father's final assurances that he was approaching his end with calm acceptance. No devout daughter would have wanted to believe otherwise.

After John Coltman's death, Elizabeth brought her mother and sister Mary Ann to Bow Bridge House to be with her. Her mother by now 'was feeling some of the encroachments of time, but retaining much sprightliness and activity'.[72] Mary Ann wrote to a friend describing a visit to Samuel's house: 'A party of friends were assembled, and I was told that my mother appeared the life of the company; she took a large share in the conversation, and discovered more animation and vivacity than any one present.' During the evening, she had even 'harangued' those present and had persuaded three to become subscribers to the Bible Society which she regarded as a 'very important and useful institution'.[73] Never an easy woman to say no to, Mrs Coltman was pleased she had 'done some good' but she lived only a few weeks more.

Elizabeth's diary (now lost) recorded the moment on 21 January 1811, between two and three in the morning, when 'the spirit of our dear mother took wing for that world where her hopes and affections had long been fixed, and for which divine grace appeared to have sweetly prepared her.'[74] She died peacefully and her passing, according to her eldest daughter, drew two of her children (probably Elizabeth herself and Mary Ann) closer to

God. Mrs Coltman was buried in Friar Lane Chapelyard, with her husband, and their young son Rowland.

Catherine Hutton, her admiring friend, wrote a warm tribute in the *Monthly Magazine,* the Dissenters' journal which was produced by the Leicester bookshop owner, Richard Phillips. This magazine regularly carried contributions from celebrated writers, including Samuel Taylor Coleridge, and was dedicated to the propagation of liberal principles.[75] Hutton's piece described Mrs Coltman as 'a woman of uncommon genius and taste' whose talents 'had been buried in private life' and who 'devoted her whole time, after her marriage, to the Service of her Maker, the duties of her family, and the mitigation of distress of those around her.'[76]

PART IV

1800–1820

Chapter 10

'The Rights of the Poor'

It was about half past five in the morning when a small group of men were removed from Leicester County Gaol and taken in a covered cart to a location near the Infirmary. They immediately began to pray and, according to a local newspaper, spent the greater part of that morning 'devoutly engaged'. At about twelve o'clock, they made their appearance on the platform, chained together by the wrist. One of the men invited the assembled crowd (estimated at about 15,000) to join with them in a hymn which he led 'in a most audible and distinct manner.' He was joined by his companions who 'sang with equally firm voices.' Then the executioner proceeded to adjust the ropes about the culprits' necks and the prisoners shook hands with each other. They 'bade a last farewell to several of their friends whom they recognised before them, throwing to each some oranges, with a request that they might be given to their children.' There were more handshakes, and then at about half past twelve one of the men 'gave a signal by stamping his foot when the fatal board fell and they were launched into eternity without much struggling…' Throughout proceedings, the six young Luddites[1] were said to have 'conducted themselves with a degree of firmness seldom witnessed on such a melancholy occasion.' They showed 'unexampled coolness,' concluded the report, and they died with 'a composure we scarcely know how to express.'[2]

It was April, 1817. Elizabeth's father, who had pioneered the use of machines in the local hosiery trade decades before and faced the wrath of his workers as a consequence,[3] had now been dead some nine years. His two sons had been left to run the business as the industrial unrest continued. The Luddites in Leicester were protesting against the introduction of wide frame machines to make one long piece of knitted fabric which was then cut up into pieces and sewn together as socks. These cheap 'cut-ups' were poor quality and unravelled easily; they flooded the market and threatened to put the traditional framework knitters out of business. Machine breaking as a form of protest was commonplace throughout the eighteenth century and Elizabeth would have remembered the factory workers' attack on her family home some thirty years before. By 1812, the law had made machine-breaking a crime punishable by death. The death sentence was cherished by the country's rulers and between 1688 and 1820 the number of capital statutes grew from about 50 to over 200. Nearly all of these statutes related to offences against property which the law openly prized above human life.[4]

If the journalists of Leicester were lost for words after the executions in 1817, the town's inhabitants were also shocked by what they witnessed. Might Elizabeth have seen the executions that day? Some years later, she recalls the 'never-to-be-forgotten spectacle' of men 'paying the forfeit of their lives' on the scaffold for demanding better wages and better living conditions for their families.[5] Leicester historian, Temple Patterson, claims that although the fear of it lived on, Luddism died with these six men on the scaffold.[6] And in the same year, Elizabeth wrote the first of her pamphlets about workers' rights. In *Exposition of one Principal Cause of the National Distress particularly in Manufacturing Districts,* she argued that since the introduction of machines and the development of large manufacturing towns, workers had 'lost the simple, frugal, healthy and comparatively virtuous habits of the peasant.'[7] She does not mention the Luddites by name but her sympathies are plain and as an attack on the family's commercial activities, it is only thinly veiled. As well as nostalgia for the past, Elizabeth held a deep dislike of industrialism and a manufacturing system that brought profound inequalities. With the industrial revolution well underway,[8] wages were falling and distress amongst framework knitters in Leicester was becoming severe as they faced a savage reduction in living standards. Such poverty was not accidental, argued Elizabeth, but caused by the greed of the rich who were 'grinding the faces of the poor'.[9]

Time and again in her pamphlets, she takes aim at the rich and privileged. By 1815, the Napoleonic Wars had come to an end and cheap imported grain was again available. The British government now sought to protect the financial interests of their landowners, including many who were members of Parliament, by imposing tariffs on the imported grain. These protectionist measures (known as the Corn Laws) kept domestic prices high and benefited land owners and farmers, but those who had to pay the higher prices to feed their families, suffered distress and increased hardship. Further, as local factory owners sought to protect their own incomes and profits, they resorted, Elizabeth claimed, to the simple expedient of reducing wages for their workers. The peasant had been lured to the town by the temptation of higher wages but these were curtailed soon after his arrival.

The story of the framework knitters' struggles to survive during the Industrial Revolution is one of the most harrowing.[10] By 1819, many workers had been reduced to wages as low as four to seven shillings a week for sixteen to eighteen hours work per day and Leicestershire framework knitters were not receiving enough to 'sustain nature'.[11] The provisions of the Poor Law provided scant relief for those most badly affected and Elizabeth witnessed poverty every day on Leicester's streets. It was said that she spent time in summer vacations living in a shepherd's cottage on a diet of potatoes 'anxious to prove for herself how life could be supported on the scanty fare to which these poor men restricted themselves'[12] and she became a passionate advocate for the poor. Although workers are nominally free, she writes, they 'are condemned to incessant labour for a scanty, wretched, and precarious subsistence'; they are 'shut out as effectually as the enslaved African, from all the common blessings and common enjoyments of existence.'[13] 'The Rights of Man - the Rights of Woman - the Rights of Brutes - have been boldly advanced,' she argues, 'but *the Rights of the Poor* still remain unadvocated.'[14]

* * *

In the same year that Elizabeth published her *Exposition,* and compared workers to slaves, the Leicester framework knitters themselves put forward a set of resolutions and like thousands of other articulate workers at the time, they questioned the social and economic structure of industrial capitalism.[15] In opposition to the facts of orthodox political economy, they placed their own facts and their own arithmetic and argued that if you reduce the wages paid to workers, to the same extent you also reduce their power to purchase and consume manufactured goods. If you pay the workers more, they will be able to support their families and buy the goods they need, which in turn keeps them in work and the factories running. In essence, this is Elizabeth's argument too. It is an early 'under-consumption theory of capitalist crisis'[16] and a challenge to the rhetoric of the free market now supported by her older brother. As one of the town's leading manufacturers, John has become a keen advocate of *laissez-faire* policies, and he has opposed the local framework knitters' demands for improved wages at every opportunity.[17] In 1812, though some workmen feared the Leicester trade was being ruined by inferior products, John Coltman had argued that the hosiers were entitled to produce anything the market required, including cheaper goods that would meet foreign competition.[18] Employment conditions deteriorated further with the end of the Napoleonic wars in 1815 when large numbers of servicemen returned and sought work in the town. If Elizabeth had discussed local employment with her brother, he would undoubtedly have pointed out that the labour market was already swollen and over-crowded. With the end of the wars, fancy hosiery for the military was no longer required and as demand for their goods diminished, in 1816-1817 the framework knitters' wages fell by 30-40 per cent.[19]

At length, what Elizabeth calls this 'spirit of trade' reached its limits. The suffering spread as more and more people found they had too little to live on. Then, in language that would have resonated with her more liberal readers, she again compares the workman's lot to that of the slave: 'He labours hard as many hours as the slave, for a subsistence as scanty, under fear of a lash which lacerates the mind, as deeply as that of the slave-driver does the body.'[20]

She goes on to appeal to the religious understandings of her contemporaries. Those who are Christian only in name, who profess their belief in the gospel but do not follow it, are guilty of hypocrisy. Both slavery and worker poverty are wrong, she writes, and both are 'directly contrary to the Divine will'.[21] It is the divine will, she explains, that instructs us to open our hands wide, to 'feed the hungry, clothe the naked, visit the sick and the prisoner.' When we submit to this Will, and learn to love our neighbours as ourselves, the sufferings of the poor will be relieved. This is the Christian principle which, if it is put into operation, will 'convert this *howling wilderness* (such is literally the present state of this country to the great mass of its population) into a blooming, fertile garden.'[22]

For Elizabeth saw the industrial crisis in spiritual and moral terms; the 'spirit of trade' was bringing the country to its knees. She mocks the *laissez-faire* merchants and manufacturers, those who (like her brother John) believe that 'Things will find their own level.' These employers will 'share in the same ruin with the workman,' and their opposition to God's law of universal love will carry its own punishment. 'The process is sometimes slow, but always sure. The laws by which the natural world is governed, are not more certain than those which govern the moral world.'[23] She wanted to see a legal minimum wage and she supported trade unions, later arguing that since labour was the only 'property' the workers possessed,[24] they were entitled to strike to protect their livelihoods.[25] She warned that worker unrest was simmering beneath the surface of everyday life: 'It may be most fallacious reasoning to conclude, that because the country has been so long tranquil, that therefore, it will remain so. A long continued and dead calm often precedes a tremendous explosion!'[26] In 1819, two years after making this prediction, Elizabeth would have been unsurprised to hear of an event that quickly became known as the Peterloo Massacre. On a sunny August day, a peaceful gathering of an estimated 100,000 people met in fields near Manchester to demand Parliamentary reform. The crowd was charged by a local force of volunteer soldiers on horseback and between ten and twenty people were killed. Hundreds were injured. Elizabeth continued to warn her readers that although popular tumults may have been suppressed, 'popular disaffection' was spreading rapidly and the great mass of the working population was starving.[27] A few months later, Samuel echoed his sister's warning in a letter home to his wife. Conduct like that of the 'cold blooded Manchester butchers' would cause rebellion. It was better, he declared, 'to be butchered and enslaved by a despot than by our own rulers.'[28]

* * *

During the 1820s, as the framework knitters' wages rose and fell, there was strong public support for their cause.[29] Elizabeth's was not a lone voice, and hundreds of pounds were raised from local sympathisers. The Combination Acts passed during the Napoleonic wars had made any sort of strike action illegal but their repeal in 1824 and 1825 (which in Leicester was opposed by John Coltman) led to a wave of strikes and renewed struggles. In 1825, Elizabeth directly addressed the hosiers of Leicester. In the midst of such long running industrial unrest,[30] and much ill-feeling both on the part of the framework knitters and their employers, Elizabeth weighed in again with an attack on those she believed were best placed to avert a calamity. The workers had been on strike, without employment or sustenance, for a considerable period; all that was needed to end their suffering was for their masters to meet their wage demands or at least to meet them half-way. 'Did it never occur to you that, between master and workmen, there are reciprocal duties?'[31]

Her passionate rebukes cannot have made easy reading for her brothers and at times, her savage accusations of hypocrisy, even immorality, might well have stung. Yet she continued to insist that it was in everyone's interest to pay the workers well. Their wages must be increased and only changes in the law could bring this about. The establishment of schools, and the building of new churches, would not increase wages for the poor; it would simply 'quicken their sense of degradation and misery'.[32] Workers' labour was being devalued by their low wages. In an essay that had first appeared in 1825 in the *Edinburgh Review* attributed to 'one of the most enlightened and philanthropic statesmen of the age' but believed now to have been written by Elizabeth,[33] she again returns to her wages theme. 'The essential interests of society require that the rate of wages should be elevated as high as possible; that a taste for comforts and enjoyments of life should be widely diffused,' she writes.[34] In general, 'high wages are the keenest

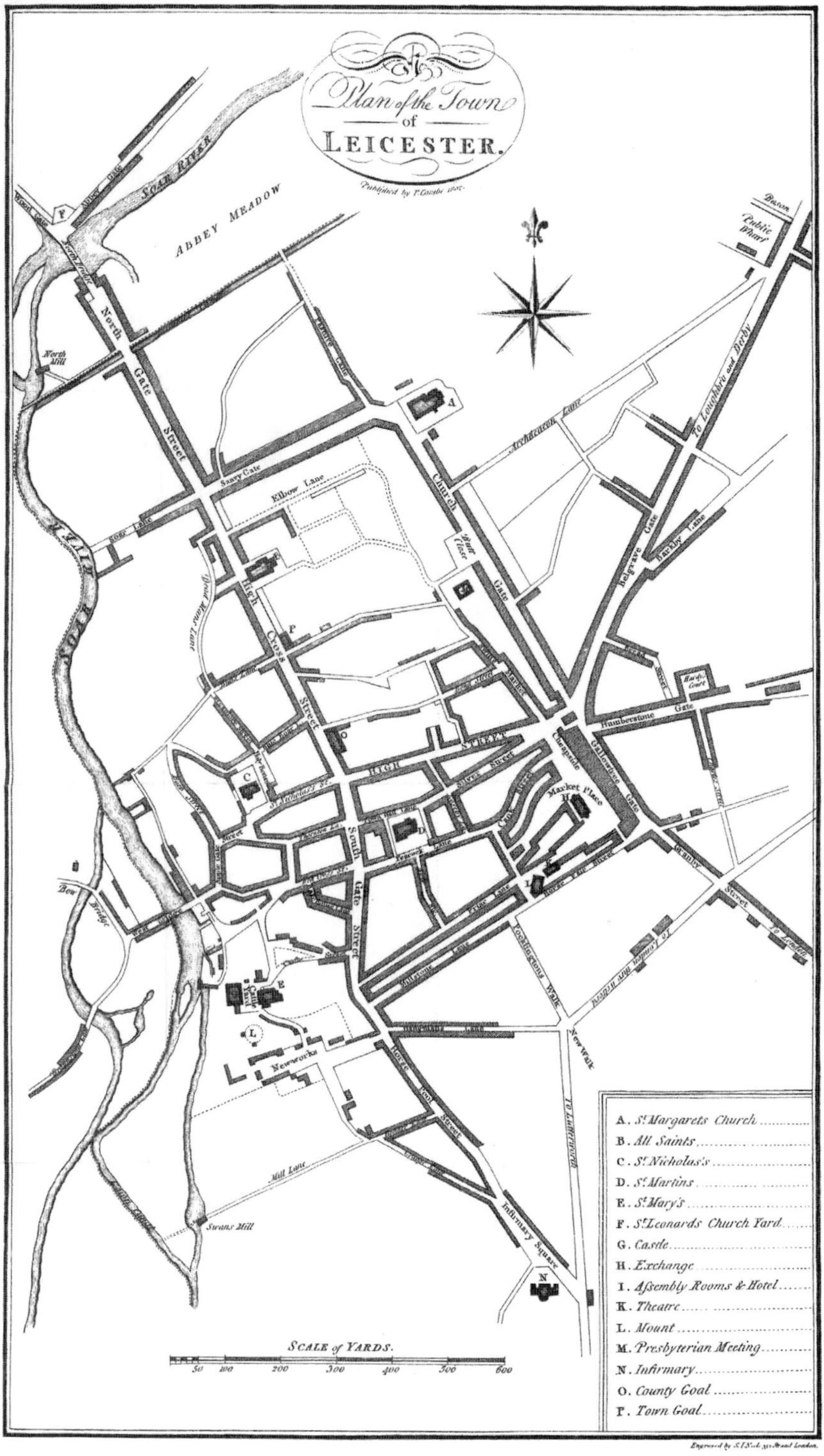

1. A plan of Leicester.

This map of the town was published in 1802 and included by Susanna Watts in her guide book 'A Walk Through Leicester.' Watts was a close friend of Elizabeth's. Unusually for the time, Watts made a living with her writing and was able to support her widowed and impoverished mother.

2. Shambles Lane, Leicester.
In an early chapter of his memoir, Elizabeth's younger brother Samuel recalls growing up on Shambles Lane. It took its name from a nearby 'shambles' or butcher's slaughter house but by the early nineteenth century, had become known as St. Nicholas Street.

Above left: **3. Portrait of Elizabeth's mother, also named Elizabeth.**

Above right: **4. Portrait of Elizabeth's father, John.** The artist of these family portraits is unknown. The style of the images suggests they were the work of an amateur, quite possibly Elizabeth herself.

Right: **5. Elizabeth's older brother John.** John and his brother Samuel inherited the hosiery business from their father. John became a staunch advocate for employers' rights in the town, opposing all efforts by the framework knitters to improve their wages.

6. Elizabeth's youngest brother, Rowland.
Notes on the reverse side of this watercolour portrait tell us that it was Elizabeth's work, completed when she herself was still a child, and without any instruction.

7. Maria at Moulines, by Angelica Kauffman (1741-1807).
This painting by Angelica Kauffman was thought to have provided inspiration for Elizabeth's needlework. As a fifteen- year-old girl, she embroidered a tiny medallion with this figure of Maria who was a character in a novel by Laurence Sterne.

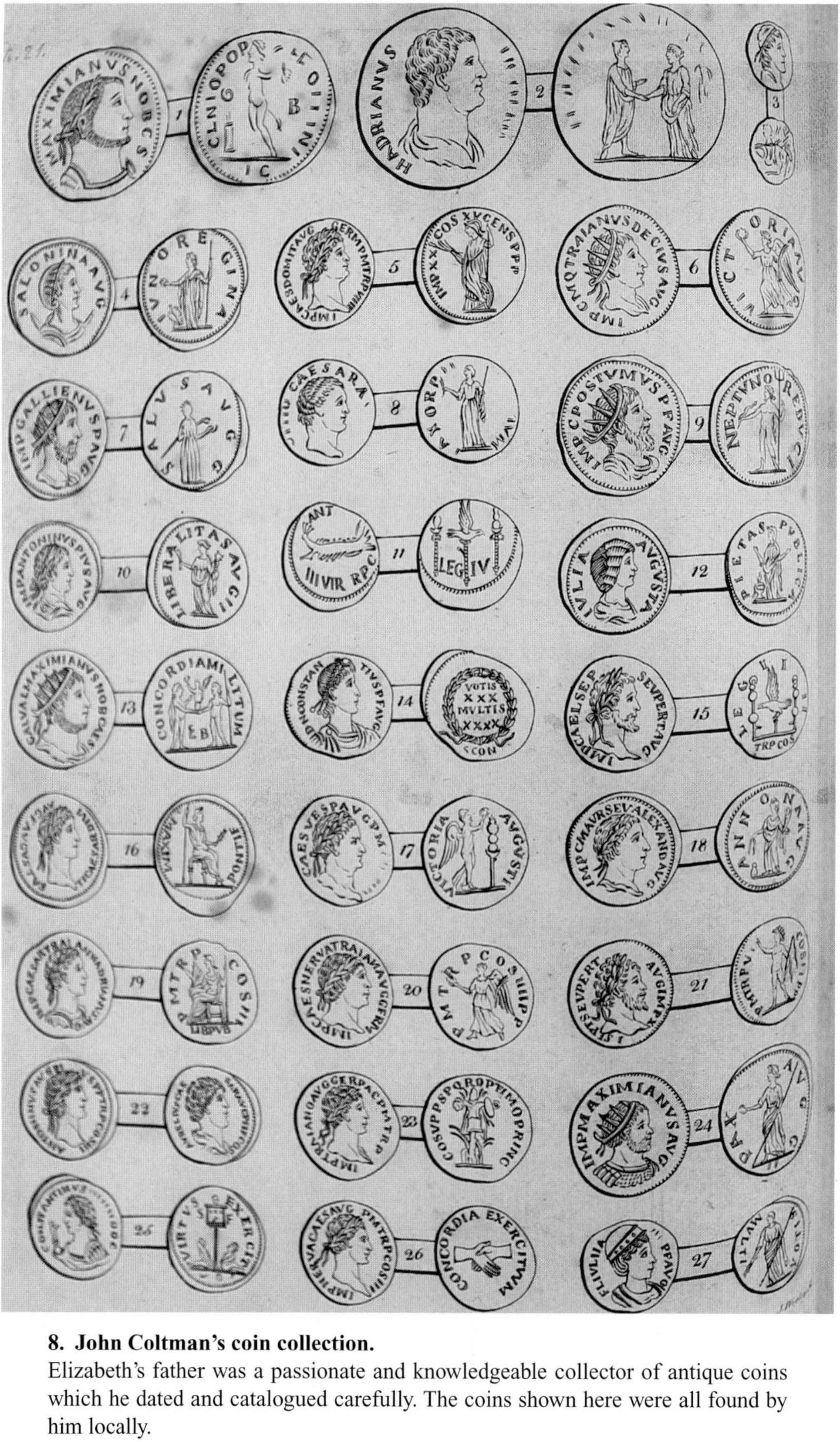

8. John Coltman's coin collection.
Elizabeth's father was a passionate and knowledgeable collector of antique coins which he dated and catalogued carefully. The coins shown here were all found by him locally.

9. St Nicholas Church.
The Anglican St Nicholas Church was opposite the Coltman family home but as religious nonconformists, they worshipped instead at the Great Meeting chapel, which was a short walk away.

10. The Jewry Wall, in front of St Nicholas church.
The Roman Jewry Wall in front of St Nicholas Church provided rich pickings for John Coltman in his search for coins.

ROTHLEY TEMPLE, LEICESTERSHIRE, THE BIRTHPLACE OF LORD MACAULAY.

11. Views of Rothley Temple in Leicestershire, which were published in 1893 in The Illustrated London News.

Rothley Temple in Leicestershire was the family home of the Babington family and in the late eighteenth century, it became a meeting place for leading abolitionists, including Zachary Macaulay, whose sister had married Thomas Babington. Zachary Macaulay became Elizabeth's sympathetic advisor.

12. 'Taste in High Life'.
The painting here was completed by William Hogarth in about 1742 and in it, he satirises fashionable society and their use of black domestic servants.

13. Framework Knitters workshop in Bonsall.
One of the early framework knitters' workshops in The Dale in Bonsall was first built in 1737. This photograph was taken in 2017, and the building has since been renovated.

***Above left*: 14. Bull stone, Bonsall.**
The bull-stone now located in the local church in Bonsall, Derbyshire, is believed to have been used to tie the bull down during his torment. On one occasion in 1809, Elizabeth freed a bull by purchasing it and then wrote her first pamphlets in which she campaigned against animal cruelty.

***Above right*: 15. Reverend Robert Throsby.**
Elizabeth's friend Susanna Watts pasted this image of the Reverend Throsby in her scrapbook after the Leicester women had rejected his attempt to join their literary society.

16. The Art of Stocking Framework Knitting.
The engraving dates from 1750. Elizabeth's father John Coltman was just embarking (albeit reluctantly) on a business career in the hosiery trade and this workshop is typical of those in Leicester at this time.

***Above left*: 17. 'Am I not a Man and a Brother?'**
This iconic image, made in about 1787, became an international symbol for the abolitionist movement. It was created by the ceramist Josiah Wedgewood and appeared on sugar bowls, brooches and medallions. The words became a famous campaign slogan.

***Above right*: 18. 'Am I not a woman and a Sister?'**
In the 1830s, in a conscious echo of the earlier image, this one appeared emphasising the impact of slavery on women. William Lloyd Garrison, American abolitionist and an admirer of Elizabeth's writing, placed the image of a female slave in chains in his newspaper 'The Liberator' in 1832.

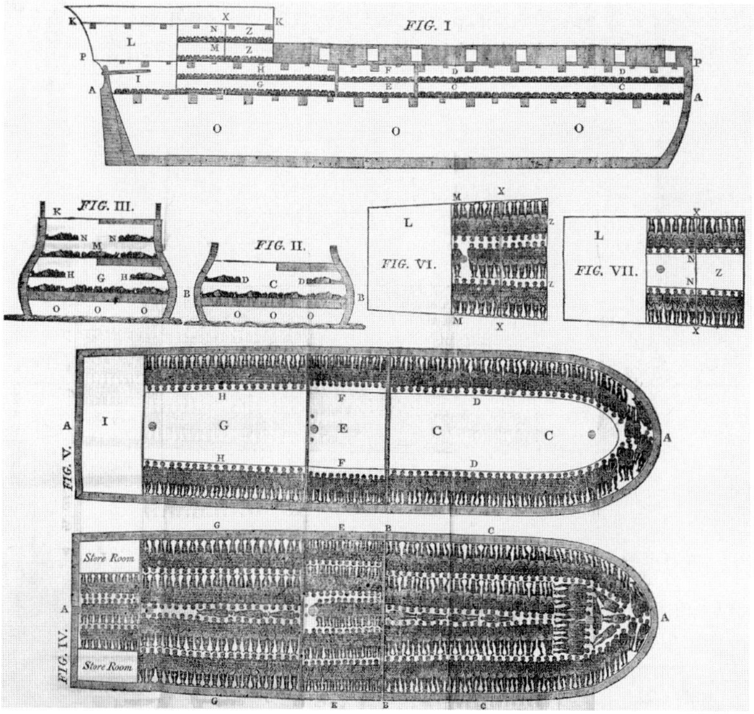

19. The Slave ship 'Brookes' of Liverpool.
This illustration was also created in 1787 and widely disseminated by abolitionists. Although only 450 slaves are shown here, the slave ship 'Brookes' was known to have carried six or seven hundred at times.

TERMINATION
OF SLAVERY
BRITANNIA, RENOWN'D O'ER THE WAVES.
FOR THE HATRED SHE EVER HAS SHOWN
AUGUST 1ST
1838
TO THE BLACK-SCEPTRED RULERS OF SLAVES.
RESOLVES TO HAVE NONE OF HER OWN.

20. Britannia giving freedom.

First published in 1798, when anti-slavery debates in Britain were at their height, this abolitionist illustration reinforces attitudes related to empire and national superiority and fails to acknowledge the role enslaved people themselves played in their emancipation.

21. The Retreat.
In York in 1796, Elizabeth's friend William Tuke established 'The Retreat.' Here he and his colleagues pioneered a humane regime for the treatment of the mentally ill.

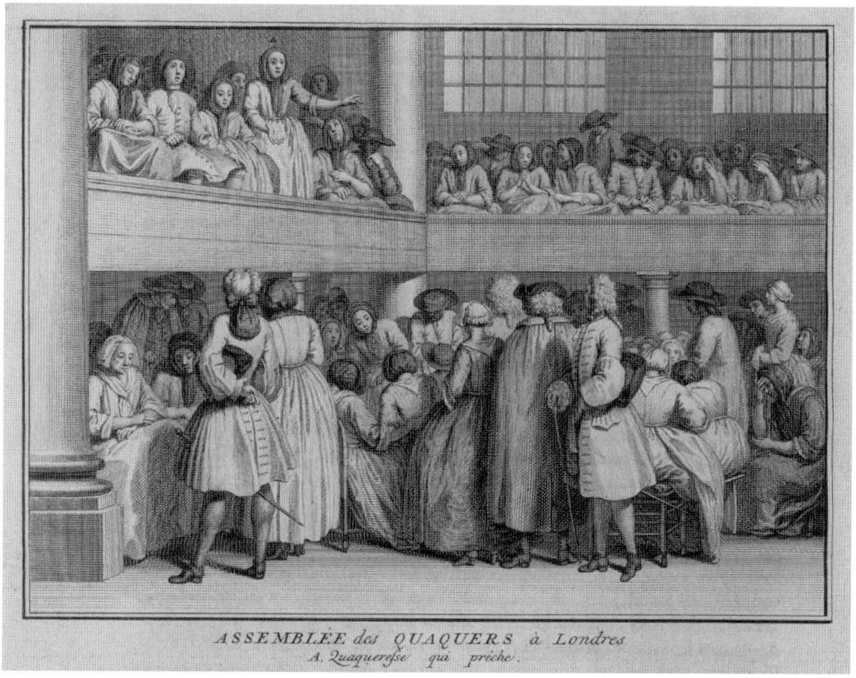
ASSEMBLÉE des QUAQUERS à Londres
A. Quaquereſse qui préche.

22. Women preaching at a meeting of Quakers.
Unusually for the time, Quakers allowed women to speak in their religious meetings, as shown in this 18th century engraving, and Elizabeth may have been drawn to them in the knowledge that she could play an active part in their anti-slavery campaign.

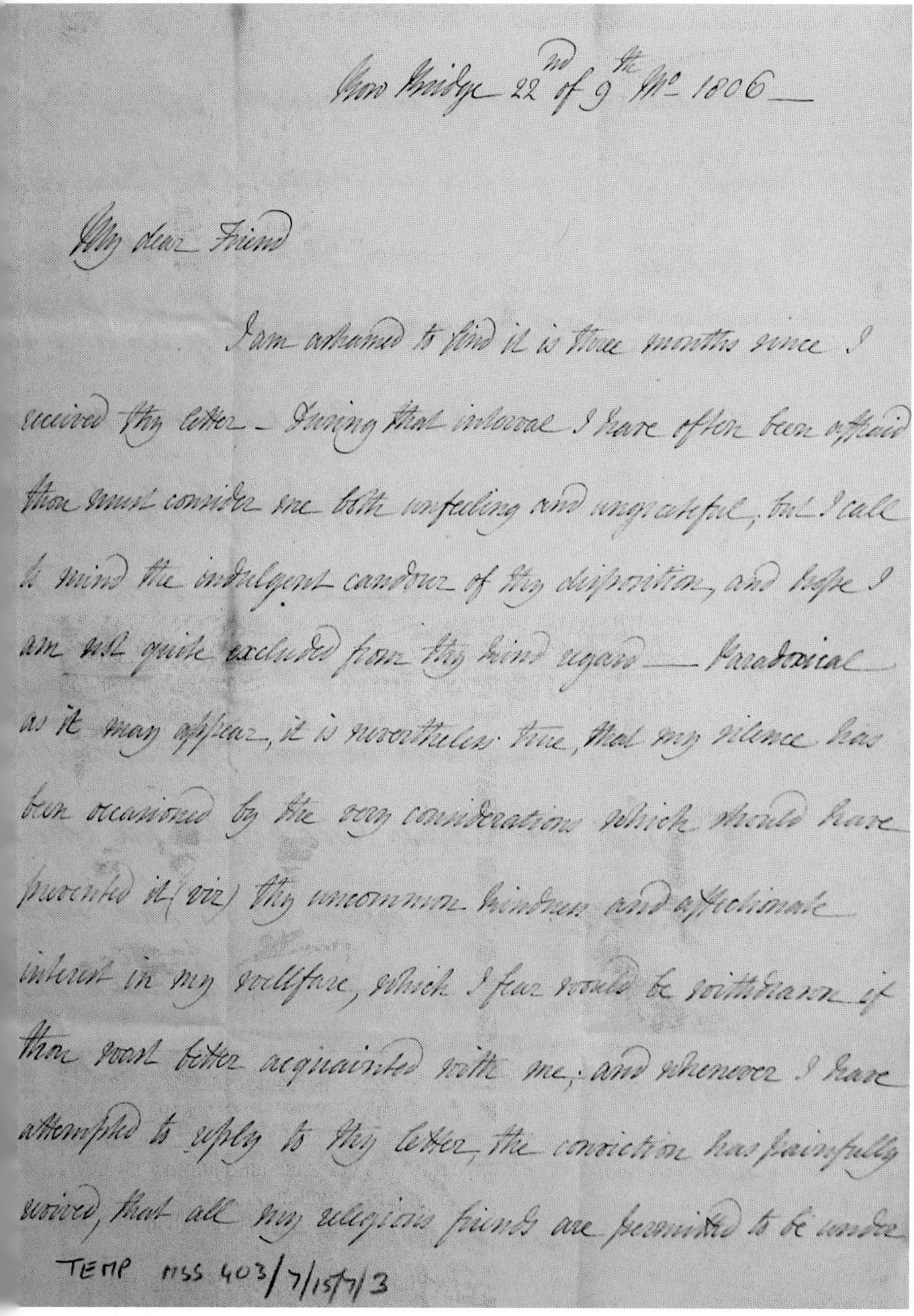

Stow Bridge 22nd of 9th Mo 1806 —

My dear Friend

I am ashamed to find it is three months since I received thy letter – During that interval I have often been afraid thou must consider me both unfeeling and ungrateful, but I call to mind the indulgent candour of thy disposition, and hope I am not quite excluded from thy kind regard — Paradoxical as it may appear, it is nevertheless true, that my silence has been occasioned by the very consideration which should have prevented it (viz) thy uncommon kindness and affectionate interest in my wellfare, which I fear would be withdrawn if thou wert better acquainted with me; and whenever I have attempted to reply to thy letter, the conviction has painfully revived, that all my religious friends are permitted to be under

***Above and overleaf*: 23. Elizabeth's letter to Mary Lloyd in 1806.**
In this letter to her Quaker friend, Mary Lloyd, Elizabeth explains the reason for her recent silence and in her anguish, seeks her friend's support.

a delusion respecting my real character and state of mind,
~~mind~~ and consequently are induced to say "peace when there is no peace" — I am however still hoping that the time will arrive when I shall be less unworthy of thy kind regard — In the mean time I hope thou wilt receive my sincere and very grateful acknowledgments for thy friendly counsel, tho' at present I can have no part in the comfort and encourage-ment it was so kindly intended to inject ——

I should have taken an early opportunity of relieving thy anxiety about Mary Price, but that soon after the receipt of thy letter, her Mother inform'd me she knew Mary intended to write to thee herself — We think her health and spirits much improved by her last excursion, but she has again left Leicester, and is gone with my sister Anne to seek for a fresh reinforcement from the air and water of Matlock —

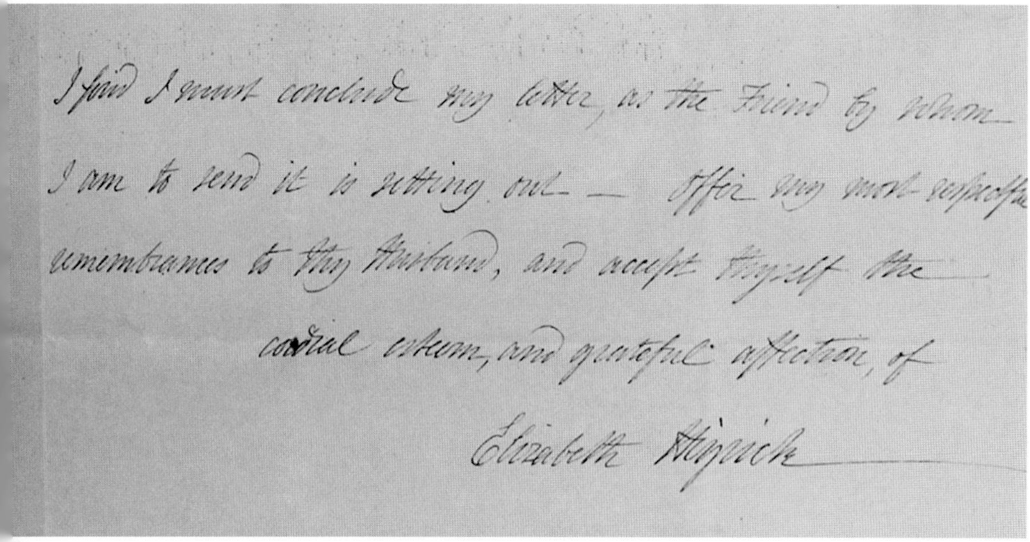

I find I must conclude my letter, as the Friend by whom I am to send it is setting out — Offer my most respectful remembrances to thy Husband, and accept thyself the

cordial esteem, and grateful affection, of

Elizabeth Heyrick

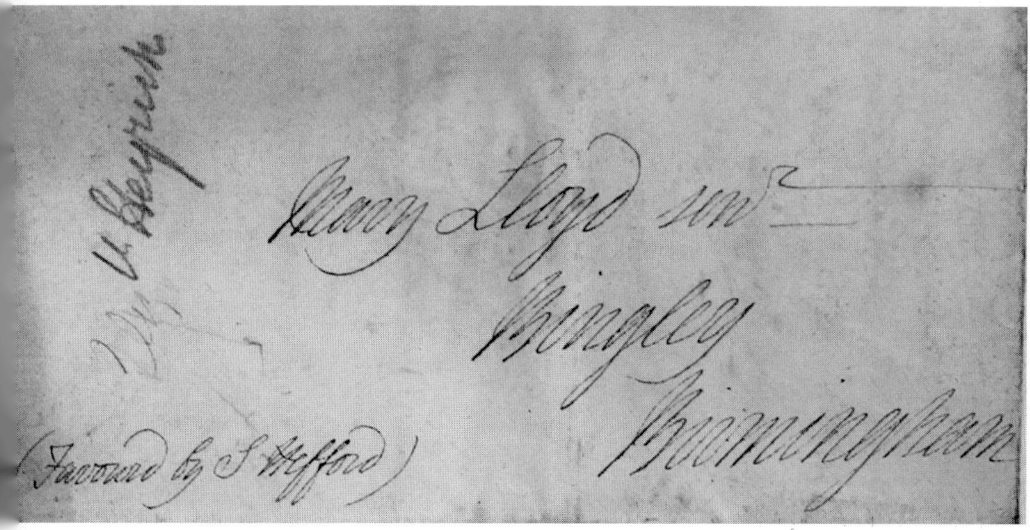

E Heyrick

Mary Lloyd senr

Bingley

Birmingham

(Favoured by S Hefford)

24. Original silhouette of Elizabeth Heyrick.
Like most Quakers at the time, Elizabeth is likely to have preferred silhouettes to painted portraits.
This one in black card, carefully preserved by her descendants, was cut in about 1824.

25. The copied silhouette of Elizabeth Heyrick.
The second silhouette of Elizabeth is an unsigned ink drawing copied from the first, probably by an amateur. It was made after her death in 1831, and kept presumably in tribute to her and as a memento of her life.

spur - the most powerful stimulus to unremitting and assiduous exertion.'[35] It is only when wages are low that you get popular unrest and riots and because society is supported by them, by their industry and ingenuity, workers should themselves be well cared for. No country, she concludes, can flourish when wages are low because labourers are 'the foundation of the social pyramid'.[36]

In the same year, Elizabeth also wrote an open and anonymous '*Letter of remonstrance from an impartial public to the Hosiers of Leicester*'. Here, she accuses the employers of showing a 'supercilious disregard'[37] for the claims made by their workers. Though she acknowledges that some hosiers are 'men of honor, of humanity, of religion', others are, she claims, 'too evidently destitute of these virtues'.[38] Which camp did she mean to place her brothers in? John Coltman was of a more sedate and a graver temperament than the younger Samuel, and more like his father. Was he similarly detached from the daily preoccupations of a business life? He was fond of art and intellectual pursuits and as a young man, he was deeply religious. He was baptised by immersion and became attached to the church of the Reverend Robert Hall. He had 'a noble and generous disposition, and entered warmly into all plans of public and private benevolence', writes Catherine Hutton.[39] She describes his political views as 'Liberal' and notes that he was highly respected in his native town.

He may have been as appalled by the Peterloo Massacre as Samuel and Elizabeth both were but in local employment disputes, he and his sister held deeply opposing views. Did John read his sister's pamphlets? Did the family know who had written them? It seems clear they did. Elizabeth's sister Mary Ann apparently sent the 1817 pamphlet to Hutton who commented: 'Her language is beautiful but I am not convinced by her arguments. It is a difficult subject for a woman to write upon; it would be difficult even for a man to take in the whole at one view. Mrs Heyrick argued from what she saw; but I think she saw only a part. Give my love to her, and either tell her this or not, as thou likest…'[40]

The historical records suggest that John may have taken Elizabeth's criticisms badly. In a letter she wrote to her brother between 1824 and 1825, Elizabeth confronts their growing estrangement. Her hurt is palpable. It is a month since they last saw each other and it would comfort her, she says 'to know that you were thinking of your absent sister half as frequently and with half as much affection as she does of you.'[41] John had accompanied her to the coach when she left but had not asked her to write and now she is apprehensive and concerned that she has fallen out of favour. She suspects she has expressed her own opinion too confidently and that John disapproves of her pamphlets. Yet however low 'may be your estimate of your sister's natural powers and capabilities her own is still lower'. She never would have ventured into the arena of public debate were it not for the urgency of the cause and however she is judged by others, she believes she was more influenced by a sense of duty than by arrogance or vanity.

By this time, Elizabeth has begun her anti-slavery writing in earnest and in this letter to John, she soon shifts her attention to a discussion of slave emancipation. Certainly, there is common ground here and her views on abolition would have been more sympathetically received than those on workers' rights. And despite Elizabeth's awareness that many are opposed to her, the woman that emerges from the 1820s is increasingly single-minded, increasingly willing to fight her corner, and fiercely focused on social and political issues. Led by her older brother, the hosiers had by now first rejected and then briefly accepted the workers' demands but by the end of 1825, prosperity had again given way to depression and employers had begun to claw back their recent concessions. Over the following year, the Leicester framework knitters' wages tumbled to starvation level.

Although low pay was a major concern at this time, working people held other grievances, too. The British electoral system was deeply unrepresentative and very few people had the right to vote. Some constituencies contained thousands of electors, others a handful. Pressure for reform was growing. Elizabeth herself does not call for Parliamentary reform though she does oppose malpractice in the local elections of 1826 and bemoans the defeat of the popular radical candidate that year.[42] She also supports emancipation for Catholics and is critical of their exclusion from Parliament. And, although she urges her readers to vote for candidates who oppose the Corn Laws, West Indian slavery, and 'every description of legal injustice and cruelty', she stops short of demanding Parliamentary reform or a more democratic franchise. As the writer Kenneth Corfield observes, she simply outlines ways in which even an unreformed Parliament would carry out its duties to the people.[43]

For Elizabeth's view of the social world is based on mutuality and moral responsibility. She rejects market competition and like many of the frame-workers themselves, she can see no fairness in a system which allows one man, or a few men, to engage in practices that bring manifest injury to their fellows.[44] As the daughter of a merchant, she might have been expected to align herself more squarely with the interests of her brothers but throughout her life, she retained a sympathy for the less privileged and for those with limited power. It is an alternative view to that held by her older brother and it cannot be reconciled with his.

Yet in the winter of 1827, long after the death of both their parents, she is not averse to advising him. After spending a wakeful night, she again writes to him. The day before, they have apparently discussed the younger Samuel and his wish to withdraw from the family's business. In courteous but insistent terms, Elizabeth now urges John to act, and to allow Samuel to leave the factory if he wants to. John, she knows, will display not just honesty but also 'disinterestedness and generosity'. She compares herself to him:

> 'Great instability of purpose and fluctuation of feeling are, you know, justly considered our family failings: the largest share of these infirmities belong I believe to yourself and to me: ought we to be surprised at discovering, or severe in censuring them in a brother or a sister?'[45]

There is no trace in the archives of John's reaction to his sister's letters and Elizabeth's opinion of the family's 'failings', their 'great instability of purpose', is hard to square with what we know now of her activities in the 1820s. As she pursues her anti-slavery work, attends Quaker meetings and writes anonymous pamphlets, she is without a direct tie to the family business and so she is free to be their conscience. The transition to new manufacturing processes that would later become known as the Industrial Revolution was the backdrop to her life, running from sometime soon after her birth until the 1840s.[46] It was not until then that its social effects began to be documented in official and unofficial literature but the Coltman family had lived through the early reality of what these changes meant to ordinary working people. And long after the family had withdrawn from the hosiery business, the Industrial Revolution continued to bring unrest to Leicester. For decades, the factory workers' struggles here and elsewhere, their poverty and desperate living conditions found a place in books, articles and pamphlets of the period. Most pamphlets were brief, cheap and openly partisan and they were Elizabeth's weapon of choice as in her biting prose, she passionately challenged both her readers and her family.

Chapter 11

'A War with beggars! An exterminating crusade against the poor and miserable!'

One day in 1824 when she was glancing at a local newspaper, Elizabeth's attention was caught by a paragraph outlining the provisions of a new Vagrant Act.[1] The Napoleonic Wars (fought by France and her allies against a range of European states including Britain)[2] had ended nine years earlier and across the country large numbers of soldiers had returned home to places like Leicester to find they had no work or accommodation. Many were now displaced. Elizabeth was horrified to read that within the terms of the new legislation, in England and Wales, all pedlars and itinerants, those who lived outdoors or in barns, no matter their injuries or deformities, were to be classified as 'rogues and vagabonds' and were now liable to be imprisoned, and even whipped.

The new legislation resonated painfully with nineteenth-century Quakers. Since the 1600s, they had had a tradition of 'travelling ministry' where itinerant preachers witnessed Quaker beliefs and nurtured members of distant meetings. They exhorted others, carried news and on both sides of the Atlantic, they reinforced a shared sense of identity. They were central to Quaker life.[3] Yet there was no formal system of support and they were dependent on the free hospitality that was offered in return for spiritual ministry. They often drew crowds of several hundred to streets and market places[4] where their social and religious differences made them an easy focus for attack. Numerous Quaker preachers were tried as vagrants. Their detractors believed they were intent on destroying the established church with their rejection of orthodox theological beliefs, their insistence that everyone had the light of God within them, that men and women were spiritual equals, and with their refusal to take legal oaths or to defer to those in authority. Dissenters had been persecuted for a long time and after the Restoration in 1660, Quakers and others were increasingly vulnerable.[5] Historical records include examples of Friends being dragged from their beds at night or apprehended on the road where their horses and goods would be seized. Many were publicly humiliated by being whipped, abused by mobs or locked in the stocks. Often they were tried alongside common thieves, vagabonds and murderers and local magistrates or judges passed severe sentences.[6] After the Toleration Act of 1688, which granted freedom of worship to Nonconformists, the official persecution of Quakers ended.

More than a hundred years later, however, when the new legislation appeared, Elizabeth was angered by how little seemed to have changed. In post-war England, in addition to those recently discharged from the military, many of them wounded and homeless, large numbers of economic migrants from Ireland and Scotland had arrived in search of work. Roy Porter observes that vagrants along with paupers, the old, the sick and unemployed were 'society's flotsam and jetsam'[7] in the eighteenth century and early evidence of Elizabeth's sympathy for the dispossessed is contained in a piece published in *Ainsworth's Magazine*.[8] Here, Catherine Hutton recalled how her friend (whom she calls here 'Elizabeth Adeling') had responded to meeting an Irish beggar dressed in tattered garments:

> 'You are able to work,'
> 'Yes', the man replied, 'but I can't get work.'
> 'Perhaps you don't like to work?'
> 'Yes, I do like work, and I don't like begging; but nobody will employ me in these rags.'
> 'What work can you do?'
> 'I work in the fields.'[9]

Elizabeth gave him a guinea from her purse so that he could clothe himself decently. It was a loan, not a gift, she said, and if ever the man was able to repay it, she would expect him to do so. The man reappeared a few days later in new apparel, so the story goes, and Elizabeth told him she had found him work as an outdoor labourer with fellow Quaker, John Ellis of Beaumont Leys.[10] After a year, the man came to Elizabeth and duly paid his debt.

Hutton gives no date for her story but vagrancy had been on the statute books in England since the fourteenth century when it was first made a criminal offence. In her study[11], the historian Audrey Eccles writes that there were official distinctions between the 'deserving settled poor' and those who were seen as the 'undeserving settled poor', as well as the 'wandering poor'[12] as numerous legislative attempts were made to control the disorderly, ensure the able bodied all worked and to keep people in their place, in every sense. From 1662, a person who was destitute because of unemployment, sickness or incapacity to work had had the right to relief but in one parish only, typically the one where they had been born, married, hired or apprenticed, or had rented a house.[13] The poor were therefore effectively immobilised in their 'settlement parish' and usually a certificate was required before they could leave it.[14] Further, officers had the power to drive 'vagabonds' back to their native parish to ensure they did not become a burden on the rates.

Yet boundaries were confused. Hutton's anecdote about Elizabeth's encounter with a local beggar carefully establishes that the man is a 'deserving' case since he doesn't like begging, is willing to work and repays his debt. Now, as she read about the new Vagrant Act that had just become law, Elizabeth's concern grew. Eventually, she sat down to record her thoughts and later that year, she published her *Protest Against the Spirit and Practice of Modern Legislation as Exhibited in the New Vagrant Act.*[15] She sent a copy of her pamphlet to the *Leicester Chronicle* whose editor recognised the 'able pen' of the anonymous person who had recently written about cruelties practised at Smithfield market in London.[16] In the interests of 'justice and humanity', he decided to print a lengthy extract from the new pamphlet.[17]

The newspaper's more progressive readers would have sympathised with Elizabeth's arguments. In 1819, in an attempt to address the problem, a Vagrant Office had been set up in Leicester where beggars could here have their cases investigated. If they were found to be in genuine need, they would receive support from the Poor Rate; if not, they could now be prosecuted under the new legislation.[18] The public had been asked to stop making donations to beggars they came across in the streets. This system would continue in Leicester until 1834 when the Poor Law was amended but, in the meantime, Elizabeth angrily took the country's authorities to task. She was, she admitted, one of those who supported these 'rogues' and 'vagabonds'. The new Act effectively branded 'misfortune with the stigma of crime'.[19] Every Christian's duty was to open their hand wide to their brother, to give bread to the hungry and to offer sanctuary to the poor. Yet this legislation, in stark contrast, decreed that the poor should receive only imprisonment and punishment. To which authority should Christians submit? The vagrant's resources had been much reduced by circumstances beyond his control, by fluctuations of trade, increased population and by the substitution of mechanical for manual labour. Why should he be stigmatised, robbed of his independence and punished? What crime has he committed? His poverty is his only crime:

> 'All his natural and political rights lie open to invasion; and he is stripped of them, one by one, without the power of resistance, or even of making his complaint in any quarter where it will be listened to.'[20]

What possible motives could the authorities have? Is it, Elizabeth wonders, that the wounds and deformities of the vagrant, their poverty and rags are unpleasant to look at? Or do they really pose a commercial threat to the livelihoods of respectable shopkeepers and regular tradesmen as some had claimed? Why has no one exposed the injustice of these persecuting measures? How is it that no one has noticed the cruel system of tyranny they will lead to? And pointedly, she asks, 'where were the great abolitionists - the sworn enemies to slavery and oppression - the detectors and exposers of petty tyranny - the great popular advocates - when this instrument of oppression was proposed to the House?'[21]

It is impossible not to hear the mockery in these words and Elizabeth's contempt for the male leaders of the abolitionist movement. The flurry of anonymous pamphlets that she produced in 1824 may well have been an audacious response to the posturing of a male establishment and anger at decision-makers who were far removed from the experiences of those they sought to control. Now, as she attacks the new vagrancy legislation, she admits that many members of Parliament, since they cannot observe the vagrancy measures in operation, presumably because they lead sheltered and privileged lives, 'are utterly ignorant of the oppressive and barbarous nature of these new enactments.'[22] Soon, in another pamphlet published that same year,[23] she would tackle head on those who had turned away from the realities of enslavement, those who having voted in 1807 to abolish the trans-Atlantic trade now resisted attempts to abolish the very institution itself. As far as she is concerned, the new Vagrant Act is 'as unjust in its nature as any which perpetuates slavery'[24] and seems to have originated in cruelty and 'in the delight of oppression for its own sake'.[25]

Elizabeth returns to her slavery theme near the end of her pamphlet with a further venomous attack on the inconsistency of legislators who, although they have abolished the foreign slave trade, with this new Vagrant Act have now 'established a system of domestic slavery'.[26] With one hand they have opened the doors of the prison, and with the other they have driven multitudes into it. Their poor fellow-creatures - who have committed no crimes and are not dangerous are being deprived of their liberty - and the worst thing of all, Elizabeth writes, is that others are informing on them. Vagrants now find themselves at risk of intimidation by paid informers from within their own communities just as the Quakers had been some two centuries before.[27]

Some informers have patriotic motives but others do not. Sometimes 'petty infringements' such as after-hours drinking could lead to punishment, or even a whipping if the threat to inform on those taking part did not successfully result in a payment.[28] These 'persons of the very worst description' are being encouraged and bribed to betray 'the friendless and destitute', and each time they do it, they receive five shillings for their trouble. By implication, Elizabeth likens their work to that of the slave holder who sells his victims on and pockets the proceeds.

The use of informers was in effect a kind of 'outsourcing' and other measures were introduced too during the late eighteenth and early nineteenth centuries as poverty grew and the costs to local parishes of administering the vagrancy law increased markedly.[29] Elizabeth would have been well aware of tensions between the local parishes in Leicester and the borough justices[30] who were given significantly more power with the new legislation. To her horror, the justices now had the discretion to inflict such punishment on vagrants as they saw fit, including whipping and imprisonment with hard labour. Who are these 'characters' she asks, and what gives them the right 'to imprison their fellow creatures' for soliciting alms and for being houseless and destitute?[31] Of course, they themselves escape the punishments that they inflict on others. Both legislators and magistrates have been 'observed to bet at horse races, and cockpits and pugilistic exhibitions,' Elizabeth remarks wryly. So, she asks, what is the intrinsic difference between lawful and unlawful games? What is it that allows those in officialdom to 'engage with impunity' in their amusements while the poor risk imprisonment and whipping?[32]

It was not the first time Elizabeth had attacked rich and powerful members of society for their hypocrisy and it would not be the last. A few years earlier she had targeted local industrialists[33] and even though she again is careful to note that there are exceptions and that not all deserve her censure, it is plain to see she is no friend to those in authority. Cuttingly, she writes that with the new legislation about vagrancy, the country's rulers have excelled themselves. Savage barbarians take vengeance on their enemies and captives but they at least are kind to the poor and needy of their own tribes. Not so the English:

> 'The honour of a crusade against beggars was reserved for England alone!- in the nineteenth century after having triumphantly terminated a twenty years war; subdued

> her political enemies at home as well as abroad - secured legitimacy and quelled innovation - It should seem as if her active enterprising genius could not rest - and rather than submit to be tame and quiet - to have no achievement - no adventure - no enemy, foreign or domestic, to vanquish - that her conquering genius, rather than endure torpid inaction, will engage in a new kind of civil or domestic war - such an one as has no precedent in all antiquity - a war with beggars! An exterminating crusade against the poor and miserable!'[34]

Irony 'in the hands of a master', remarks the writer Charles Mullett, may be 'so convincing that no other weapon is needed'.[35] In his pamphlet, *A Modest Proposal,* published in 1724, the satirist Jonathan Swift (1667-1745) had used irony to devastating effect when he suggested that Irish poverty could be alleviated if the children of the poor were butchered and sold as food to wealthy English landlords. A hundred years later, Elizabeth adopts a similarly bitter tone but then she pauses and checks herself. This is a subject that is 'too serious for satire,' she admits. For the new vagrancy laws represent a monstrous evil, 'a deep stain on our justice'.[36] No law should forbid us from helping those in need but this persecution of beggars is 'in strict accordance with the fashion of the times'[37] for the current age is not humane, charitable or beneficent; some individuals may have these qualities but the society as a whole is so taken up with its ambition and its wants, its vanity and selfishness that there is nothing left for others. And beggars have rights, too. When they suffer, they have the right to complain; when they are in need, they have the right to solicit relief. Poverty and homelessness, wretchedness and vice all strengthen a person's claims on a Christian's sympathy.

Further, the poor have a right to liberty, and to travel on foot, just as the rich have a right to ride on horseback or in splendid carriages. So long as they do no harm, why not leave them alone? For the rich need the poor and cannot live without them. 'The world depends for its subsistence on the plough, the sickle and the flail'; the rich 'have never supported the poor but the poor have first supported them.'[38] As she had argued in relation to Leicester's impoverished hosiery workers,[39] all members of society have a moral responsibility to care for the disadvantaged and all benefit when workers are properly remunerated. Vagrants, the wandering poor, beggars and enslaved people everywhere deserve care and respect and her underpinning argument is again a religious one. She sets aside her scorching sarcasm. 'Honour all men - not because they are noble, rich or wise, or even good but because they are made in the image of God, and are probationers for eternity.'[40]

Belief in an afterlife was not, of course, the preserve of Quakers alone but in her writings, Elizabeth returns time and again to the Quaker conviction that personal behaviour in this life will have eternal consequences.[41] The 1820s saw the emergence of doctrinal differences particularly within American Quakerism[42] and some also saw a growing evangelicalism within the London Yearly Meeting[43] that Elizabeth is thought to have attended.[44] At this time, these meetings were held in Devonshire House in Bishopsgate. The Society's administrative system had a tree-like structure, which allowed local worshipping groups to send representatives to a Monthly Meeting. From here, further representatives would go to a Quarterly Meeting which would in turn send them to the London Yearly Meeting.[45] After a long period of controversy, a separate women's yearly meeting had been established in London in 1784. The women, who were led by Elizabeth's friend Esther Tuke from York,[46] had argued long and hard for their own meeting and were finally given permission on the condition they did not attempt to make any rules. Many male Friends remained reluctant to cede any authority to a woman[47] and women were not officially recognised as equal to men and eligible to serve on the Meeting for Sufferings, which was the Quaker executive body, until 1896.[48]

Evangelical Friends placed emphasis on the scriptures and Elizabeth too, frequently appeals to biblical texts. Writing again in 1827, at more length, she asks if the magistrates who sentenced a convicted local vagrant to be imprisoned for three months with hard labour (and during that time to be publicly whipped) had ever read the gospel according to St Matthew? She quotes the relevant verse: 'I was a stranger and ye took me in; naked and ye clothed me, &c. In as much as ye did it unto one of the least of these, ye did it unto me.'[49] God, the supreme Judge, will see to it that miscreants and all those who oppose His 'law of universal love' are punished. We are only stewards, she writes, 'who must shortly be summoned before the great Lord of the universal household, to render an account of our stewardship.'[50]

Punishments must be proportionate and to be salutary, they must be just. Elizabeth had been shocked by a recent event in Leicester's marketplace reported in the local newspaper:

> 'John Wilson, convicted at our last Borough Sessions, of stealing a hat; and John Cryton, for obtaining money under false pretences, by a sham certificate, purporting that he has been shipwrecked and had lost a considerable sum of money, &c. underwent the punishment of public whipping in our market place, on Saturday last, pursuant to their

> sentence - Cryton seemed to writhe under the infliction and called upon Jack Ketch to spare him. Wilson, on the contrary, never once shrunk from the punishment, nor suffered an expression to escape him, except at its conclusion, when he desired some of the crowd about him to refrain from hooting at the executioner, for having exercised what they considered an unfair severity towards him. Wilson's sentence was that he should be severely whipped. He appeared to be gnawing something whilst undergoing the flagellation.'[51]

She quotes the newspaper article in full but perhaps in deference to her genteel readers she omits the final chilling sentence. Corporal punishment is barbarous and cruel and the public is rightly disgusted by it. Capital punishment is to be preferred she argues, since it is accompanied by a certain solemnity[52] whereas a public whipping simply damages those who witness it. The 'vulgar rabble' are 'converted into a ferocious, blood thirsty mob'. 'Humanity sickens at the picture'.[53] And what have the crowd gained from it, she asks? Returning to her argument about the need to give vagrants the chance to work, she asks what if the culprit instead of being whipped and discharged had been detained in custody, and set to labour till he had acquired habits of industry and been compelled to repay those he had robbed the amount of their losses? And what if he had 'received the instructions of patient and compassionate friends, and been restored to liberty under circumstances of credit and decency'? Surely the public would have benefited more.[54]

In a footnote, Elizabeth acknowledges her source for these ideas as one William Roscoe (1753-1831), an English penal reformer, who during a brief spell in Parliament had voted with those seeking to abolish the slave trade.[55] In his writings, he advocated milder punishments for law breakers believing that such treatments would reform the criminal and that this would be in everyone's interests. Kindness and decency would do more for them (and for us) than harsh punishments. His proposals are strikingly modern and even in the twenty-first century, when contemporary prisons are full to over-flowing[56] schemes for prisoner training, rehabilitation and restorative justice are not universally supported.

Elizabeth's own experiences of punishment as a young schoolgirl at Hartshill were not documented but are unlikely to have been severe. Her mother's focus on decorum and modesty[57] and the Quaker school's emphasis on cleanliness, orderly quiet and courtesy[58] may well have been more formative but physical beatings were common in Quaker schools elsewhere in the early nineteenth century. At Ackworth, a Quaker school in Yorkshire, in about 1820, punishments were described as harsh 'if not barbarous' and one boy at Sidcot Quaker school, established in 1808, was repeatedly caned causing thirty or forty cuts on the palm of his hand.[59] As she came to frame her arguments about punishment, Elizabeth was more likely to have remembered the radical and compassionate approaches to mental illness pioneered by her friend William Tuke in York[60] and the humanity and discipline underpinning Roscoe's proposals obviously resonated with her. Incredibly, the legislation that Elizabeth took exception to in 1824 was not finally removed from the UK statute books until 2022. Well ahead of her time, she argued that reason, compassion and justice should govern penal policy and that the treatment of offenders and vagrants, like the treatment of all enslaved people, should be determined fairly and in full accordance with their human rights.

Chapter 12

'...by a train of most exquisite reasoning'

In Jane Austen's novel *Mansfield Park,* published in 1814, the heroine Fanny, aged only 10, is staying with her better-off cousins when her uncle, Sir Thomas Bertram, returns from a business trip to Antigua. The Bertram family are financed by the income from their Antigua estate, and Sir Thomas is an absentee plantation owner, as well as a member of Parliament. Fanny tells her cousin Edmund that she could listen to her uncle talking about the West Indies for hours but at the mention of slaves, he dries up:

> 'Did you not hear me ask him about the slave trade last night?'
>
> 'I did - and was in hopes the question would be followed up by others. It would have pleased your uncle to be inquired of further.'
>
> 'And I longed to do it - but there was such a dead silence!'[1]

The much discussed 'dead silence' of the Bertrams speaks volumes. Clearly, the young Fanny is learning that the topic of slavery could lead to some uncomfortable conversations in the drawing rooms of the gentry and in Austen's novel, she is presented unmistakably as 'a friend of the abolition'.[2] Following the passing in 1807 of the Act for the Abolition of the Slave Trade, which had prohibited the trade in the British Empire,[3] the practice of slavery itself had nevertheless continued and when the novel was published, it was still 'a burning issue'.[4] Much as they yearned for the liberation of all British slaves, abolitionists were left dreaming of this long-imagined goal and nothing seemed to bring it closer.[5] British warships now patrolled the Atlantic in an attempt to stop competitors from continuing in the lucrative trade but it would be decades more before the institution of slavery itself was banned.[6]

Elizabeth's own publications at about this time were centred on the rights and conditions of industrial workers[7] but slavery was always in the back of her mind. On numerous occasions, she draws parallels between workers and enslaved people[8] and by 1824, she is ready to turn her attention fully to the scandalous institution that had been encouraged and sanctioned for 250 years.

Again, her pen is her weapon of choice. The tract that would become her most celebrated work on the subject appeared in 1824, entitled *Immediate not gradual abolition: Or an inquiry into the shortest, safest and most effectual means of getting rid of West Indian slavery.*[9] It is now acknowledged to have been one of the first and most forceful texts to argue for an immediate end to slavery and against gradualism.[10] Before she had finished writing it, however, Elizabeth heard news of events in Demerara (now part of Guyana) that left her deeply shocked. As she drafted the final few pages, she raged. A year before, several thousand enslaved Africans had rebelled against their owners and Elizabeth spares her reader nothing as she recounts the punishments meted out. Some insurgents had been hanged, dismembered or decapitated; others had received or were yet to receive corporal punishment amounting to one thousand lashes, after which they were condemned to work in chains for the rest of their shortened lives. Three times in the space of a few pages, and always in capital letters, she repeats the words 'ONE THOUSAND LASHES' determined to have her reader understand the full horror of the retribution. What had warranted such 'frightful vengeance' she asks. 'What horrible crimes could have instigated man to sentence his fellow man to a punishment so tremendous? To doom his brother to undergo the protracted torture of a THOUSAND LASHES? To have his quivering flesh mangled and torn from his living body? And to labour through life under the galling and ignominious weight of chains! It was insurrection.'

Guyana is located in the north eastern corner of South America. Its coastline is laced with mangrove swamps and mudflats and a blistering tropical sun beats down. The indigenous inhabitants gave the country its name which is derived from their word *guiana* (meaning 'land of water') and with its fertile soil and its canal and river networks, it was ripe for European exploitation.

Demerara was one of three colonies acquired by the British from the Dutch in 1814 and it was the most productive. Since then, declining sugar prices had brought economies of scale and the plantation system had intensified. The abolition of the British transatlantic slave trade in 1807 that Elizabeth and her family had long campaigned for had been a major achievement but it brought about a shortage of labour. When, in 1815, colonists switched their Demerara plantations from cotton to sugar production, pressure increased.[11] Planters were no longer able to replenish their enslaved labour force by purchasing Africans and they had to rethink their management systems. They began to shuffle their slaves around from one property to another, changing established work systems, so that their broader economic interests could be protected.[12] The slaves bore the brunt of these changes and when, in 1816, a young missionary named John Smith arrived in the colony, with his wife Jane, he found himself in a fully-fledged 'slave society' where terror ruled, the whip was used unsparingly and neglect and ill-treatment were commonplace.

In these societies, slavery was the central institution and the master-slave relationship shaped all aspects of life. John Smith was shocked by the cruelty he observed. In his journal, he writes about an African slave named Quamina, who worked as a carpenter and lived on one of the plantations in Demerara. He was Smith's deacon and widely respected within his own community. For nearly twenty years, he had lived with Peggy, a freed black woman who worked as a domestic. When Peggy became so ill that it was feared she had little time to live, Quamina was sent to work in a distant part of the plantation and refused leave to see her, other than during his few off duty hours. On Peggy's final day, he arrived back at their house an hour after she had died.[13]

If Smith struggled to square this life with the one he was accustomed to back in England, Mary Prince who was born a slave in Bermuda in about 1788, also grappled with the differences she observed when she eventually found herself living in England in 1828:

> 'Since I have been here I have often wondered how English people can go out into the West Indies and act in such a beastly manner. But when they go to the West Indies, they forget God and all feelings of shame, I think, since they can see and do such things.'[14]

Prince's story, and others like hers, revealed the institutionalised brutality of a slave's life. Smith believed that as well as systematically mistreating their slaves, the planters were demanding 'immoderate labour' from them. They had refused to implement reforms sought by the British Colonial Office to reduce the severity of punishments and they had stopped the slaves from attending religious services.[15] There was little love lost between the planters and the missionaries who saw the colonial world in very different ways. Some of the planters were more enlightened than others but most believed that it was dangerous to encourage slaves to become Christians; teaching them anything other than their 'duties' to their masters would surely bring about the destruction of the entire colony.

Elizabeth would have known that disturbances amongst slaves in the West Indies were becoming more frequent. In both 1823 and 1824, *The Christian Observer* (a journal edited by her friend and advisor Zachary Macaulay) carried sympathetic pieces about slave insurrections in the colonies[16] and their resistance to enslavement which, as James Walvin explains, took many forms from quiet, unspoken truculence and foot dragging to explosive revolt.[17]

Under Governor Murray, who administered the colony from 1813 to 1824, Demerara was, in effect, a crude 'plantocracy'.[18] Murray was himself a planter and although the colony was nominally ruled from Westminster, the planters were the dominant class. Yet slaves outnumbered whites by twenty to one and rebellions were something of a tradition. So, too, were the particularly barbaric and inhuman forms of retribution inherited from the Dutch. Torture, beheadings and being burnt alive on a stake were some of the punishments that might follow an insurrection.[19] Then, as tensions rose in the early nineteenth century, word reached the enslaved population of Demerara that plans were being drawn up in England to grant them their freedom. Hochschild comments wryly that they believed the King of England was about to set them free - and that William Wilberforce was next in line for the throne.[20]

In fact, what had happened was that on 31 January 1823, a group of men had met at the King's Head Tavern in the City of London and agreed to call themselves 'The London Society for Mitigating and Gradually Abolishing the State of Slavery Throughout the British Dominions.'[21] There were some here who had been part of the old 1787 abolition committee[22] like William Wilberforce but others were new. Once again, women were not invited and the group's carefully worded title was at once a source of particular aggravation to Elizabeth – as well as a spur to her activism.

In Guyana, though the rumours of emancipation quickly came to nothing, the planters were becoming increasingly wary of the anti-slavery lobby back in England and amongst the slaves themselves, frustrations were building. Soon after his arrival and without telling the planters, John Smith had begun teaching reading to some of the slave children. He had been warned by his missionary masters in London not to create dissatisfaction and not to encourage the slave community to question their status. The planters usually saw missionaries as 'meddlesome do-gooders'[23] and Smith knew he needed to be careful. A particular bone of contention was the slaves' use of Sundays, their one official day of rest, to cultivate their own produce which they could then take to market. Smith regarded this as an ungodly breaking of the Sabbath but growing food on the allotments cut down on the need for issued provisions and served the interests of the slave economy. It left the missionary with a dilemma and as the size of his Sunday congregation grew, he became more and more convinced of the incompatibility of the plantation system with the moral and spiritual wellbeing of the slaves.[24] When drums started beating on the night of 17 August and shell-horns were heard blaring, he knew a rebellion had begun.

Quamina had initially tried to stop the uprising, arguing instead for a peaceful strike and Smith, for his part, now refused to take up arms against the slaves. The historian, Michael Craton, gives a detailed account of the insurrection in his book *Testing the Chains*[25] and it appears Smith was to some extent unwittingly caught up in it. Yet he was soon arrested and subjected to an 'elaborate travesty' of a trial. He was found guilty of complicity though not of inciting the rebellion. At his trial, the missionary laid the blame squarely at the door of the planters and their hirelings. Already very ill with consumption, he was condemned to death by hanging with a recommendation for mercy. A reprieve signed in England by King George IV came too late to save him and his death in a Demerara prison cell outraged British abolitionists.

* * *

Back in England, the title the men had chosen for their new anti-slavery society was an immediate source of provocation. The setting up of an organisation that was officially committed to the *gradual* abolition of slavery was not a cause for celebration since its title suggested that emancipation was still as far away as ever. Vehemently, Elizabeth attacks this 'very masterpiece of satanic policy' which presents immediate emancipation as harmful and injurious to the slaves themselves. The abolitionist who argues in that way, she claims, has drastically undermined the cause. He insists that bringing the slave into the light after 'whole years of total darkness', offering him a banquet when he is 'half famished' and his digestion 'feeble' or exposing him to 'fervid heat' when he is 'half frozen with cold' are profoundly damaging to the individual:

> 'Thus by a train of most exquisite reasoning, has he brought the abolitionists to the conclusion that the interests of the poor, degraded and oppressed slave, as that of his master, will be best secured by his *remaining in slavery.*'[26]

The pamphlet is heavy with irony, and it will prove to be her most memorable contribution to the movement. Towards the end of it, when she turns to the news from Demerara, like John Smith she blames the planters for provoking their slaves 'beyond human endurance'. It is one year on from the King's Head meeting and she will write three more fiercely argued anti-slavery tracts before its close.[27]

* * *

The uprising at Demerara was not an isolated event but it was one of the largest slave rebellions in Western history, involving some nine to twelve thousand insurgents. In all, about 250 slaves died and only three whites.[28] Typically, remarks Craton, British emancipationists regarded the ordeal of the young missionary as far outweighing the slaughter of more than 200 slaves. Certainly, the news of Smith's death strengthened the abolitionist movement and in another tract from 1824 Elizabeth herself mentions his treatment. She briefly describes 'this excellent man' who 'had been illegally tried, unjustly condemned'[29] and she is scandalised by the colonial authorities' treatment of him, as well as their religious intolerance. Yet her firmest sympathies lie with the slaves themselves for the brutal treatment they have received in Demerara and in other parts of the West Indies.

She spells it out. Her Quaker belief that all people were equal before God meant that she found no grounds for setting one above another. 'The slave has a right to his liberty, a right which it is a crime to withhold,'[30] wrote Elizabeth. Doubtless slave holders had rights too, but these paled into insignificance alongside those of people who had been cheated of their freedom. Too much delicacy and tenderness had already been shown towards the West Indian proprietors, claimed Elizabeth, and too much accommodation that had allowed them to prosper at the expense of others.

Who was she talking about? Who had shown 'too much delicacy and tenderness' towards the proprietors? It was 1824 and seventeen years had passed since the trans-Atlantic slave trade had been abolished by Parliament. Elizabeth bitterly bemoans the lack of progress towards the ending of slavery itself but acknowledges the strengths of the opposition:

> 'The advocates of slavery are more alert and successful in insinuating into the public mind, doubts and fears, coldness and apathy on the subject of emancipation than the abolitionists are in countering such hostile influence…..'[31]

Who were these advocates of slavery? Why were they so successful in opposing emancipation for so long? In her writing, Elizabeth overtly and repeatedly targeted the 'abolitionists', those like Wilberforce who opposed an immediate end to slavery and the West Indian slave owners themselves but she also hints darkly at the existence of others behind the scenes, 'a mighty host of powerful interests and deep-rooted prejudices' that continue to uphold slavery.[32]

In fact, some of the 'mighty hosts' were to be found in the British Parliament where there was a strong pro-slavery lobby. Like the fictional Thomas Bertram in *Mansfield Park*, many of these individuals had ties to the Caribbean trade and some, like Charles Ellis (1771-1845), were apologists for it. Ellis was present in the House of Commons when in May 1823, a debate on abolition was introduced by Thomas Fowell Buxton (1786-1845). Buxton was the Member for Weymouth and had recently been asked by Wilberforce to join him in the Parliamentary campaign against slavery.[33] Buxton's mother was a Quaker and as a politician, he had several humanitarian concerns. A few years before, Elizabeth had taken up her pen to write to him about the suffering of working people in distressed manufacturing districts, like Leicester. She was aware of his sympathies, probably also his Quaker background, and she knew that he was 'zealously disposed' to investigate social injustices.[34]

In the House at this time, there was seating for just over half of the MPs and when an important debate occurred, they were crammed together, many not being able even to find standing room. Up to fourteen women at a time were permitted to view proceedings from the attic space above the chamber from where they could see nothing and hear very little.[35] It was unbearably hot and members suffered in their fitted waistcoats and high cravats. If he had been wearing a hat, Thomas Buxton would have been required to remove it as he got to his feet to open the debate: 'It is a crime,' he declared, 'to go to Africa, and steal a man, and make him a slave.' One million British subjects were currently victims of this 'most intolerable enormity', an injustice and a crime that has been licensed by British law. At the end of his speech, Buxton moved that since the state of slavery was 'repugnant' to the principles of the British constitution and those of Christian religion, 'it ought to be gradually abolished' throughout the British colonies.[36] Despite their shared commitment to abolition, Elizabeth, if she had been present, would not have been surprised to hear Buxton insist that he was advocating 'expedition' but not immediate emancipation which he believed would be reckless.

Soon, it was the turn of Charles Ellis. He was a frequent Parliamentary speaker on West Indian affairs, and he was both prominent and influential.[37] He argued that if they were set free, Negroes would have no 'stimulus to work'. They would be likely to revert 'to their former habits of savage life', and to abandon 'the habits of peaceful industry'.[38] To characterise life on a West Indian sugar plantation as 'peaceful industry' was certainly to stretch a point but Ellis persisted. Early the following year, in the *Quarterly Review,* he published a piece that he had written with Robert Wilmot-Horton of the Colonial Office.[39] Here, the authors openly pitted themselves against the abolitionists. They acknowledged that sugar production in hot climates was intense but argued that 'it is the nature of the African to be indolent.' Without fear of punishment, how can the free Negro be persuaded 'to perform the task of sugar cultivation with that energy and continuity which can alone render his labour beneficial to the planter?'[40]

Slavery can be justified, in other words, because it generates profits. Though it may be regarded as 'distasteful' in some quarters, and may eventually be abolished, Ellis and Horton rejected the idea of immediate abolition as a 'fatal gift'.[41] Like the abolitionists in the new London anti-slavery society, and like Elizabeth's own brothers, these men argued that emancipation was likely to bring violence and bloodshed unless it was undertaken gradually. Many of those who supported gradualism had commercial interests in the plantations and were deeply involved in financial services. They sought to prolong forced labour in order to avoid the collapse of the sugar industry. Gradual emancipation would give time, as the author Scanlan puts it, 'to transform by degrees their murderers into their employers'.[42]

In the nineteenth century, anti-slavery was made up of competing interests. There were those like Wilberforce for whom it was an imperial project, intended to reform rather than destroy the empire. Some believed that their interests could be better protected if time was taken to teach enslaved people how to be Christian small holders. Elizabeth herself concedes that freed slaves would need protection and that the rule of law would still be required to prevent disorder and 'restrain and punish crime' in black communities as in white populations[43] but she nevertheless holds fast to her belief that emancipation is urgent. The influential Wilmot-Horton held liberal views on trade and religion but he was firmly convinced that slave emancipation was dangerous and impracticable. At the Colonial Office, he and his friend Thomas Moody (1779-1849) spread a toxic and contagious gospel of racial difference and, as the historian Michael Taylor reveals, they created there a 'bastion of pro-slavery ideology'.[44]

These then were some of the 'powerful interests' that Elizabeth was up against. As Horton and his colleagues played on people's prejudices and fears in the 1820s, so she continued to appeal to her compatriots' moral sense, their understanding of fairness and belief in a just God. What she sees clearly is that this is a debate about vested interests; she believes that the difficulties and dangers of emancipation have been over-stated by those who have benefited for too long from the gains of oppression. Greed is being elevated over human life. Elizabeth is unlikely to have met officials like Wilmot-Horton and Moody in person but she has certainly read poisonous pro-slavery tracts like theirs and though she does not name any West Indian planters, she has followed reports of their meetings. She continues to attack the hypocrisy of the pro-slavery lobby in her pamphlets, once again urging a boycott of slave-produced sugar, and by the end of 1824, she has also found time to co-produce a ground breaking anti-slavery periodical, edited solely by women.

For away from Westminster, the anti-slavery campaigners were again rallying. The authors of the journal called *The Hummingbird* describe themselves as 'an ancient Sisterhood' who have been so united 'that no man may put us asunder'. Though they do not give their names, Elizabeth, her sister Mary Ann, and friend Susanna Watts are thought to have together established, written and edited the journal.[45] Like other literary women of the time, they found friendship, inspiration and strength in one another's company.[46] The title, they explain, is intended to convey the contrast between the lives of slaves, driven to their labour by a whip, and the little humming bird, 'buzzing like a feathered bee, free and happy to her voluntary labour'.[47] The journal itself is an assemblage, containing some pieces that are redolent of Elizabeth at her combative best, and others, most likely written by Watts, which are spikey and playful, poetic and full of classical allusions. A poem by Watts appears on the publication's 1824 masthead:

As the small Bird, that flutt'ring roves,
Among Jamaica's plantain groves,
A feather'd busy Bee
In note scarce rising to a song,
Incessant, hums the whole day long
In Slavery's Island, free!

So shall 'A still small voice' be heard
Though humble as the Humming Bird,
In Britain's groves of oak;
And to the Peasant from the King
In ev'ry ear shall ceaseless sing
'Free Afric from the yoke!'[48]

The journal's authors insist that everyone can do something to help bring slavery to an end. The people can petition Parliament; they can refuse to consume the produce of slavery; they can spread accurate information about it and if 'the whole nation sets to work in this manner, the great task will be accomplished.'[49] For Man is 'subject to the laws of his Creator', argued the Leicester women, and it is God's will that we should hurt no one. Yet through the slave trade, we 'sanction the oppression and misery of millions'[50] because we see African slavery as we see death, far away, and not directly before our eyes.

As Christians, the women believed it was their duty to oppose the slave trade. The question was a religious one. In emphasising Christian morality and in placing stress on slavery as a mortal sin, the women set themselves apart from their male counterparts. Many male anti-slavery societies drew on religious rhetoric to support their case, as the academics James and Shuttleworth explain, but mostly these arguments were 'tempered by an awareness of economic and political practicalities'.[51] The women were not unaware or unconcerned about the practicalities but they believed only a principled stand would maintain public support for the anti-slavery cause.[52] Throughout the rest of her life, Elizabeth held fast to her belief that, *whatever* the practicalities, slavery should be immediately abolished. Though many had assumed that the ending of the transatlantic trade in 1807[53] would bring about an end to slavery itself, by the 1820s it was clear to Elizabeth and her Leicester friends, amongst others, that while there was still a market for the products of slave labour, especially sugar, slavery would continue.

There was an alternative to slave-produced sugar, however, that by this time was being actively promoted as a more ethical option. Charlotte Townsend, the daughter of Elizabeth's friend Lucy, wrote a pamphlet for children in which she asked them if they knew where sugar came from. It comes from a country far away, she explains.

> 'It is not planted, and gathered in, as wheat is here, by free people who are paid for their work.' Rather it is 'cultivated by slaves, by poor black Africans, who are bought and sold like brute beasts, who are compelled to labour without wages, under the lash of a cart-whip; and who are marked with red hot irons, flogged and chained at the pleasure of their owners.'[54]

Consumers had a choice, explains the young writer. They could continue to eat West Indian sugar and so support slavery or they could purchase East Indian sugar instead, which was 'cultivated by free men, who are paid for their work, and who cannot be used ill as the slaves are.'[55] Thanks to the activities of the East India Company, this 'free' sugar was widely available but it was made more expensive for consumers at home by the imposition of heavy duties. In this way, the interests of West Indian planters were being protected. Elizabeth was not alone in arguing for the removal of these duties which she believed would lead quickly to the collapse of slavery.

Ironically, history does not give the East India Company a completely clean bill of health either. It was formed in 1600 under Royal Charter to establish trade links with India and China and was immensely powerful, having its own army, ships and fortresses which it used aggressively to protect its trade monopoly. The historian William Dalrymple writes about the company's brutal reign[56] and academic Andrea Major points out that East India sugar was routinely produced under conditions that were far from 'free'.[57] From the early 1620s, the company had transported enslaved people from East Africa to India and Indonesia to work in its facilities and this practice did not end until the 1770s. Whether Elizabeth was aware of the historical background or not, by the 1820s, she was impatient for reform. As she renewed the fight to persuade her fellow citizens to boycott West Indian sugar, she alluded to the contributions William Fox and Martha Gurney had made in the 1790s.[58] About thirty years ago, she writes, we could have done this, when 'the public attention was so generally roused to the enormities of the slave trade'. She issued this challenge to the male leaders of the anti-slavery movement: 'Too much time has already been lost in declamation and argument, in petitions and remonstrances against British slavery. The cause of emancipation calls for something more decisive, more efficient than words.'[59] A small and seemingly insignificant sacrifice would 'give the death blow to West Indian slavery' if only people could be persuaded. It would take just a tenth of the population to do this, she claimed, but 'none are so blind as those who will not see'.[60]

No longer concerned to make allowances or concessions to those with influence and power, Elizabeth now launched a full-frontal attack on the male leaders of the anti-slavery movement. After publishing *Immediate not Gradual* she produced several more anti-slavery pamphlets[61] and took out a subscription to the Leicester Auxiliary Anti-Slavery Society. The membership of this Society was exclusively male but women could show their support by subscribing to these organisations and many did so.[62] Both John and Samuel Coltman held office in the Leicester Society[63] and in 1824, they too produced a pamphlet.[64] Here they stated their aim to 'ameliorate' the treatment of enslaved people, to 'soften the rigour of their bondage' and to develop their character through religious and moral instruction.

For although slavery was 'most iniquitous', they did not seek a 'sudden revolution'. In siding with the 'gradualists' and with the new Anti-slavery Society led by Wilberforce, Elizabeth's brothers again set themselves firmly at odds with their sister. Was she provoked into writing her *Immediate not Gradual* pamphlet in that year? Or was it a coincidence? Regardless of her brothers' discomfort, she now had the bit between her teeth as with fierce optimism, she set about reinvigorating the sugar boycott campaign. Two more of the pamphlets she published in 1824[65] appealed directly to the people to put an end to slavery by refusing to consume its produce. 'Have nothing to do with their sugar; refuse it admission into your houses; let it perish, or be cast into the sea as a libation to the fishes; let the slave holders know that your resolution is inviolable, that you will never swerve from your solemn purpose to be contaminated no longer with their blood stained merchandise.'[66] She mocks her opponents - 'the right noble and right honourable sugar planters of both Houses of Parliament'[67] – as she urges the people to do what government are refusing to do. Let governments learn that 'WHEN THEY FAIL TO DO THEIR OWN DUTY, THE PEOPLE WILL DO IT FOR THEM.'[68] It was the following year that she formally joined forces with women in the female branch of the anti-slavery movement, and she was soon to become one of its most radical activists.

PART V

1820–1830

Chapter 13

'Let compensation be made in the first place where it is most due'

In 1787, nearly forty years before Elizabeth and her Leicester friends published *The Hummingbird*, a little-known African writer, named Quobna Ottobah Cugoano, had produced his autobiography. In it, he described how he had been enslaved as a child:

> 'I was early snatched away from my native country, with about 18 or 20 more boys and girls, as we were playing in a field… Some of us attempted in vain to run away, but pistols and cutlasses were soon introduced, threatening that if we offered to stir, we should all lie dead on the spot.'[1]

Once he was freed, Cugoano had called for an end to slavery and the slave trade. His was the first British publication in which an African writer had argued for immediate emancipation and the first book also to press for reparations to be made to African nations for the loss of their people and the impact of so much human trafficking. More radical and more outspoken than most of his white counterparts, Cugoano goes on to elaborate his proposal in some detail. Universal emancipation must begin at once, following a proclamation that should be sent to all courts and nations in Europe. It must be made illegal 'for any man to buy or sell another man'; there must be an end to that 'horrible iniquity of making merchandize of us'.[2]

The hurt and pain of being bought and sold 'like sheep or cattle' in a Bermuda market-place is also recalled by Mary Prince (1788-1833):

> 'I was soon surrounded by strange men, who examined and handled me in the same manner that a butcher would a calf or a lamb he was about to purchase and who talked about my shape and size in like words - as if I could no more understand their meaning than the dumb beasts.'[3]

Though her fate is unknown, she was the first black British woman to walk away from slavery to claim her freedom and her story which was published in 1831[4] became a valuable document in the abolitionists' struggle (as Cugoano's had been more than fifty years before). Prince calls for people to 'know the truth' and compares the status of slaves to that of English servants who are far better off because they have 'proper treatment and proper wages'- and they have their liberty.

How then were the slaves in the Caribbean going to achieve their freedom? The islands were in a depressing state in the early 1820s, and the slave population was in decline. Enslaved people were controlled more tightly than ever, and violence and brutality were commonplace. 'Slave resistance begat violent repression on a scale that contemporaries in Britain could barely believe,' comments James Walvin.[5] Increasingly, the slave islands looked 'like survivors from a lost epoch'[6] and despite the lack of progress in Parliament, British abolitionists from far and wide took heart. By the mid-1820s, planters were on the defensive and abolitionists knew they had support from all parts of the country. Between 1823 and 1831, the Society for the Mitigation and Gradual Abolition of Slavery published more than three million anti-slavery tracts[7] and hundreds of anti-slavery societies were formed. For abolition was now considered imperative not just on moral and religious grounds but also economic ones.[8] Slave grown sugar was subsidised and without the sugar duties, it could not be competitive.[9] Take those away, argued Elizabeth, expose slave-grown sugar to free competition, and it would simply collapse from its own inefficiencies. Other cheaper sugars were available in shops and consumers could purchase them knowing that by doing so they were not helping to sustain the slave economy. Surely no-one would want to pay more simply to keep slavery going.

Having to prove both the moral and the economic benefits of slavery, the West Indian lobby now found itself with an impossible task. Towards the end of her tract, Elizabeth hones in on the money question. The duty put on East India sugar to keep up the 'unnatural price' of West India sugar was two million pounds annually, she writes. And the planters were asking for still more 'to bolster up their tottering system'.[10] The case for abstaining from West Indian sugar, and for substituting it with cheaper East India sugar, was growing stronger by the day and news about the way insurgents in Demerara had been treated only added to the moral pressure.

To Elizabeth's chagrin, the Commons agreed in 1823 to press for the key principle of gradual abolition[11] and now questions about how that emancipation should be accomplished were beginning to surface. Cugoano's proposal more than thirty years before had attempted to describe how the transition from slavery to freedom might be achieved and intriguingly, his proposals are not so different from the terms of emancipation that were eventually decreed by the British Parliament. Cugoano had believed that after emancipation, the liberated slaves should remain in 'lawful servitude' and receive 'reasonable wages' for a period of seven years. If they behaved honestly and decently, acquired knowledge of the Christian religion and the laws of civilisation, and showed themselves to be obedient and useful labourers, his view was that they should then go free since they would have repaid their owner more than enough with their labour.[12]

Although the Slavery Abolition Act that would eventually be passed in 1833 made no provision for 'reasonable wages' to be paid to former slaves, or for compensation to African nations, in order to soften the blow to planters, Parliament did decide that emancipation should happen in two stages, with slaves first becoming 'apprentices'. The length of their apprenticeship was a sticking point in Parliamentary debates but after a great deal of wrangling amongst abolitionists of various persuasions, some wanting to remove the apprenticeship altogether, eventually agreement was reached.[13] For a term of six years for field workers and four for those working indoors, the slaves were required to labour full-time for their owners without pay. In reality, it was little different from slavery[14] and we can be certain that had Elizabeth lived to hear of it, she would have been outraged.

* * *

Many years after Cugoano had published his views on reparations, and about ten years before Britain made any legislative attempt to address the question of compensation, Elizabeth again took up the cudgels. In her 1824 pamphlet *Immediate not Gradual* she acknowledges that the planter has an interest in the emancipation question but insists that this interest is of a different order and completely distinct from the right of the slave to their freedom. If 'the West Indian gentlemen' are to be compensated for the loss of their slaves, justice demands that the slaves themselves be first to receive recompense for their 'long years of uncompensated labour, degradation and suffering'.[15] As ever, it is the principles that concern Elizabeth and she will not allow herself to be distracted from her primary goal. Though she does not name him, she echoes Cugoano's call for immediate abolition but unlike him, she sets no conditions. A slave is entitled to their freedom and it is a crime to withhold it, no matter what the consequences may be to the planter.

The problem for the emancipationists, however, was that slaves, whether bought or inherited, were widely regarded as property, as were their off-spring.

No legislation was ever passed in England that legalised slavery but Elizabeth had grown up in a country where private property was sacred, and she understood its centrality. As the daughter of a prosperous merchant, whose brothers had inherited the family business, she knew that property rights were embedded by tradition and law, and that the loss of property entitled the owner to compensation. Yet, as Michael Taylor notes, to pay slave holders for the confiscation of their 'property' was to concede that slavery was legal.[16]

Like many of her fellow abolitionists, Elizabeth abhorred the notion that slaves might be made equivalent in law to personal property. Her Quaker belief that everyone had a direct relationship with God meant that all were equal before Him and none could be the 'property' of another since all belonged to God. Her opposition to the payment of compensation to slave holders is consistent with her religious principles; slaves are human beings, not chattels.[17] Many abolitionists railed against the proposal that the planters should be compensated. Petitions were sent and anti-slavery members of Parliament spoke out vehemently against it. As for Elizabeth, she also turned her fire on the 'abolitionists', referring again to the male leaders of the movement, who had tried to please everyone. Slavery would never die a natural death, she argued. 'It must be crushed at once, or not at all.'[18] In her tract *An Enquiry which of the two parties is best entitled to freedom? The slave or the slave-holder? From an impartial examination of the conduct of each party, at the bar of public justice* also published anonymously in 1824, she argues that the only way to end the kind of cruelty shown to the enslaved people in Demerara was to emancipate the slaves and to do so at once. As she returns to her case for immediate abolition, and again advocates sugar abstinence as the most effective way to achieve it, her language is strident. 'Away then with puerile cant about gradual emancipation'.[19] Furiously, she goes head-to-head with the gradualists as she launches her counter-attack. While they are reasoning and declaiming and petitioning, 'let them remember that the miseries they deplore remain unmitigated - the crimes they execrate are still perpetuated; still the tyrant frowns, and the slave trembles; the cart whip still plies at the will of the inhuman driver, and the hopeless victim still writhes under its lash.'[20] Why rely on 'the slow and solemn process of Parliamentary discussion' when a refusal to consume 'one single article of luxury' would 'sign the death warrant of West Indian slavery' and 'eight hundred thousand of our fellow creatures' would be saved?[21] When the slave-holders see that slave produce is no longer marketable, then they will cease to offer it. When 'they substitute equitable wages for the stimulant of the cart whip,' when they restore the slave to liberty, 'when they regard him as a fellow creature, treat him no longer as a brute, but as a rational intelligent being, then we will open fresh accounts with them, and give them the right hand of fellowship.' Until then, she writes, 'we shall consider them as robbers and outlaws' and, in clear reference to the treatment meted out to slaves themselves, 'although there are no gibbets, chains, or ingenious bodily tortures prepared FOR THEM, we shall nevertheless, as in duty bound, exhibit them to the public, as having, by their late conduct, BRANDED THEMSELVES WITH INFAMY AND INVITED UNIVERSAL REPROBATION.'[22]

Writing in capital letters (as if shouting) Elizabeth is incandescent. Angrily, she upbraids the slave holders. Her brothers are also in the firing line. Both were sympathetic to the gradualists' cause and John, along with her brother-in-law William Heyrick, belonged to the Leicester Auxiliary Anti-Slavery Society.[23] This group followed the policy of the main London organisation and in the same year as Elizabeth was accusing male abolitionists of 'puerile cant', the Leicester society put out an 'address to the public' that argued against immediate emancipation. Slavery was deplorable and iniquitous but 'inveterate diseases admit only of a slow and gradual cure'.[24] As well as 'an amelioration' of their treatment, the Leicester men wanted to see provision for the slaves to receive moral and religious instruction since 'developing their faculties and improving their character, may ultimately qualify them for the possession of the freedom of which they have been cruelly deprived.'[25]

Such thinking was complete anathema to Elizabeth. The notion that a slave needed to 'earn' their freedom or somehow 'prove' their humanity was alien to someone who believed unconditionally in the humanity of all enslaved peoples. Both brothers were now taking the gradualists' line and Samuel urged his wife to communicate his thoughts to his 'Sister Heyrick'. In his view, the Spanish approach to abolition, which allowed slaves to purchase their freedom one day at a time was 'the best and most efficacious' way forward. This would be 'a stimulus to industry and prevent any violent change' either to the slaves or their owners. For some feared that emancipated black people might abuse their freedom and seek pay-back for years of violent oppression.

To support her case, Elizabeth now refers to evidence gathered by Thomas Clarkson from the island of St Domingo where he had found no instances of bad behaviour amongst freed slaves. Clarkson had published his report[26] the year before Elizabeth's pamphlet appeared, and he described how in far more unfavourable circumstances, including war and invasion, and without notice or preparation, almost 500,000 slaves had been liberated by the French authorities in St Domingo in 1793. This was almost as many as the total number of slaves in the British West Indies at the time and Clarkson, keen to anticipate objections from his opponents, describes some of the measures that were taken to ensure peaceful change. A code of rules was drawn up to be observed on the plantations and these were publicly distributed. Labourers were obliged to hire themselves to their masters for a minimum period of one year and they received a third of the estate's produce as recompense for their labour. Questions about compensation were yet to be fully resolved by the British government and Samuel was not alone in fearing the social upheaval abolition might bring. Racism underpinned much of the debate and Elizabeth was one of the few who were ready to contest the abolitionists' implicit use of racial stereotypes. In another pamphlet written in 1824, she addresses her reader directly:

> 'All of you may not know what it is to be a slave, a West Indian or a British slave. We will therefore tell you. A West Indian or British slave is distinguished from his master by his *black skin,* and is considered and treated by him, not as human being, but as a beast of burden, whom he buys and sells like cattle in a market; whom he drives and keeps to labour, all year round, with a heavy cart whip- applied without mercy and without distinction upon the trembling bodies of women and girls, as well as men, at the will of the brutal driver. Few slaves are to be seen, of either sex, without deep and shocking marks of this terrible instrument of torture upon their bodies, and they are often compelled to labour in chains with their wounds bleeding. Moreover, these white-skinn'd tyrants disfigure the bodies of their slaves with brand-marks, stamped on their flesh, by their purchasers, with red-hot irons.'[27]

She wanted to confront readers with the realities of enslavement and she understood that abolitionism did not go hand in hand with a belief in racial equality. Abolitionists themselves held a variety of racial stereotypes. Some saw black people as meek victims or as grateful survivors welcoming opportunities for self-improvement.[28] Not all believed as Elizabeth did that all men were equal. Other more illustrious abolitionists, like William Wilberforce, held views that were less egalitarian. At a dinner he hosted for the African and Asiatic Society, Wilberforce sat his guests of colour behind a screen.[29] He believed that freed Africans belonged to the lowest ranks in society and would eventually come to be regarded as 'a grateful peasantry'. And for his part, Zachary Macaulay, Elizabeth's one-time adviser, deeply disapproved of miscegenation which he described as 'degraded concubinage'. Leading abolitionists of Elizabeth's day, in other words, though they hated slavery, as Taylor remarks, never once considered Africans to be their equals.[30]

Chapter 14

'Finish the great work'

In 1825, the year after Elizabeth had published her pamphlet *Immediate not Gradual Abolition*, a woman named Lucy Townsend (1781-1847) took up her pen to write to Thomas Clarkson. He had inspired her as a girl and now she sought his advice about forming a women's anti-slavery society. Clarkson replied with unrestrained enthusiasm, claiming that he had 'long been of opinion that such committees would, in time, finish the great work'.[1] Townsend later preserved an extract from Clarkson's letter in her *Scrapbook on Negro Slaves*.

Lucy Townsend's family were members of the Church of England and her father, William Jesse, was an Evangelical clergyman. Her Conformist background contrasted sharply with Elizabeth's and she was more than ten years Elizabeth's junior but by the 1820s, the two women were friends. Though Clarkson rejected 'immediatism' and still subscribed to the 'gradualist' school of anti-slavery thought, he was generally supportive of women believing, unusually for his time, that they deserved a full education and a role in public life. He wholeheartedly approved of the Quakers who allowed women to speak at their meetings and he objected to the fact that women were 'still weighted in a different scale from men'.[2] Though women were excluded from full membership of the main anti-slavery organisations, and barred from holding office, they were accepted as subscribers and many took out paid subscriptions in support of the campaign. It was unusual for women to organise independently but encouraged by Clarkson's response, Townsend now set about convening the first meeting of the first ladies' anti-slavery society in the country at her West Bromwich home near Birmingham.[3]

It was a landmark occasion, described in the minutes as 'a very large and respectable' gathering of ladies.[4] Elizabeth was amongst those present. Townsend and her friend, the Quaker Mary Lloyd (née Honeychurch, 1795-1865)[5] now became the first joint secretaries of the Birmingham society. A committee of District Treasurers was also formed and Elizabeth was appointed District Treasurer for Leicester.[6] A few months after the Society's inaugural meeting in Birmingham, Elizabeth and Susanna Watts established a local affiliated branch in Leicester, called the Leicester Ladies Anti-Slavery Society, but no records of this group have survived.

The Birmingham society was from the outset independent of both the national Anti-Slavery Society and the local men's anti-slavery society.[7] All its members were urged to proselytize, to awaken in other women 'a lively sense of injustice' concerning slavery[8] and in addition, the District Treasurers were tasked with collecting money from their local members and bringing it to the Society. Women came from Birmingham, Coventry and Manchester, as well as places further afield, including London and Cornwall and when they produced their First Report in 1826, the group called themselves the Female Society for the Relief of British Negro Slaves.[9] By 1833, over seventy-three such societies had been established.[10] The total membership of these groups probably never exceeded ten thousand and most of the women were drawn from the gentry and the families of prosperous tradesmen, industrialists, bankers and farmers,[11] from social backgrounds like Elizabeth's, in other words. Many were younger than her. They came from a variety of religious denominations, including evangelical Anglicans, Baptists, and Unitarians. Many activists were Quakers and the Birmingham group's early records are peppered with the names of prominent Quaker families, such as Lloyd, Cadbury, Sturge and Rowntree.[12] Hutton may have disapproved of Elizabeth's conversion to Quakerism[13] but she was never Elizabeth's most ardent supporter and the Society of Friends had now a pivotal role within the abolition movement. Theirs had been a lonely, pioneering voice in the wilderness for many years, says the historian James Walvin, but now abolition was 'a popular force in the land' and the Quakers 'had exercised a profound influence out of all proportion to their numbers'.[14]

The Birmingham Society's committee met once a quarter and there was also an Annual Meeting of all members where the accounts were presented. Funds were needed for the fight and the Society resolved from the outset to seek an annual subscription of 12s from each of its members.[15] It was one of the largest local donors to central funds and records show that for the year 1825 to 1826 the women paid the men's National Anti-slavery Society £80[16] equivalent to about £7000 in terms of today's purchasing power.[17] Together, in 1829, women's associations supplied over one fifth of the national society's total income.[18]

The Birmingham women made clear their aims in their First Report. They would, they said, 'endeavour to awaken (at least in the bosom of English *women*) a deep and lasting compassion, not only for the bodily sufferings of female slaves, but for their '*moral degradation....*'[19] The italics were for deliberate emphasis. The women hoped that once English '*gentlemen*' also understood that Negro women had 'no one in the land of their captivity to plead for them', no one to hear their 'piercing cries' then they would lend their sympathy and assistance. The Birmingham society functioned as the hub of a developing national network of female anti-slavery societies and it also had important international connections with organisations in America.[20] Elizabeth found her niche here, just as she had with the Leicester writing group,[21] in a gathering of likeminded women who shared her values and ambitions. Local intellectual friendships were important, especially for single women[22] and Elizabeth herself knew from her Leicester book society days[23] that they could make their voices heard.

Felicity James and Rebecca Shuttleworth have written engagingly about the richness and creativity of female networks like these in the Midlands at this time.[24] They describe how, through collaboration and conversation, the women were able to clarify their activist role in society and to offer kindness and support to each other. As well as collecting subscriptions and donations, the women distributed poems and raised money from the sale of anti-slavery workbags. New and distinctive versions of the slave medallion that had been produced by Josiah Wedgwood in 1787[25] now appeared. In one, the male slave is replaced by a kneeling woman, who holds her manacled hands up in supplication. The female figure of Justice reaches towards her and in conscious reference to the earlier medallion, the inscription now reads 'Am I not a Woman and a Sister?' These images were central to the abolition campaigns in both Britain and America and were used on banners, cameos, brooches, snuff boxes and even hairpins. Innovative and distinctively female forms of anti-slavery activity flourished under the leadership of Townsend and Lloyd.[26] They put the emphasis on the suffering of enslaved women and the English campaigners systematically highlighted their shared sisterhood with those in captivity. Yet Elizabeth was virtually alone, comments Hochschild, in celebrating the slave rebels who were not on their knees.[27]

At one point, the women in Birmingham arranged for 300 copies of William Cowper's poem *The Morning Dream* (1788) to be printed for distribution.[28] Campaigners had for many years circulated poetry to promote their cause and Cowper's anti-slavery poems were some of the most favoured.[29] The ballad chosen by the Birmingham women was intended to be sung. In it, the narrator describes a dream in which he finds himself sailing westwards with a 'goddess-like woman' who goes 'to make Freemen of Slaves'. On an unnamed 'slave-cultur'd' island, she is confronted by her enemy 'Oppression' who sickens and dies at the sight of her. The narrator awakes then, reflecting that Britannia because she so much hates oppression will resolve to have nothing to do with the slave trade.

Women were not represented in Parliament but strategies such as the sugar boycott,[30] the anti-slavery poems and the biting prose that Elizabeth adopted in her pamphlets were tools to challenge entrenched views like those of the gradualists and this they did, despite the existence of family and local links. In Leicester, William Wilberforce's friend the MP Thomas Babington, who had been elected on an anti-slavery platform,[31] was a member of the same anti-slavery society as Elizabeth's brother John and her brother-in-law, William Heyrick. Susanna Watts includes an image of Wilberforce and a watercolour of Rothley Temple, Babington's Leicestershire home, in her scrapbook suggesting that despite their deep differences with men in the Wilberforce circle, the women were prepared to fight their corner. Watts gleefully challenges their male opponents:

> 'On a gentleman saying that some ladies, who were zealous in the anti-slavery cause, were <u>brazen-faced</u>:
>
> Thanks for your thought-it seems to say,
> When ladies walk in Duty's way
> They should wear <u>arms of proof</u>
> To blunt the shafts of manly wit-
> To ward off censure's galling hit
> And keep reproach aloof:-
> And when a <u>righteous cause</u> demands
> The labour of their hearts and hands
> Right onward they must pass
> Cas'd in strong armour, for the field-
> With casque and corselet, spear and shield,
> Invulnerable <u>brass</u>.'[32]

In the country, as in the Coltman family, anti-slavery opinion was often divided along gender lines. The popular belief in Georgian times was that women were more sympathetic, more able to support those who suffered and closer to the innocent and purest conception of God. Their experience of the family gave many of them a special interest in the abolition movement for slavery represented an attack' on their self-image, and their intense involvement in the cause was rooted in this understanding. 'All those who were enslaved suffered', notes the author Edith Hurwitz, 'but women suffered still more'.[33] Torn away from their families, most enslaved women were deprived of their roles as mothers, grandmothers and wives and from their first days in captivity, they were likely to be taken advantage of. The slave trader John Newton later admitted in his memoirs that as a young ship's captain he had routinely and savagely assaulted women and girls and though he is better known now as the author of the hymn 'Amazing Grace' which he wrote following his conversion to evangelical Christianity, his earlier writings are testament to the cruel treatment often meted out to female captives.[34]

Women were markedly more sympathetic to the cause of immediate abolition than their male counterparts just as they had more enthusiastically campaigned for the sugar boycott.[35] They were also more inclined to take a moral stance. The Sheffield Female Anti-slavery Society in 1827 was the first to take up Elizabeth's call for immediate abolition: 'We ought to obey God rather than Man. Confidence here is not at variance with humility. On principles like these, the simple need not fear to confront the sage; nor a female society to take their stand against the united wisdom of this world.'[36] Writing again in 1828, Elizabeth bemoaned the lack of progress towards abolition and recognised the special qualities a woman might bring to the cause: 'The peculiar texture of her mind, her strong feelings and quick sensibilities, especially qualify her, not only to sympathise with suffering, but also to plead for the oppressed, and there is no calculating the extent and importance of the moral reformations which might be effected through the combined exertion of her gentle influence and steady resolution.'[37]

In directly addressing her women readers, Elizabeth emphasises the role they can play in the struggle for abolition. More than thirty years before, Mary Wollstonecraft had advocated full educational opportunities and equality for women[38] but as she pleads for women's particular attributes to be recognised and employed in the campaign against slavery, Elizabeth seems content with rather less. A woman can 'exert a powerful influence' without 'violating that retiring delicacy which constitutes one of her loveliest ornaments,'[39] she writes. Such sentiments may sit uneasily with modern feminists but Elizabeth's single and unwavering focus was the anti-slavery campaign. She seeks to inspire her female readers, and as Adam Hochschild comments, in doing so, it is as if she gives them permission to speak.[40] As the number of ladies' anti-slavery societies mushroomed throughout the 1820s, Elizabeth called for women 'of cultivated minds' to use their talents to influence other women 'on this momentous question'.[41] Would it not be a sin to refuse?

Further, she understood that most genteel women of her era were not confined to their household and family. This was not the limit of their horizons.[42] There was no clear separation of a private, domestic sphere from the wider world and, as we saw with the Coltman family, a variety of interactions regularly took place within the home that linked families to others, such as employers, neighbours, landowners, colleagues and kinsfolk. As a widow, with no dependents and a family to give her financial support, Elizabeth had more time than most of her peers for her writing and campaigning. And her stance on the position of other contemporary women is clearer now. After years of misattribution, Timothy Whelan enables us to see that our Elizabeth is less concerned, for example, with domestic duty and the rearing of children than her namesake who takes a more conservative view of a woman's role.[43]

Although Elizabeth and her peers had to navigate tensions between competing interests with some care[44] and their activities caused Wilberforce considerable unease,[45] they were able to draw strength from each other and within local religious contexts, to adopt a combative approach. Though abused by some for daring to speak their minds in support of the anti-slavery cause, women continued through the 1820s to grow in confidence and reach. Elizabeth, in particular, with her furious energy, her use of graphic detail and uncompromising language to convey the suffering of enslaved people and her contempt for male abolitionists who persisted in arguing for gradualism, emerges now as a fierce advocate of fairness and equality. Yet she wrote also about her personal suffering at this time and in an extract from a poem that was initialled by her and published in *The Hummingbird* in 1825 she seems even to yearn for death:

'Be mine a broken, contrite heart,
Which God will not despise;
That meekness which devoid of art
On heaven alone relies.

A soul to dwell on things divine,
To love the sacred page;
Oh! Jesus, grant that these be mine,
From youth to latest age.

Fit me, my God, to dwell with thee
And may an angel come,
Whenever death shall summon me,
To guide to heaven my home.
'My God! My Friend! Thy will is best;

> For thankfulness I pray,
> But yet I long for heavenly rest,
> Nor wish for tresses grey.
>
> The sooner, sweeter will it be,
> To leave this house of clay;
> But thou canst make earth heaven to me,
> For peace of mind I pray.'[46]

All Elizabeth's anti-slavery pamphlets were written in the 1820s, and these were the years of her most intense engagement with the abolitionist cause. Yet her work does not seem to lift her spirits or give her hope; instead, her writings reveal a deep and persistent despondency that goes hand in hand with her activism. There were those, however, with whom she could share her personal desolation and in 1826 she confided in her admired Birmingham friend, Lucy Townsend:

> 'Your steady zeal and unwearied labours in the great cause of humanity would reanimate and stimulate my own if anything human could have the effect- but nothing human can dispel that despairing torpor into which I have been plunging deeper and deeper for many months past…..I have done nothing and I am doing nothing to any good purpose. All my anti-slavery zeal seems to have flashed out in an unprofitable flare.'[47]

It is possible that, as Adam Hochschild speculates, Elizabeth's despair had been caused by the political failure to end slavery.[48] Yet we know from her few surviving diary entries that she had suffered all her life from depression[49] and it is remarkable that despite her personal anguish, she was still able to harness her energies and passions to become one of the Birmingham society's most effective members. She was not afraid to take sides in local debates, even though many of the people involved would have been known to her and her family. During the 1826 local elections in Leicester, over ten days of polling, Elizabeth and her fellow residents witnessed widespread upheaval and some violence. The corporation's preferred candidates won the vote but in doing so, they incurred crippling expenses which left the town in serious financial difficulties for some years. Elizabeth's favoured candidate was a reformer named William Evans, a cotton manufacturer who had been proposed by Thomas Babington and seconded by Elizabeth's brother, John. Evans had denounced slavery and the Corn Laws[50] and after his defeat, the town's opposition began a 'campaign of exposure' with the intention of discrediting their rivals.[51]

In a pamphlet that can be read as a contribution to this campaign, Elizabeth makes an outspoken attack on the town's authorities. In '*Animadversions on the Late Contested Election for the Borough of Leicester*' published in 1826, she accuses them of greed and corruption and although she does not argue specifically for women to be represented in public life or to have the vote, we can see her clearly here as a supporter of political reform. She regards it as her duty to expose 'public and private mischiefs', the 'undetected, unexposed machinations' of those in Leicester who are 'fortified by the bulwarks of office'.[52] The free expression of public opinion provides an essential check on abuses, she argues, and she rages here at the loss of principle and honour just as she does in her anti-slavery writings.

* * *

In their first annual report in 1826, the Birmingham women describe Elizabeth, though they do not name her, as a 'most powerful, and consistent, advocate of our enslaved fellow-subjects'.[53] However, the new London anti-slavery society that had been set up in 1823 had largely ignored her tract on immediate abolition and Wilberforce instructed members not to speak to the ladies' societies, continuing his campaign against them until at least July, 1826.[54]

Despite this, some copies of Elizabeth's work were distributed and it generated interest amongst a number of provincial campaigners as well as some in Scotland and America.[55] It was also favourably reviewed by two major religious periodicals, the *Baptist Magazine* and the *Christian Observer*[56] and quotations from it were given in the House of Commons where, on account of its 'vigorous style', it was assumed to be the work of a man.[57] By 1826, some of the men in the national anti-slavery society were increasingly willing to break ranks and by this time, Zachary Macaulay (whose brother had married John Heyrick's sister, Ann) was in correspondence with the lawyer and politician Henry Brougham (1778–1868). The men both agreed that women were their powerful allies in the cause and that their involvement was crucial.[58] In the same year, Macaulay wrote to Elizabeth assuring her that he was anxious to see her new work and would promote its circulation as far as he could.[59] Such contacts were helpful, of course, but the women wanted radical change and in 1830, the Birmingham Society's records indicate that they decided to take their campaign up a gear.

It was Maundy Thursday, 8 April in 1830 when the society convened their annual meeting. This was a cold, wet week across the country, with a chance of snow, and Elizabeth's journey from Leicester to Birmingham in a horse-drawn coach would have taken her nearly six hours. Rail travel here was still a few years away and although some of the passengers were lucky enough to be seated inside the coach on these services, most were outside. Elizabeth would have been relieved to reach her destination and there is little doubt that as on previous occasions, she would have stayed in Birmingham before making the return journey. The Easter holiday was approaching and her relative Catherine Hutton lived at nearby Bennett's Hill. She had called in to see Hutton on other visits to Birmingham and her parents had stayed there in 1802.[60] The meeting was held in West Bromwich, probably again at the home of Lucy Townsend where the society had first come together in 1825. Now, mindful of the position adopted by the leaders of the anti-slavery movement, they were ready to act, and to flex their financial muscle. Being 'anxious not to compromise their own principles' they would, they said, donate £50 to the Gentlemen's Anti-Slavery Society when the men were willing to give up their use of the word 'gradual' in their title.[61] They now voted to submit their resolution to the National Conference of the main anti-slavery society. This meeting was convened on Saturday 15 May 1830 when about two thousand men gathered in Freemason's Hall in central London.[62]

George Stephen (1794-1879), a prominent Society member, was there and later recalled that the 'enormous hall was crammed to suffocation' and that hundreds were turned away at the doors.[63] The ensuing debate was characterised by the same earnest insistence and timid resolution that had been the hallmarks of the abolition campaign for so long,[64] until Henry Pownall (a conservative lawyer) rose to his feet. Exasperated at the leadership's procrastination, he called for the emancipation of all slaves born in the British dominions to take effect from the beginning of that year. Stephen remembers the uproar that followed in the Hall, 'the shouts, the tumult of applause' such as he had never heard before. Repeatedly, their leaders called for calm. Wilberforce waved his hand for silence but no sooner had the noise begun to subside, than it rose again as others took over the shouts until 'with a burst of exalting triumph that would have made the Falls of Niagara inaudible' Pownall's amendment was carried.[65]

About ten days later on 25 May 1830, records show that a small sub-committee (which included the rebellious Henry Pownall) met to consider the National Society's next step. They were reinvigorated in the aftermath of the Conference, and now they put their minds to making themselves more effective. What arrangements could they make to implement their plans better? The first thing they decided to do must have delighted Elizabeth and her Birmingham colleagues. In the absence of any written constitution or rules that might constrain them, the sub-committee now recommended the formal adoption of a new title for their organisation. From now on, they would be known as 'The Society for the Abolition of Slavery throughout the British Dominions' with all reference to 'gradual mitigation' and 'amelioration' finally removed.[66] There is no mention in the national Society's records of the Birmingham women's ultimatum and no acknowledgement that it had been received or discussed but the fact remains that seven weeks after the women had moved to force their hand, the men decided to drop the offending words from their organisation's title. As the academic Claire Midgley remarks, though pressure from male delegates at the Freemason's Hall that day was clearly a significant factor, a threat to withhold funding from one of their largest local donors could hardly be ignored.[67] The Birmingham Ladies Society upheld their end of the bargain a few months later when they donated £50 to central funds.

The national Society's decision to change their name in 1830 might seem now like a small victory but the removal of the word 'gradual' from their title brought a new emphasis to the campaign for abolition, a new focus on direct and immediate action. The women had asserted their independence and though they did not claim equal rights in the abolition movement, they set out a clear alternative to the official view and in doing so, publicly questioned male authority. Voices calling for a sugar boycott were again raised, particularly by the women, and Elizabeth herself must have felt considerable satisfaction that her stalwart opposition to the principle of gradualism had finally succeeded.

Chapter 15

'A burning passion for justice'

A year later, the end came. Elizabeth had suffered from indigestion and stomach discomfort for some time; 'my old malady', she called it. According to her death notice, she died at her house in Friar's Causeway (off Highcross Street) near the centre of Leicester and a short distance from the house in St Nicholas Street where she had been born more than sixty years before. It was also a short distance from the church where she had married John Heyrick in 1789. In her will, she left money and furniture from a house in London Road to her siblings, suggesting that she had retained a property there as well.

On 26 September 1831, she wrote to her sister who was again staying in Birmingham with Catherine Hutton. In the letter, she addresses Mary Ann as 'thou' (a term used by Quakers to address everyone regardless of their social status.) Yet her particular fondness for her sister is clear. 'Farewell my dear, dear sister,' she writes. 'Pray do not be long without writing.'[1] It is the last of her letters that we still have and she did not publish any more pamphlets. Yet when she died on 18 October, aged 62, she knew at least that, as George Stephen recollects, the anti-slavery nation was waking.[2]

Writing to his absent wife a few days later, Samuel describes his sister's final days:

> 'My beloved sister continued to linger between life and death till Tuesday 4 o'clock when respiration gradually ceased, indeed the hand of death was upon her from the time of the discharge of blood from her stomach, upon that time I am glad to learn her bodily suffering appeared to cease. Her mind was perfectly composed and tranquil at her end, such as all her best friends would have wished, her spirit being resigned to God and the mercy of an omnipotent saviour.'[3]

Probably, Elizabeth had suffered a perforated stomach ulcer. Without recourse to effective medical procedures, there would have been no way to save her but Mary Ann arrived back in Leicester in time to be at her sister's bedside.

The last words and deathbed testimonies of pious friends were often collected[4] but although she was comforted by the presence of her sister, Elizabeth was by now beyond speech. For a woman to whom words had meant so much, this must have been painful indeed. The Lord could give a dying person ease and friends often prayed for that, as Elizabeth had prayed for her father. A dying person might feel the Lord's arms underneath them, offering support and comfort, and though Samuel was not a Quaker, he stressed his sister's resignation at the end and affirmed his belief that her 'beatified spirit was now in communion with the blessed'.[5] Catherine Hutton recalled how watching friends had seen Elizabeth's 'serene expression,' one that told of 'the settled peace that reigned within'.[6]

Elizabeth's death passed with little comment from those outside her immediate circle. There was a brief notice in the *Leicester Journal* three days later[7] and a more generous tribute appeared a day after that in the *Leicester Chronicle:*

> 'By her death, the poor have lost a kind and most benevolent friend, and the negro a zealous advocate, as the various forcibly written pamphlets, published at her own expense, most amply testify.'[8]

She was buried in the graveyard of the Gallowtree Gate Congregational Chapel, in the centre of the town. Eventually, her three surviving siblings would be buried here, too. The chapel had been built in 1823 as an additional place of worship for Nonconformists, whose numbers were increasing.[9] Now one of the main shopping streets in Leicester, Gallowtree Gate was originally located outside the city wall and some who made their way along it knew of course that they were walking to their death.

After Elizabeth's relatives had deposited her remains in the family vault, Samuel returned home and wrote to his wife:

> 'I could not help a shuddering feeling of dread on taking a last view of the vault where my remains may possibly be deposited, that those blessed regions where they are now inhabitants of, may be for ever closed against me. But there was still a hope for the thief upon the Cross and I will not despair.'[10]

In fact, Samuel lived for another thirty years and late into his eighties, he was still working on his memoirs.[11] These included significant extracts that had been copied from Elizabeth's now missing diaries. He is open about the woman he respectfully calls 'Sister Heyrick' and about the difficulties of having such a sister. Yet there is a sense, too, that as the years have passed, he is coming to understand her achievements, even to admire her. And now that she was gone, it was left to others to guard her reputation. In a letter to his brother John written in 1841, shortly after the tenth anniversary of Elizabeth's death, Samuel admits that the occasion has led 'to much serious reflection'. He 'could not help contrasting the actively useful life she led' with his own. How unselfish she had been, always acting from duty or a hope of benefitting others. If she had been less ardent, he concludes, she might have lived a longer life 'but she might not have been equally useful'.[12]

Other family tributes were diligently collected by Catherine Hutton in her memoirs and there are letters there from John Heyrick's brother, William, and from his sister, Anne Macaulay.[13] The family had sent Anne a miniature of her late brother that had clearly been in Elizabeth's possession and she asks now for a memento, 'some trifling remembrance' of her sister-in-law, in return. William Heyrick laments his loss deeply 'since she was one of the *very few* whom I thought of with very high respect and affectionate regard'.[14]

After their initial commendation, the *Leicester Chronicle* published a much warmer appreciation a few days later. The Reverend Charles Berry (1783-1877), minister of the Great Meeting since 1803 and Elizabeth's friend of nearly thirty years, feeling that a little more should be added about her 'excellent qualities', writes that he has never known anyone 'more pure in motive, and more ardent in charity'. He elaborates: 'Her time and her talents, her tongue and her pen, her labours and anxieties were unceasingly employed in giving effect to the benevolence of her heart.' Berry admits that her religious views differed from his, that she was sometimes mistaken and 'unreasonable in her expectations, almost Quixotic in her attempts' but 'where she erred, it was from an exuberance of fine feeling such as those who were disposed to sneer at and undervalue her, never possessed and therefore could not comprehend. If she went astray,' he continues 'it was by a light from Heaven to which they were insensible. Had she enjoyed the advantages of a more exact and learned education, her intellectual stores might have been greater, her judgement more mature, her imagination less predominant but I question whether her character would have been improved or her usefulness increased thereby.' He concludes: 'If ever the oppressed lost an advocate, or the destitute a friend, who expected no other reward than that of an approving conscience and an eternal crown, they have suffered that loss in the removal of Mrs Heyrick.'[15]

It is heart-felt praise but Berry is one of very few who were willing to speak out. Elizabeth is barely mentioned in the memoirs of contemporary abolitionists and the committee of the national Society did not notice her death.[16] Decades later, the campaigning journal titled *The Slave*, published a call for all readers to wash their hands of any connection with slavery. On the journal's masthead there appeared two slogans that Elizabeth would have warmly endorsed: 'Slavery is sustained by the purchase of its productions' and 'If there were no consumers of slave produce, there would be no slaves.' Then, in a column about what is here called The Free Labour Movement, Elizabeth is remembered. She had 'stood almost alone in declaring a negro's right to immediate emancipation', though she had been heavily criticised:

> 'She might be considered a fanatic: she might be stigmatised, even by faithful abolitionists, as a woman of one idea, and that idea as incorrect and injudicious; but never did this affect the clearness of her vision or lead her in any way to change her course. She was faithful to her convictions of truth and duty; and she carried these even to the portals of the eternal world.'[17]

Here, as in the *Leicester Chronicle* obituary, we glimpse again the darker side of Elizabeth's life. Why was she sneered at and undervalued? And who by? The loyal Charles Berry offers some intriguing insights into her character and reputation at the time she died and clearly, her demeanour and opinions had brought her into some disrepute.

Yet if she was despised in some quarters, elsewhere people saw her in a more favourable light. None of her Leicester friends would have been surprised that Susanna Watts immediately picked up her pen to celebrate Elizabeth's life in verse:

TO THE MEMORY OF ELIZABETH HEYRICK, WHO DIED OCT. 18, 1831

> 'Friend of the Slave! Of Afric's countless train,
> Tramped for ages by nations round
> With noble zeal she strove to burst the chain,
> In whose vast rim a continent was bound.
> Friend of the Brute! Of those that smarting feel
> The scourge of human tyranny below,

With generous courage and unveiled zeal,
She stood betwixt the animal and woe.

And friend of all who in this vale of woe
Are found 'mid mis'rys varied scenes,
Thither with hand and heart she loved to go,
And self-denial lent the liberal means.

Deep tender feeling, wide expanse of heart,
And intellectual strength to her were given,
And best of gifts that Mercy can import,
The will to dedicate them all to Heaven.

But spare the Dead! They reach the judgement seat
(Their conscious souls reject approving lays);
They go the sentence of their God to meet
The "poor in spirit" should be all their praise.

Yet who shall say what further deeds of love
Engage on high the spirits of the Blest;
Errands of mercy 'mid the worlds above
Heaven is not idleness and empty rest.

In the full glories of that holy place,
FAITH shall be lost, and HOPE shall find no room;
But with new life and renovated grace
Immortal CHARITY shall ever bloom.[18]

Watts wrote the poem in the same year that her friend died. This was also the year that the second silhouette was created, an ink drawing rather than a cut-out, and although the precise date is not known, nor whether it was made before or after her death, it seems likely now that it was intended as a tribute to Elizabeth, a mark of her good standing in Quaker circles. The practice of copying previously produced artwork has existed for centuries, one of the most common means being the creation of lithographs from famous oil paintings.[19] The minor differences between the two artefacts in this story may suggest that the later one was the work of an amateur, a Quaker friend perhaps who wanted to keep Elizabeth's image 'alive' for future generations, just as Mary Ann did. Further the creator of the second silhouette must surely have had access to the first for the copy to be so detailed and precise. Intriguingly, records show the ink silhouette was donated to the Friends' Library in 1903 by the family of George Stacey Gibson (1818-1883),[20] a Quaker who in 1845 had married into the Tuke family of York. This family are likely to have remembered Elizabeth from her visit there in 1802[21] and they would certainly have known of her role in the anti-slavery movement.

Female abolitionists were particularly mindful of Elizabeth's contribution to the abolitionist cause. As it happened, about six months before her death, the general election of May 1831 had returned a reform-minded Parliament and in 1832, following the passing of the Representation of the People Act (or the Great Reform Act), a further general election, based on reorganised boroughs and constituencies, created a parliamentary climate that was favourable for the abolitionists.[22] The electorate was now larger, more independent and more inclined to elect those who wanted to see an end to slavery. Further, the interests of West Indian planters in the new Parliament were significantly reduced.[23] Though some wanted the legislation to go further and women were still formally excluded from voting in Parliamentary elections, Elizabeth would surely have applauded the reforms. This was a Parliament that was more likely to reflect the country's reviving anti-slavery sentiments. There were long and complex negotiations still to come, about compensation payments and apprenticeships[24] but when the Emancipation Act finally came into effect in August 1834, there were celebrations in Leicester and both Elizabeth's and Susanna's names were put up in lights.[25] There was regret that she had not lived to see the end of slavery but as the years passed, references to her work (most of them still anonymous) kept appearing, like ripples on a pond, and were published on both sides of the Atlantic.

Links between British anti-slavery women and those in America had been building steadily during the last decade of Elizabeth's life. The abolition of slavery would not be achieved for another thirty years in America but as 'the transatlantic sisterhood' grew,[26] Elizabeth's work circulated and in abolitionist circles, the unknown author of *Immediate not Gradual Abolition* was widely celebrated. One of the most prominent American abolitionists at this time was William Lloyd Garrison (1805-1879), who is now remembered for his radicalism and his commitment to immediatism. In 1831, in Boston Massachusetts, he began publishing his anti-slavery journal *The Liberator*. By then, he had read Elizabeth's work and, in 1846, when he embarked on a speaking tour of Scotland, several times he named her. Catherine Hutton, apparently now more willing to acknowledge her friend's achievements, recorded his words in her memoir:

> 'Who first gave to the world the doctrine of immediate emancipation? It was a woman of England, Elizabeth Heyrick.'

By way of explanation, and presumably in case his Glasgow audience had never heard of her, a footnote was attached:

> 'Mrs Heyrick was the highly respected, talented and uncompromising friend of liberty. As an eloquent advocate of the total and immediate abolition of negro-slavery, her fame has gone through the length and breadth of the land, to the shores of the American and Western world. 'Immediate, *not gradual*, abolition' was her motto, and under that title hundreds of thousands of copies of a pamphlet from her pen were printed and circulated, the influence of which was everywhere felt, while the Anti-slavery Society, and nearly all the friends of abolition were opposed to her views.'[27]

In Edinburgh too, a newspaper reported Garrison's tribute to the English woman he admired:

> 'It was not the published opinions of Clarkson, Wilberforce or Buxton, and other champions of emancipation that hurried slavery to its eternal overthrow in the West India colonies; but it was the pamphlet of a woman connected with the Society of Friends, Elizabeth Heyrick which, urging immediate emancipation, electrified the country, and sent forth advocates to plead the immediate freedom of the slave. She ought to be remembered on every occasion on which the friends of the slavery cause were gathered together.'[28]

Garrison echoed Elizabeth in his opinions but also in his language which was every bit as vigorous and uncompromising as hers. On the first page of the first edition of *The Liberator* he admitted that he knew his language caused discomfort in some quarters:

> 'I am aware, that many object to the severity of my language; but is there not cause for severity? I will be as harsh as truth, and as uncompromising as justice. On this subject, I do not wish to think, or speak, or write, with moderation. No, no! Tell a man whose house is on fire to give a moderate alarm; tell him

> to moderately rescue his wife from the hands of the ravisher; tell the mother to gradually extricate her babe from the fire into which it has fallen; - but urge me not to use moderation in a cause like the present. I am in earnest; I will not equivocate- I will not excuse-I will not retreat a single inch- AND I WILL BE HEARD.'[29]

Garrison's tone and delivery evoked Elizabeth's at her most strident. Another American abolitionist, also an admirer of hers, was an associate of Garrison's named Benjamin Lundy (1789-1839). Like Elizabeth, Lundy was a Quaker[30] and in 1821 had founded a newspaper named the *Genius of Universal Emancipation.* Lundy and Garrison differed in their approach to abolition, with Garrison being the more radical. In the early 1820s, Lundy was amongst abolitionist leaders in the American South to present gradualism as a means to end slavery[31] but Garrison advocated immediate emancipation and used his 'flamboyant rhetoric'[32] just as Elizabeth had used hers to argue the case. Both men admired Elizabeth's work though she would die without ever meeting either of them. Lundy was particularly impressed with her 'moral absolutism', her emphasis on individual responsibility and he also enjoyed her forthright statement of both the problem and the solution, all expressed, he wrote, in language very 'unlike the milk-and-water style of some writers on this side of the Atlantic'.[33]

Lundy made that observation in 1824, soon after the publication of *Immediate not Gradual*, at a time when so many of Elizabeth's compatriots were discomforted by her writing and prepared to ignore it. Yet from the other side of the Atlantic the ripples kept coming, and they persisted long after Elizabeth's death. In 1853, during a visit to England, the writer Harriet Beecher Stowe (1811-1896), best remembered now as the author of *Uncle Tom's Cabin,* was celebrated by Ladies of the Surrey Chapel, a Nonconformist church located in what is now Blackfriars, in London. They proudly acknowledged their compatriot:

> 'It is not a little gratifying to us to recollect that an honoured female in the Society of Friends was the first to propose immediate abolition as the proper remedy for the wrongs inflicted on slaves then held by England in her colonies. In this sentiment we heartily concur with respect to the slaves in America.'[34]

Slavery was not formally abolished in America until 1865 when, following the Civil War, the 13th Amendment was adopted as part of the United States

Constitution. And Elizabeth was not the first person to propose immediate abolition - Ottobah Cugoano must have that accolade[35]- but she was the first woman to do so and she was certainly the policy's most insistent advocate. More than twenty years after her death, and despite not naming her, the women of the Surrey Chapel certainly knew who their 'honoured female' was.

Why was her identity such a vexed concern? Why is it still the case that so few have heard of her? The question of female authorship at this time is discussed by Timothy Whelan[36] who explains that members of writing circles (like the Leicester one) were not interested in acquiring fame through print so much as in the recognition and pleasure their writing gave others. Writing anonymously or under a pseudonym, he argues, was part of an authorial tradition that was not connected to social standards of female modesty, and was not an attempt to avoid trespassing on male territory. Rather, these female literary networks functioned to enrich and sustain the 'social, intellectual and aesthetic lives of their members'.[37] Although Elizabeth's pamphlets were all anonymous, it was always clear to her family, friends and supporters that they came from her pen, and equally clear that she did not suffer fools gladly. When she sent her anonymous pamphlet about the new vagrant act to the *Leicester Chronicle* in 1824[38] she was doubtless seeking the wider dissemination of her strongly held views and she risked having her cover blown. Her strident, challenging language caused discomfort, even outrage, amongst some of those closest to her, and there were certainly some (like her brothers) who believed she had transgressed contemporary understandings of the way women from the gentry should behave. After her sister's death, Mary Ann is believed to have cut some pages from Samuel's memoirs (leaving the sharp edges still evident in the archives), and to have burned her sister's accumulated letters and diaries,[39] either because she felt compelled or had been instructed to do so. We can only speculate because the younger sister emerges much less clearly from historical sources than any of her siblings. It is thanks to Catherine Hutton, who was Mary Ann's close confidante and affectionate friend, and her decision to include a lengthy account of Mary Ann written by Miss Alicia Cooper in her memoirs[40] that we do know a little about Mary Ann's life and beliefs. She outlived all her siblings and survived into her nineties but she left few words of her own, probably because from birth she had suffered from dismally poor eyesight. After six operations to correct it, without chloroform, eventually one of her eyes had to be removed. She was nine years younger than Elizabeth, tall, loyal and devout, with 'a gentle fearlessness in rebuking wrong'. Though she belonged to no religious society, she wished at the end to be 'considered as dying in union with Friends' as her sister had.

And Mary Ann saw herself as the guardian of the family's reputation and secrets. In the front of the family's collection of letters which she had carefully transcribed, before handing them over to her great nephew in 1861, she wrote that it was 'her earnest request that this memorial of his ancestors may never pass out of his family'.[41] Her concern with the family's privacy was picked up by Hutton too, who used pseudonyms when she later wrote about the Coltmans in her published work.

Why did those close to Elizabeth make such concerted efforts after her death to conceal or obscure truths, to hide details relating to her private life? What were her mistakes and her missteps? The Reverend Berry is one of the first to hint at flaws in Elizabeth's character and misjudgements in her dealings with others, without elaborating. Did the family wish to dissociate themselves from Elizabeth's radical views? And in destroying so many records, was Mary Ann simply trying to protect her beloved sister's reputation? If so, why would she lend the family's cut silhouette to the unknown artist of the ink drawn one, if indeed she did?

Some puzzles remain. Yet Elizabeth's words have been clearly preserved and her pamphlets are uncompromising. For she had always been willing to speak out when others held back, often prioritising their own interests and allegiances. At times, her behaviour must have seemed eccentric, as when she adopted the lowly life of a peasant spending nights in a shepherd's cottage[42] or when, after the end of her brief marriage, she withdrew completely and berated herself endlessly, for somehow being responsible for her husband's demise. Samuel may have believed her grief to be well beyond the bounds of what might normally have been expected from a young woman in her situation but there was an intensity in all her dealings and interactions with others. Her brother also believed that her lifelong depression was a family trait, one to which she was 'constitutionally liable' and had inherited from her father.[43] Before her husband's death, she had written about it:

> 'I have suffered little from the loss of friends, health or outward prosperity; but some latent source of dissatisfaction and regret has been ever open to embitter all my enjoyments and produce apathy and discontent in the midst of every outward prosperity.'[44]

Yet what is singular about her story is that despite her misfortunes, or perhaps because of them, she was always willing to contest the dominant view, and to set beside it her compassion for others and deep devotion to what she believed was a just God. In other words, she was motivated less by a wish to reform and, for example, to improve the position of women within society than by a very real set of religious imperatives.[45] Religion was a powerful force within the abolition movement and Elizabeth's life bears testimony to this. Yet to challenge the religious orthodoxy, the authority of brothers, the senior hierarchy of the anti-slavery movement was in itself a questioning of male authority.[46] And not many women dared then to put their heads above the parapet in the way Elizabeth did. She stepped determinedly out of her social milieu and deviated from the orthodox path, by forcibly challenging those she disagreed with.

In 1833, when abolition came, there were celebrations in a tavern called the Crown and Anchor, in Arundel Street off the Strand in central London. It is unlikely women were invited. Elizabeth, described by Michael Taylor in his recent book as 'the Leicester firebrand' was of course no longer alive and William Wilberforce had also died, just a few days earlier. Though their contributions and beliefs differed markedly and Wilberforce (then as now) was seen as the movement's figurehead, both deserved a place at the table, says Taylor, and both were missed.[47] It has taken nearly two hundred years for Elizabeth to make her presence felt as a radical abolitionist, to become known as the fierce 'enemy of compromise'. In debates about the emancipation of slaves, she was always ahead of the curve but as her friend Charles Berry suggested, all she wanted was to do the right thing, and to have others do it too.

Endnotes

Searching for Elizabeth Heyrick

1. The academic, Clare Midgley, published an influential account in 1992 of women's role in British anti-slavery campaigns and Elizabeth Heyrick's contribution is described there. See Midgley, C. (1992) *Women Against Slavery: The British Campaigns, 1780-1870,* (London and New York, Routledge). Other women discussed include Elizabeth's friends, Susanna Watts and Lucy Townsend, as well as women who came later, such as Anne Knight (1786-1872) and Elizabeth Pease (1807-1897). They remain overshadowed and far less well known than most male abolitionists.
2. See Manuscript VI, Gibson Collection, MS vol 339/237, LSF.
3. I am grateful to the family for their generosity in allowing me access to their private collection of papers.
4. Samuel Coltman's journal is entitled *Times Stepping Stones or some memorials of Four Generations of a family by an Octogenarian of the same* and is contained in three volumes, dated 1772-1857. It was dictated by him and written by his wife Mrs Anne Coltman. See ROLLR, 15D57/448-450. For a typescript version of the journal, see M1153. For ease of use, the typescript version is referred to throughout this book since it has clear page numbering. The collection 15D57 also contains a large number of letters and other papers relating to the Coltman family.
5. See Beale, C (ed.) (1895) *Catherine Hutton and Her Friends* (Birmingham, Cornish Brothers).
6. I am indebted to Jess Jenkins and to Melissa Atkinson for their astute observations about the two artefacts.
7. McKechnie, S. (1978) *British Silhouette Artists and their Work 1760-1860* (London, Philip Wilson Publishers for Sotheby Park Bernet Publications).
8. Clark, J. (2011) 'Quaker silhouettes' in *The Friend*, 28th July. Homan, R. (2013) 'Quakers and Visual Culture' in: *The Oxford Handbook of*

Quaker Studies, Angell, S. & Dandelion, P. (eds) (Oxford University Press), p.492-506.

9. Catherine Hutton had no such qualms and portraits of her can be found in the Library of Birmingham and online. There is also a stipple engraving of her, by William Read, dated 1824, that is held by the National Portrait Gallery in London.
10. See Whelan, T. (2015) *Other British Voices: Women, Poetry and Religion 1766-1840 (New York, Palgrave Macmillan)*. (Chapter 6 focuses on Elizabeth Coltman (1761-1838) and distinguishes her clearly from Elizabeth Heyrick (née Coltman) who lived nearby and was a friend.)
11. Wykes, D. (1995) 'The reluctant businessman: John Coltman of St Nicholas Street, Leicester (1727-1808)' in: *Transactions: Leicestershire Archaeological and Historical Society*, vol.69, pp.71-85. See note 3.
12. Beale, *Hutton and Friends,* p.244.
13. Vickery, A. (1999) *The Gentleman's Daughter: Women's Lives in Georgian England* (New Haven & London, Yale University Press), p.13.
14. Beale, *Hutton and Friends,* p. 215.
15. See Appendix 1, Pamphlets by Elizabeth Heyrick (née Coltman).

Backdrop

1. *Modern Language Notes,* 35, 7, pp. 413-417. In London, the play was produced under the direction of David Garrick, who was nearing the end of his career as an actor and theatre manager and is remembered for bringing Shakespeare to contemporary audiences.
2. Olusoga, D. (2016) *Black and British: A Forgotten History* (London, Macmillan), p.76
3. Cumberland, R. (1771) *The West Indian: a comedy.* (London, Griffin), p.4.
4. ibid, p.7.
5. 'Critique on the West-Indian,' *The Lady's Magazine,* February 1771, pp. 310-312.
6. Hochschild, A. (2006) *Bury the Chains: The British Struggle to Abolish Slavery* (Pan Macmillan Ltd., London).
7. For a clear account of the origins of slavery see Walvin, J (2007) *A Short History of Slavery* (London, Penguin).
8. But see Olusoga, *Black and British,* for reference to earlier activities by English slave traders operating from abroad.

9. Little, K. (1972) *Negroes in Britain: A Study of Racial Relations in English Society* (London & Boston, Routledge and Kegan Paul), p. 191.
10. For a full discussion of the Somerset Ruling and its impact, see Olusoga, *Black and British,* pp.134-145.
11. Brontë, E. (1847) *Wuthering Heights* (republished by Macdonald, London, 1955), p.37-38. Although the novel was first published well after the passing of the Slavery Abolition Act in 1833, the story opens long before when the struggle for emancipation was just beginning.
12. See von Sneidern, M. (1995) 'Wuthering Heights and the Liverpool Slave Trade', *English Literary History,* 62, 1, pp.171-196.
13. 'Jamaica St James 546 (Providence)', *Legacies of British Slave-ownership database, http://wwwdepts-live.ucl.ac.uk/lbs/claim/view/24026* (accessed 10th July 2018).
14. Lyon, K. (1985) *The Dentdale Brontë Trail* (Lyon Equipment, Dent). Thanks to Sally Griffin for alerting me to this story.
15. Gawthrop, H. (2013) 'Slavery: *Idée Fixe* of Emily and Charlotte Brontë *Brontë Studies*, 38, 4, pp.281-289.
16. Nonconformists were Protestants who Dissented from the established Church of England.
17. Walvin, J. (2008) 'Slavery, The Slave Trade and the Churches', *Quaker Studies,* 12, 2, pp.189-195.
18. Benezet, A. (1766) *A Caution and Warning to Great Britain and Her Colonies,* (Philadelphia).
19. ibid, p.3.
20. Benezet, *A Caution and Warning,* p.35.
21. Williams, G. (1897) *History of the Liverpool Privateers* (London, William Heineman), p.678.
22. Shields, J. (2008) 'Wheatley, Phillis (c.1753-1784)' *Oxford Dictionary of National Biography, www.oxforddnb-com* (accessed 7/2/23).
23. Little, *Negroes in Britain.*
24. Chater, K. (2009) *Untold Histories: black people in England and Wales during the period of the British slave trade, c 1660—1807* (Manchester University Press.), p.94.
25. See the panel entitled 'The Juba Family from servant to freeman' in the exhibition 'The Long Road to Freedom' produced by ROLLR in 2007, *www.antislavery.ac.uk* (accessed 7/2/23).
26. From *Williamson's Advertiser*, 8 September, 1758, quoted in Williams, G. (1897) *History of the Liverpool Privateers* (London, William Heineman), p.475.

27. Chater, *Untold Histories,* p.99.
28. Little, *Negroes in Britain*, p.192.
29. ibid.

PART I: 1760-1770

Chapter 1: '.....in hopeless disaccord'

1. Thompson, J. (1871) *The history of Leicester in the eighteenth century* (Leicester, Crossley and Clarke), p.140-1
2. Wykes, D. (1995) 'The reluctant businessman: John Coltman of St Nicholas Street, Leicester (1727-1808)' in: *Transactions: Leicestershire Archaeological and Historical Society*, vol.69, pp.71-85.
3. Schofield. R. (2013) 'Joseph Priestley, 1733-1804' *Oxford Dictionary of National Biography, www.oxforddnb.com* (accessed 7/2/23).
4. Porter, R. (1991) *English Society in the 18th Century*, (London, Penguin Books) (revised edition.) p.181.
5. Coltman, S. *Time's Stepping Stones - or some memorial of four generations of a family by an octogenarian of the same,* 3 vols., 1772-1857, ROLLR, M1153, p.2.
6. Gardiner, W. (1838-1853) *Music and Friends, or pleasant recollections of a dilettante* (London), vol. III, p.32-3.
7. Porter, *English Society.*
8. Vickery, A. (1999) *The Gentleman's Daughter: Women's Lives in Georgian England* (New Haven & London, Yale University Press), p.95.
9. Patterson, A. Temple (1954) *Radical Leicester: A History of Leicester 1780-1850* (Leicester, University College) p.12.
10. Beale, *Hutton and Friends*, p.65-6.
11. Skillington, S.H. (1923) *A History of Leicester* (Leicester, Edgar Backus), p.133.
12. Gordon, A. 'Worthington, Hugh (1752-1813)' *Oxford Dictionary of National Biography, www.oxforddnb.com.* (accessed 26/07/23)
13. Beale, *Hutton and Friends,* p.68.
14. Chadwick, R (2004) 'Hall, Robert (1764-1831)' *Oxford Dictionary of National Biography, www.oxforddnb.com.* (accessed 26/07/23)
15. Woods, M. (2010) *The Story of England: A Village and its People through the whole of English History* (London, Viking), p.310ff.
16. Coltman, S., *Time's Stepping Stones,* p.17.

17. Routley, E. (1960) *English Religious Dissent*, (Cambridge, The University Press).
18. Wykes, D. (1995) 'The reluctant businessman: John Coltman of St Nicholas Street, Leicester (1727-1808)' in: *Transactions: Leicestershire Archaeological and Historical Society*, vol.69, pp.71-85.
19. Woods, M. (2010) *The Story of England: A Village and its People through the whole of English History* (London, Viking), p.328. After a feminist reappraisal in the 1970s, Barbauld's biographer notes that she is now seen as a leading writer of Romanticism. See William McCarthy (2004) 'Barbauld (nee Aikin) Anna Letitia' *Oxford Dictionary of National Biography,* www.oxforddnb.*com* (accessed 7/2/23).
20. Yeoman farmers were a class of lesser freeholders, below the gentry, who cultivated their own land.
21. Jenkins, J. (2007) 'Elizabeth Heyrick (1769-1831) "Friend of the Poor" *Leicestershire Historian*, no. 43, p.37.
22. Coltman, S. *Time's Stepping Stones,* p.9.
23. Beale, *Hutton and Friends,* p.151.
24. ibid.
25. ibid.
26. Presumably this was a reference to Queen Charlotte (1744-1818) who was married to George III at the time.

Chapter 2: 'I will not be trifled with'

1. The courtship letters are contained in Samuel Coltman's memoirs: *Time's Stepping Stones – or some memorial of four generations of a family by an octogenarian of the same.* Samuel (Elizabeth's younger brother) dictated his memoirs to his wife when he was in his eighties and the quotations in these chapters are taken from the typescript version held in ROLLR, reference M1153. The courtship letters begin in Chapter 2 and (mixed with other material) continue through to Chapter 12. Catherine Hutton used the letters as a key source for her reminiscences. See Beale *Hutton and Friends*.
2. This is the original spelling of the title. The book later became known as *The Prince of Abyssinia: A Tale.*
3. Coltman, *Times Stepping Stones,* p.15.
4. ibid, p.16
5. ibid, p.22.
6. ibid.

7. ibid. p.22.
8. ibid, p.23.
9. ibid, p.24.
10. Beale, *Hutton and Friends.*
11. Coltman, *Times Stepping Stones*, p.25.
12. ibid, p.29.
13. ibid, p.30.
14. ibid, p.40.
15. ibid, p.42. (Underlining in the original.)
16. ibid, p.43.
17. ibid, p.45.
18. Porter, *English Society.*
19. Coltman S, *Time's Stepping Stones,* p.54.
20. See Olsen, K. (1999) *Daily Life in 18th Century England* (Connecticut & London, Greenwood Press). Olsen notes that life expectancy fluctuated throughout the eighteenth century but usually hovered in the low to mid-thirties.
21. Coltman, *Time's Stepping Stones,* p.57.
22. Austen J. (1813) *Pride and Prejudice,* (republished by Penguin Popular Classics, London, 1994), p.150-1.
23. Coltman, *Times Stepping Stones,* p.58.
24. ibid, p.63.
25. ibid, p.64.
26. Porter, *English Society.*
27. Coltman, *Times Stepping Stones,* p.66.
28. ibid.
29. ibid, p.67.
30. ibid, p.69
31. ibid, p.69.
32. ibid, p.70.
33. ibid.
34. Olsen, K. (1999) *Daily Life in 18th Century England* (Connecticut & London, Greenwood Press).
35. Coltman, *Time's Stepping Stones,* p.71.
36. ibid, p.72.
37. ibid, p.75.
38. ibid, p.76.
39. ibid, p.78.
40. See Mitchell, R. (2004) 'Hutton, Catherine (1756-1846)' *Oxford Dictionary of National Biography, www.oxforddnb.com* (accessed 7/2/23).

41. Originally titled *'Oakwood House'* the novel was serialised in 1812 and published in a monthly women's magazine *La Belle Assemblée*.
42. Hutton, C. (1819) *Oakwood Hall, A Novel: including a description of the Lakes of Cumberland and Westmoreland, and A Part of South Wales*, 3 volumes, (London).
43. Wilson, C. (2015) 'Something like mine': Catherine Hutton, Jane Austen, and Feminist Recovery Work', *The Eighteenth Century,* vol.56, no.2, pp.151-164.

Chapter 3: '…the prettiest and the ugliest of the litter should both be preserved'

1. Coltman, *Times Stepping Stones,* p.104.
2. Beale, *Hutton and Friends,* p.186.
3. Gardiner, W. (1853) *Music and Friends or Pleasant Recollections of a Dilettante* (London, Longmans et al) vol. III, p.3.
4. Crook, Z, and Simon, B. (1968) 'Private Schools in Leicester and the County 1780-1840' in: *Education in Leicestershire 1540-1940,* B. Simon (ed.) (Leicester, Leicester University Press) p.108.
5. Allen, J. *The Nathaniel Newton Foundation School, Hartshill, Warwickshire: 1742-1895.* [Place of publication, publisher and date of publication not identified]
6. ibid, p.13.
7. Coltman, *Time's Stepping Stones.*
8. Olsen, *Daily Life,* p.226.
9. Allen, *The Nathaniel Newton Foundation School,* p.12.
10. Aucott, S. (2007) *Elizabeth Heyrick 1769-1831: The Leicester Quaker who Demanded the Immediate Emancipation of Slaves in the British Colonies* (Leicester, Shirley Aucott), p.4.
11. Beale, *Hutton and Friends,* p.192-3
12. Coltman, *Time's Stepping Stones,* p.106.
13. Olsen, *Daily Life,* p.105ff.
14. Hutton, C. (1844) 'A Sketch of a Family of Originals, by an original, their friend' *Ainsworth's Magazine* vol.5, p.61. (Though published anonymously this article is believed to be by Catherine Hutton, who uses pseudonyms for some of the story's key protagonists.)Angelica Kauffman (1741-1807) was a talented portrait painter and one of the founder members of the Royal Academy in 1768.
15. At the time, Freestone was a small sea bathing place in Lincolnshire.

16. Coltman, *Time's Stepping Stones,* p.120-121.
17. Jenkins, 'Elizabeth Heyrick', p.37.
18. Richardson, S. (1740) *Pamela* (Edition first published as Oxford World's Classics paperback in 2001, reissued 2008), p.20.
19. Vickery, *The Gentleman's Daughter,* p.113.
20. Beale, *Hutton and Friends,* p.188-189.
21. Olsen, *Daily Life,* p.161-2.
22. Vickery, *The Gentleman's Daughter,* p.113.
23. Quoted in Porter, *English Society,* p. 308.
24. Porter, *English Society,* p.249.
25. Sterne, L. (1760) *The Sermons of Mr Yorick,* vol.II, Sermon X, (London, R. & J. Dodsley) p.98-9.
26. Extract of letter from Sterne to Sancho, from Coxwould near York, dated 27 July 1766, available at *www. brycchancarey.com/sancho/ letter1.htm* (accessed 8/2/23).
27. Carretta V. (2004) 'Sancho, (Charles) Ignatius (1729-1780)' *Oxford Dictionary of National Biography, wwwoxforddnb.com* (accessed 8/2/23).

PART II: 1780-1790

Chapter 4: 'No Presbyterians, no machines'

1. Letter from Mrs Coltman to Miss Gifford, Leicester, December 18th, 1787, in private family papers.
2. Thompson, J. (1871) *The History of Leicester in the Eighteenth Century* (Leicester, Crossley & Clarke; London, Hamilton, Adams & Co.), p.188.
3. ibid.
4. ibid.
5. The Worshipful Company of Framework Knitters was incorporated as a London chartered company to regulate the trade in 1657. It was not concerned with the protection of workers' rights so much as with collecting fees from its members and preventing those who were not properly trained from entering the trade. By the time of the Leicester riots, however, its authority, especially in the Midlands, was being widely flouted. For further background, see Wykes, D. (1992) 'The Origins and Development of the Leicestershire Hosiery Trade' *Textile History,* 23, 1, p.23-54.

6. The Riot Act was passed by the British Parliament in 1714 in response to rebellion and unrest, and in the belief that existing laws were insufficient.
7. Letter from Coltman to Gifford.
8. ibid.
9. Wykes, 'The Reluctant Businessman', pp.71-85.
10. ibid.
11. Wigston Framework Knitters Museum (1999) *Notes on Framework Knitting* (Leicestershire).
12. Wykes, 'The Reluctant Businessman,' p.85.
13. Unable to exercise their traditional grazing rights, with no secure employment, and constrained by the provisions of the Poor Law to stay within the confines of the parish where they received financial assistance, many of the rural poor were reduced to pauperdom. For further discussion of the impacts of enclosure, see Porter, *English Society,* pp.209-13.
14. Porter, *English Society,* p.212.
15. Victoria County History, *www.history.ac.uk,* Vol. 4, p.166ff.
16. Thompson, *The History of Leicester,* p.257.
17. Wykes, D. (1978-79) 'The Leicester Riots of 1773 and 1787: a study of the victims of popular protest,' *Transactions of the Leicestershire Archaeological & Historical Society*, vol 54, pp.39-50.
18. ibid.
19. Porter, *English Society,* p.103.
20. Wykes, 'The Leicester Riots', pp.39-50.
21. Wykes, 'The Reluctant Businessman,' p.71-85.
22. Obituary of John Coltman, *The Gentleman's Magazine*, 78, 1808, p.181-2.
23. Gardiner, *Music and Friends,* vol.1, p.61.
24. Temple Patterson, *Radical Leicester,* p.71-73.
25. ibid, p.68.
26. Gardiner, *Music and Friends,* vol.1, p.74.
27. Wykes, 'The Reluctant Businessman', pp.71-85.
28. Some historians argue that the history of civil society stretches back hundreds of years. See Savage, O. with Pratt, B. (2013) 'The history of UK civil society', Briefing Paper 38, International NGO Training and Research Centre, *www.intrac.org* (accessed 8/2/23).
29. Coltman, *Time's Stepping Stones,* p.138.
30. Savage with Pratt, 'The history of UK civil society'.
31. ibid.

32. Wykes, The Reluctant Businessman,' pp.71-85.
33. Gardiner, *Music and Friends,* vol. 1, p.61.
34. Letter to Richard Pulteney, quoted in Wykes (1995).
35. Obituary of John Coltman, *The Gentleman's Magazine*, 78, 1808, p.181-2.
36. Wykes, 'The Reluctant Businessman.' According to the website *www.measuringworth.com*, the relative value of £3000 in 2019 was £312,200.00, calculated in terms of its purchasing power.
37. Wykes, 'The Reluctant Businessman', p.82.
38. Hutton, C. (1844) 'A Sketch of a Family of Originals', *Ainsworth's Magazine,* vol.5, January, pp.56-63. (The quote is taken from p.59 of the article which was published anonymously with pseudonyms for the key protagonists but is now attributed to Hutton.)
39. 1817 *'Exposition of one principal cause of the National Distress particularly in Manufacturing Districts with some suggestions for its removal'*; 1819 *'Enquiry into the consequences of the present depreciated value of human labour' in Letters to Thomas Fowell Buxton, Esq. MP;* 1825 *'On the advantages of a high remunerating price for labour'*; 1825 *'A Letter of remonstrance from an impartial public to the hosiers of Leicester.'*

Chapter 5: 'Never daring even to think of it'

1. J. Hector St John (1782) *Letters from an American Farmer* (Dublin, John Exshaw).
2. Beale, *Hutton and Friends,* p.85.
3. Hector St John, *Letters,* p.189.
4. For a comprehensive account of these events, see James Walvin's book *The Zong*, published in 2011 by Yale University Press (New Haven and London). J.M.W. Turner's celebrated painting *'Slave Ship'*, dated 1840 and now held at the Museum of Fine Arts in Boston, was inspired by the *Zong* massacre.
5. Calculated using the website 'Measuring Worth' *www.measuringworth.com,* (accessed on 8/6/23).
6. *Morning Chronicle and London Advertiser,* Tuesday March 18, 1783, issue 4316.
7. Quoted in Olusoga, *Black and British,* p.205.
8. Gardiner, *Music and Friends*, see Chapter XVII, vol III.

9. Hurwitz, E. (1973) *Politics and the Public Conscience: Slave Emancipation and the Abolitionist Movement in Britain* (London, George Allen & Unwin Ltd. & New York, Barnes and Noble Books), p.22-4.
10. Williams, *Liverpool Privateers,* p.678-9.
11. Hochschild, *Bury the Chains,* p.156.
12. Beale, C.H. (ed.) (1891) *Reminiscences of a Gentlewoman of the Last Century, letters of Catherine Hutton*, (Birmingham, Cornish Bros.) p.132.
13. Mintz, Stephen, 'The Middle Passage', *www.digitalhistory.uh.edu* (accessed on 8/6/23).
14. Equiano, O. (1789) *The Interesting Narrative of the Life of Olaudah, or Gustavus Vassa, the African.* Revised edition. (Simon and Brown, 2012).
15. Hochschild, *Bury the Chains.*
16. Beale, *Hutton and Friends,* p.146.
17. Hochschild, *Bury the Chains,* p.137. The figure represents about 1 per cent of the country's population at the time.
18. ibid, p.138.
19. Thompson, *The History of Leicester,* p.190.
20. *List of the Society, instituted in 1787, for the purpose of effecting the abolition of the slave trade* (London, 1788).
21. Oldfield, J.R. (2004) 'Macaulay, Zachary (1768-1838)' *Oxford Dictionary of National Biography, www.oxforddnb.com* (accessed 26/07/23)
22. Morris, C., Wilberforce, S., Wilberforce, R. Isaac. (1857) *The life of William Wilberforce.* (New York: Protestant Episcopal Society for the Promotion of Evangelical Knowledge). p.701.
23. See I Corinthians, 14: 34-35.
24. See Timeline in The Fight for the Abolition of British Slavery, p.xiii. For further background to Parliamentary debates at this time, see Hochschild, A. (2005) *Bury the Chains,* ch.21 'A Side Wind' and Walvin, J. (2007) *A Short History of Slavery*, ch.10 'Abolishing the Slave Trade'.
25. Heyrick, E. (1824) *No British Slavery or an Invitation to the People to Put A Speedy End To It* (London), p.7.
26. Hurwitz, E. (1973) *Politics and the Public Conscience: Slave Emancipation and the Abolitionist Movement in Britain* (London, George Allen & Unwin Ltd. & New York, Barnes and Noble Books), p. 82.
27. *List of the Society for abolition of slave trade,* 1788.

28. Midgley, C. (1992) *Women Against Slavery: The British Campaigns, 1780-1870,* (London and New York, Routledge), p.17-18.
29. Coltman, *Time's Stepping Stones,* p.138.
30. The Clapham Sect was a group of evangelical Christians who were active from about 1790 to 1830. They campaigned for the abolition of slavery (amongst other things) and were mostly wealthy and politically conservative Anglicans. They believed in preserving rank and order within society and preached paternalistic benevolence. For a full account, see Howse, E. (1952) *Saints in Politics: The Clapham Sect and the Growth of Freedom* (London, George Allen & Unwin Ltd.)
31. Controversy still exists about the extent to which some of the black poor were coerced into joining the scheme but David Olusoga is clear that the settlement was never 'a dumping ground for unwanted black people.' (See Olusoga, *Black and British,* p.197). When the group finally set sail, they were also joined by some white colonists, looking to make their fortunes overseas. David Olusoga gives a full and lucid discussion of the Sierra Leone experiments in *Black and British,* (Chapter Five 'Province of Freedom').
32. Peterson, J. (1969) *Province of Freedom: A History of Sierra Leone 1787-1870* (London, Faber and Faber) p.26-7.
33. Initially called the St George's Bay Company.
34. Fyfe, C.(1962) *A History of Sierra Leone* (London, Oxford University Press) p.27.
35. Coltman, *Time's Stepping Stones,* p.138.
36. *Free English Territory in Africa* (An Account of the district purchased for the settlement at Sierra Leone) (London, 1790).
37. Peterson, *Province of Freedom,* p.27.
38. Calculated using the website *www.measuringworth.com*
39. Peterson, *Province of Freedom,* p.28.
40. Fyfe, *A History of Sierra Leone,* p.59-60.
41. Wykes, 'The reluctant businessman,' p.71-85; Coltman, *Times Stepping Stones*. Amongst the other events causing anxiety to his parents at the time, Samuel mentions threats of invasion, emigration of friends to America and riots.
42. More, H. (1788) *Slavery, A Poem* (London, Cadell), *www.brycchancarey.com* (accessed 28/06/23)
43. See Howse, E. (1952) *Saints in Politics: The 'Clapham Sect' and the Growth of Freedom* (London, George Allen & Unwin)
44. The full text of the poem is available at *www.brycchancarey.com* where there is a range of useful and interesting material related to slavery and abolition (accessed 28/06/23)

45. Hochschild, *Bury the Chains,* p.159.
46. Olusoga, *Black and British,* p.232.
47. Heyrick, E. (1824) *An Appeal Not to the Government But to the People of England on the subject of West Indian Slavery,* p.7.
48. Heyrick, E (1824) *No British Slavery or an Invitation to the People to Put A Speedy End to it,* p.3.
49. ibid, p.4.
50. See *www.brycchaney.com* (accessed 28/06/23)
51. William Cowper's work was popular and his poems 'Charity' (1783) and 'The Negro's Complaint' (1783) were widely read. William Blake's poem 'The Little Black Boy' (1789) is often interpreted as one of his first abolitionist texts. See also Chapter Eleven for the use made by the Birmingham Ladies Anti-Slavery Society of Cowper's poem 'The Morning Dream'.
52. Hurwitz, *Politics and the Public Conscience,* p.88-90.

Chapter 6: 'All the work of a moment'

1. Gardiner, *Music and Friends,* p.129.
2. ibid.
3. Hutton, C. (1844) 'A Sketch of a Family of Originals' *Ainsworth's Magazine* January, vol.5, p.56-63.
4. Vickery, *The Gentleman's Daughter,* p.56.
5. Beale, *Hutton and Friends,* p.190.
6. Vickery, *The Gentleman's Daughter,* p.56.
7. Thompson, *The History of Leicester,* p.218.
8. Hutton, C. (1802) *A Hasty Sketch of the Coltman Family,* ROLLR, 15D57/387; p.3.
9. Gardiner, *Music and Friends,* p.130.
10. Coltman, *Time's Stepping Stones,* p.121.
11. Midgley, C. (2011) 'The Dissenting Voice of Elizabeth Heyrick: An Exploration of the links between Gender, Religious Dissent, and Anti-slavery Radicalism' in: Clapp, E. & Jeffrey, J. (eds) *Women, Dissent, and Anti-slavery in Britain and America, 1790-1865,* (Oxford, New York: Oxford University Press) pp.88-110.
12. Porter, *English Society,* p.146-7.
13. St Nicholas church still stands in central Leicester, behind the ruins of the Roman Jewry Wall. Some of the bricks from the wall were used in the construction of the church.

14. The Marriage Act of 1836 eventually removed this restriction and allowed Nonconformists to be married in their own places of worship.
15. See Reid, R. (1864) *Old Glasgow and its Environs* (Glasgow, D. Robertson), p.53-55.
16. The poem is 'To the Virgins, To Make Much of Time', in *The Poems of Robert Herrick,* The World's Classics no.16, Henry Frowde (London, New York, Toronto, Melbourne, Oxford University Press), p.81.
17. Heyrick, John (1797) *First Flights, containing pieces in verse on various occasions* (London).
18. Hutton, *A Hasty Sketch,* p.3.
19. Gardiner, *Music and Friends,* p.130.
20. Coltman, *Time's Stepping Stones,* p.128.
21. Beale, *Hutton and Friends,* p.191.
22. Bow Bridge (also known as King Richard's Bridge) spans the River Soar and was first constructed before 1485. King Richard III is known to have led his troops to battle over the bridge and after his death, his body was brought back tied on a horse. The bridge was rebuilt in Victorian times several decades after Elizabeth's death.
23. Coltman, *Time's Stepping Stones,* p.130.
24. Beale, *Hutton and Friends,* p.92.
25. Coltman, *Time's Stepping Stones,* p.130.
26. Thompson, *The History of Leicester,* p.218.
27. ibid, p204.
28. Thompson, *The History of Leicester,* p.214.
29. Beale, *Hutton and Friends,* p.191.
30. Porter, *English Society,* p.238.
31. ibid, p. 139.
32. Coltman, *Time's Stepping Stones,* p.131.
33. Heyrick, John (1797) 'To Eliza, A Love Elegy' in: *First Flights, containing pieces in verse on various occasions* (London), p.31
34. ibid, p.32.
35. Vickery, *The Gentleman's Daughter,* p.11.
36. Coltman, *Time's Stepping Stones,* p.127.
37. Chapone, H. (1829) *Letters on the Improvement of the Mind* (Chiswick: printed by C. Whittingham), p.45.
38. Hague, W. (2008) *William Wilberforce: the Life of the Great Anti-slave Trade Campaigner* (London, Harper Perennial) p.210.
39. See Banks, S. (2012) *Duels and Duelling* (Oxford, Shire Publications) for further background.
40. Vickery, *The Gentleman's Daughter,* p.73.

41. Coltman, *Time's Stepping Stones,* p.170.
42. ibid, p.175.
43. Hutton, *A Hasty Sketch,* p.4.
44. Olsen, *Daily Life,* p.134
45. Coltman, *Time's Stepping Stones,* p.174.
46. Wollstonecraft, M. (2015) *A Vindication of the Rights of Woman* (abridged edition) (London, Vintage Books), p.5.
47. Chapone, *Letters*, p.73.
48. ibid.
49. Wollstonecraft, M. (1798) *Maria: or, The Wrongs of Woman,* available at *https://www.gutenberg.org/files/134/134-h/134-h.htm#link2HCH0009* (accessed 9/2/23).
50. St Martin's had long been regarded as the principal church in the borough. This was not where the couple had married in 1789 but there were strong links between this church and the town's corporation in which the Heyrick family were prominent. In the seventeenth century, the Church contained a chapel known as Herrick's or Reynold's Chapel. In the early 1600s, Alderman Robert Herrick, a mayor of Leicester and one of John Heyrick's forebears, built a mansion house and garden in which (as we now know) King Richard III was buried. The garden was eventually paved over and turned into a car park.
51. Coltman, *Time's Stepping Stones,* p.147.
52. ibid, p.149.

PART III: 1790-1800

Chapter 7: '...an emblem of the Wise'

1. *Scrapbook compiled by Susanna Watts* (c1817-1839), ROLLR, DE8170, p.545.
2. ibid.
3. The term was used in the eighteenth century to describe women who shared literary interests and held 'conversations' to which aristocratic or learned men were invited. It is now applied derisively to scholarly or intellectual women.
4. Porter, *English Society,* p.31.
5. Coltman, *Time's Stepping Stones,* p.129.
6. See Porter, *English Society,* pp.168-184.
7. Beale, *Hutton and Friends,* p.191.

8. Chapone, *Letters,* p.75.
9. Grundy, Isobel (2010) 'Susanna Watts 1768-1842' *Oxford Dictionary of National Biography https://doi-org.lonlib.idm.oclc.org/10.1093/ref:odnb/38113* (accessed 9/2/23).
10. 'Letter from Maria Edgeworth to Mary Sneyd, 12 September 1802' *Scrapbook compiled by Susanna Watts,* ROLLR, p.91-94.
11. Anonymous, (1842) *Hymns and Poems of the Late Susanna Watts with a few Recollections of her Life* (printed and published by J Waddington, Booksellers, Leicester).
12. Aucott, S. (2004) *Susanna Watts 1768-1842 Author of Leicester's First Guide, Abolitionist and Bluestocking* (Leicester, Shirley Aucott).
13. Simmons, J. (1967) 'Introduction' *A Walk Through Leicester* by Susanna Watts (Third edition) (Leicester University Press) p.vii.
14. James, F. and Shuttleworth, R. (2017) 'Susanna Watts and Elizabeth Heyrick: Collaborative Campaigning in the Midlands 1820-34' in: *Women's Literary Networks and Romanticism: "a tribe of authoresses"* edited by Andrew Winkles & Angela Rehbein (Liverpool University Press).
15. ibid, p.47.
16. *Scrapbook compiled by Susanna Watts,* p.504.
17. See Whelan, T. (2015) *Other British Voices: Women, Poetry and Religion 1766-1840 (New York, Palgrave Macmillan)*. Chapter 6 focuses on Elizabeth Coltman (1761-1838) and distinguishes her clearly from our Elizabeth Heyrick (née Coltman) who lived nearby and was a friend. Both these women published pamphlets and had interests in common, including religion, politics and the hosiery trade.
18. Vickery, *The Gentleman's Daughter,* p.259.
19. Olsen, *Daily Life,* p.160.
20. Vickery, *The Gentleman's Daughter,* p.86.
21. ibid, p.60.
22. Hays, M. (1796) *Memoirs of Emma Courtney,* (republished in 1996 by Oxford University Press), p.32.
23. ibid, p.39.
24. Vickery, *The Gentleman's Daughter,* p.287.
25. See Whelan, *Other British Voices*.
26. See complete list of pamphlets attributed to Elizabeth Heyrick in Appendix 1.
27. 'Framework Knitting and Other Industries of Bonsall' Pamphlet produced by the Bonsall History Project, *www.bonsallhistory.org.uk* (accessed 9/2/23).
28. Beale, *Hutton and Friends,* p.200.

29. 'Heyrick, E. (1808) '*Bull-baiting: a village dialogue between Tom Brown and John Sims'*, (London: printed and sold by Darton and Harvey) p.5.
30. ibid, p.6.
31. Heyrick, E. (1809) *Bull-baiting: A Christmas Box, for the Advocates of Bull-baiting* (London, printed by Darton and Harvey), p.7.
32. ibid, p.4.
33. ibid, p.15.
34. ibid, p.20.
35. ibid, p.21.
36. Beale, *Hutton and Friends,* p. 201.
37. A report in the *Derbyshire Courier* on 2 August 1834 claims that a few days earlier, some locals in Bonsall had assembled and were about to begin baiting a bull when the rector Robert Grenville interrupted them and for the price of a guinea purchased the animal and led it to safety. Later, several fights broke out in the village.
38. See Bunting, J. (1998) 'Take a Look at Bullrings' *The Peak Advertiser*, 14 September.
39. Heyrick, E. (1823) *Cursory Remarks on the Evil Tendency of Unrestrained Cruelty Particularly on that Practised in Smithfield Market* (London, Harvey and Darton), p.4.
40. ibid, p.7.
41. ibid, p.7-8.
42. ibid, p.8.
43. ibid.
44. ibid, p.15.

Chapter 8: 'If we purchase the commodity, we participate in the crime'

1. See '*The Poems of William Cowper'* (1905) (edited by J.C.Bailey) (London, Methuen and Co), p.455-456.
2. See Chapter 5 'Never daring to think of it'.
3. Glasse's cookbook was a best seller for over 100 years but its success did not save her from Marshalsea prison where she was sent as a debtor some eleven years later.
4. Glasse, H. (1805) *The Art of Cookery Made Plain and Easy* (republished in 2015 by Dover Publications, New York) p.123.
5. Hochschild, *Bury the Chains,* p.194-5.

6. Sussman, C. (1994) 'Women and the Politics of Sugar, 1792' *Representations,* Autumn 1994, no.48, pp.48-69.
7. Slare, Frederick (1714) *A Vindication of Sugars against the Charge of Dr Willis, other Physicians and common prejudices* (Epsom).
8. ibid, 'Dedication' at E4.
9. ibid.
10. Hochschild, *Bury the Chains,* p. 54-5.
11. Saint-Domingue was a French colony on the Caribbean island of Hispaniola. The island now hosts two countries, the Dominican Republic and Haiti.
12. Taylor, M. (2020) *The Interest: How the British Establishment Resisted the Abolition of Slavery* (London, The Bodley Head), p.4.
13. Walvin, *A Short History of Slavery,* p.154.
14. Midgley, *Women Against Slavery,* p.23-5.
15. Jones, M. (1998) '*The mobilisation of public opinion against the slave trade and slavery: Popular abolitionism in national and regional politics, 1787-1838.*' (University of York, unpublished D. Phil thesis,) p.68.
16. Hochschild, *Bury the Chains,* p.7.
17. See Cugoano, Quobna Ottobah (1787) *Thoughts and Sentiments on the Evils of Slavery and other writings* (republished by Penguin Books, New York, 1999.)
18. ibid, p.16.
19. Olusoga, *Black and British,* p.211.
20. Hague, W. (2008) *William Wilberforce: The Life of the Great Anti-slave Trade Campaigner* (London & New York, Harper Perennial), p.149.
21. See Chapter 5 'Never daring to think of it'.
22. Hague, *William Wilberforce,* p.149.
23. Porter, *English Society,* see Chapter Nine 'Conclusion'.
24. See Chapter Four 'No Presbyterians, no machines'.
25. Beale, *Hutton and Friends,* p.124.
26. Whelan, T. (2009) 'William Fox, Martha Gurney, and the Radical Discourse of the 1790s' *Eighteenth Century Studies,* vo.42, no.3, pp.397-411.
27. Confusingly there were three other men with the same name living at about this time. Again, Timothy Whelan has untangled the historical confusions and as a result of his meticulous investigations, William Fox, the bookseller, (whose birth and death dates are not known) has now some overdue recognition for his contribution to the anti-slavery movement. See Whelan, 'William Fox, Martha Gurney, and Radical Discourse'.

28. Whelan, 'William Fox, Martha Gurney, and Radical Discourse'.
29. Fox, William (1792) 'An Address to the People of Great Britain on the Propriety of Abstaining from West India Sugar and Rum' (10th edition, p.4)
30. ibid, p.9-10.
31. ibid, p.10.
32. Olusoga, *Black and British.*
33. Whelan, T. (2011) 'Martha Gurney and the Anti-slave Trade Movement' in: *Women, Dissent & Anti-slavery in Britain & America, 1790-1865*, edited by Elizabeth Clapp & Julie Roy Jeffrey, (Oxford University Press).
34. Hochschild, *Bury the Chains,* p.195.
35. See Chapter Twelve 'By a train of most exquisite reasoning'.
36. Norton, M.B. (1980) *Liberty's Daughters: The Revolutionary Experience of American Women, 1750-1800* (Boston, Toronto: Little Brown and Company). See Chapter Six.
37. ibid, p.161.
38. Midgley, C. (2007) 'Sweetness and Power: the domestic woman and anti-slavery politics' in: *Feminism and Empire: Women activists in Imperial Britain 1790-1865* (London, Routledge).
39. Temple Patterson, *Radical Leicester,* see Chapter V.
40. Beale, *Hutton and Friends*, p.206.
41. Taylor, B. (2004) 'Wollstonecraft (married name Godwin), Mary (1759-1797)' *Oxford Dictionary of National Biography, www.oxforddnb-com* (accessed 9/2/23).
42. ibid.
43. Wollstonecraft, M. (1792) *A Vindication of the Rights of Woman with strictures on political and moral subjects* London (2nd edition) Volume 1, Chapter Two, p.44.
44. ibid, Chapter Nine, p.330.
45. Williams, Z. (2015) 'Introduction' *A Vindication of the Rights of Woman* (London, Vintage Books) (Abridged edition) p.x.
46. Midgley, 'Sweetness and Power'.
47. Heyrick, E. (1824) *Immediate not Gradual Abolition: Or an inquiry into the shortest, safest, and most effectual means of getting rid of West Indian Slavery* (London, J. Hatchard & Son).
48. Later, Elizabeth acknowledges that women have a special role to play in the abolition movement but this is because of their 'strong feelings' and 'quick sensibilities' which make them especially able to sympathise with those who suffer. See her pamphlet *Appeal to the Hearts and Consciences of British Women,* published in 1828.

49. See Taylor, B. (2004) 'Wollstonecraft (married name Godwin), Mary (1759-1797)' *Oxford Dictionary of National Biography, www. oxforddnb-com*) (accessed 9/2/23).
50. See Chapter Six 'All the Work of a Moment' for a discussion of tensions in Elizabeth's marriage.
51. Temple Patterson, *Radical Leicester,* p.91-92.
52. Whelan, 'Martha Gurney and Anti-slave Trade'.
53. Porter, *English Society,* p. 350.

Chapter 9: 'Peace - when there is no peace'

1. The extract from Elizabeth's diaries is quoted in Jenkins, J (2007), 'Elizabeth Heyrick (1769-1831) "Friend of the Poor", *Leicestershire Historian*, p.38.
2. Skidmore, G. (2004) 'Gurney, Priscilla Hannah (1757-1828)' *Oxford Dictionary of National Biography, www.oxforddnb.com* (accessed 9/2/23).
3. ibid.
4. Anon (1862) 'A Brief Sketch of the Life and Labours of Mrs Elizabeth Heyrick' (Leicester), p.15.
5. Porter, *English Society,* p.291.
6. Jenkins, 'Elizabeth Heyrick', p.36-41.
7. Heyrick, E. (1827) *Observations on the offensive and injurious effect of Corporal punishment on the unequal administration of penal justice; and on the pre-eminent advantages of the mild and reformatory over the vindictive system of punishment,* (London, Hatchard and Son).
8. Porter, *English Society,* see chapter 3.
9. Sadly, Elizabeth's diaries did not survive intact. Fragments were preserved by some of those who were close to her, such as her brother Samuel and the family relative Catherine Hutton who both clearly had access to them at some point.
10. Desforges, J. (2001) 'Satisfaction and Improvement: A Study of Reading in a small Quaker Community, 1770-1820' *Publishing History, vol.49, p.5-47.*
11. ibid.
12. Hutton, *A Hasty Sketch,* p.4.
13. Midgley, 'The Dissenting Voice of Elizabeth Heyrick.'
14. Anon, *A Brief Sketch,* p.9.
15. Temple Patterson, *Radical Leicester,* p.17.

16. Aucott, *Elizabeth Heyrick,* p.3-4. See also Chapter Three 'The prettiest and the ugliest'.
17. Beale, *Hutton and Friends,* p.235.
18. Porter, *English Society,* p.182-3.
19. See Chapter Seven '…an emblem of the Wise'.
20. *Victoria County History www.british-history.ac.uk/vch/city-of-york* (accessed 9/2/23).
21. Wright, S. (1995) *Friends in York: The Dynamics of Quaker Revival 1780-1860* (Keele University Press), p.13.
22. ibid.
23. ibid, p.16.
24. Digby, A. (2004) 'Tuke, William (1732-1822)' *Oxford Dictionary of National Biography, www.oxforddnb.com* accessed 9/2/23.
25. Digby, A. (1985) *Madness, Morality and Medicine* (Cambridge, Cambridge University Press), p.15.
26. Tuke, Samuel (1813) *Description of The Retreat, an Institution near York for Insane Persons of the Society of Friends* (York, printed for W. Alexander) p.40-41.
27. See Chapter Eight 'If we purchase the commodity we participate in the crime'.
28. Digby, A. (1985) *Madness, Morality and Medicine* (Cambridge, Cambridge University Press), p.29.
29. Digby, *Madness, Morality and Medicine.* For an informative discussion on the approach taken at The Retreat, see Chapter 3 'Moral Treatment.'
30. The Retreat closed in 2018 and the site was sold for development. A York-based mental health charity known as the Tuke Centre took over its outpatient work.
31. Letter from Dr Gilbert Thompson of Worcester, November 1827, Admission Papers 25 June 1796-22, The Retreat Archive, BIA, RET/6/1/1.
32. See Chapter Six 'All the Work of a Moment'.
33. Digby, *Madness, Morality and Medicine,* p.30.
34. ibid, p.33.
35. Letter from Elizabeth Heyrick to her mother, 1802, Letters of the Coltman Family, ROLLR, 15D57/64.
36. Letters of William Murray Tuke, Correspondence, other letters received by William Tuke, 1837-1901, Tuke Family Collection, BIA, TUKE/1/30/2/2/68.
37. Wright, S. (1995) *Friends in York: The Dynamics of Quaker Revival 1780-1860* (Keele University Press), p.12. The school was closed in 1814 but reopened in 1835 to become The Mount Girls' School which still exists and, according to its website, has an ethos that reflects

Quaker values of simplicity, truth, equality, peace, social justice and sustainability. See *https://www.mountschoolyork.co.uk/about-the-mount-school/ethos-aims/* (accessed 9/2/23).

38. Eddington, A. (1934) 'Prison Visiting in 1819' *Journal of the Friends' Historical Society,* vol. 31, pp.61-68.
39. ibid.
40. See Chapter Eleven 'A War with beggars! An exterminating crusade against the poor and miserable!'
41. Letter from Elizabeth Heyrick to her mother in 1802, Letters of the Coltman Family, ROLLR, 15D57/64.
42. ibid.
43. Porter, *English Society,* p. 164-5.
44. See Chapter One '..in hopeless disaccord'.
45. Letter from Elizabeth Heyrick to her mother in 1802, Letters of the Coltman Family, ROLLR, 15D57/64.
46. Jenkins, 'Elizabeth Heyrick.'
47. Letter to Susanna Watts from Elizabeth, Letters of the Coltman Family, ROLLR 15D57/81.
48. Tieken-Boon van Ostade, I. (2010) 'Murray, Lindley (1745-1826)' *Oxford Dictionary of National Biography, www.oxforddnb.com* (accessed 9/2/23).
49. ibid.
50. Beale, *Hutton and Friends,* p.195.
51. ibid, p.197.
52. ibid, p.195.
53. Isabella's story is contained in the private family papers which were compiled by Mary Ann Coltman in 1861.
54. Brown, R. (2009) 'Way, Lewis (1772-1840)' *Oxford Dictionary of National Biography, www.oxforddnb.com* (accessed 9/2/23).
55. Private family papers, compiled by Mary Ann Coltman in 1861.
56. ibid.
57. Letter from Elizabeth Heyrick to Mary Lloyd, 22 September 1806, LSF, TEMP MSS 403/7/15/7/3.
58. Fyfe, C. (2004) 'Lloyd, Charles (1748-1828)' *Oxford Dictionary of National Biography, oxforddnb.com* (accessed 9/2/23).
59. A second, younger and related Mary Lloyd was born Mary Honeychurch in 1795, married Samuel Lloyd in 1823, and died in 1865. She was also a contact of our Elizabeth's and is best known now as the co-secretary of the first women's anti-slavery society in Britain. See Midgley, C. (2004) 'Lloyd, (née Honeychurch) Mary (1795-1865)' *Oxford Dictionary of National Biography, www.oxforddnb.com* (accessed 09.02.23)

60. Beale, *Hutton and Friends,* p.196.
61. See Chapter Five 'Never daring even to think of it'.
62. Hochschild, *Bury the Chains,* p.307-8.
63. Minutes of the Leicester, Hinkley & Oakham Women's Monthly Meeting of the Society of Friends, ROLLR 12D39/126.
64. Brontë, C. (1847) *Jane Eyre* (republished in 1994 by Penguin Books), Chapter 24.
65. Beale, *Hutton and Friends,* p.135.
66. ibid, p.152.
67. Carey, B. and Plank, G. (eds) (2018) 'Introduction' in: *Quakers and Abolition* (Urbana, Chicago and Springfield, University of Illinois Press). Some opposition to slavery began to surface in Quaker essays published in America in the late seventeenth century but it was not until the 1750s, that the Friends' Society on both sides of the Atlantic began to marshal and promote anti-slavery arguments more formally.
68. Turner, M. (2010) 'A Good Death' in: Thomas Hamm (ed.) *Quaker Writings: An Anthology,1650-1920* (New York, Penguin Books), p.197.
69. Private family papers.
70. 'Obituary of John Coltman' *The Gentleman's Magazine,* 78, 1808, pp.181-2.
71. Private family papers.
72. Beale, *Hutton and Friends,* p.146.
73. ibid, p.148.
74. ibid, p.149.
75. Carnall, G. (1954) 'The *Monthly Magazine' The Review of English Studies,* vol.5 no.18, pp.158-164.
76. Beale, *Hutton and Friends,* p.151.

PART IV: 1800-1820

Chapter 10: 'The Rights of the Poor'

1. 'Luddites' were named after Edward Ludlam, a pauper born in Anstey near Leicester. His name sometimes abbreviated to 'Ned Ludd' appears regularly in parish records and contemporary sources suggest that he was a 'lunatic' who went berserk and smashed a frame. He was chosen by protesters in Nottingham as their fictitious leader.
2. *Leicester Chronicle*, Saturday 19 April 1817, p.4.
3. See Chapter Four 'No Presbyterians, no machines'.

4. Hay, D., Linebaugh, P. Rule, J.G., Thompson, E. P, Winslow, C. (1977) *Albion's Fatal Tree* (London, Peregrine Books) p.17-19.
5. Heyrick, E. (1825) '*A Letter of Remonstrance from an Impartial Public to the Hosiers of Leicester*' (Leicester, Cockshaw), p.12.
6. Temple Patterson, *Radical Leicester,* p.114.
7. Heyrick, E. (1817) *Exposition of one Principal Cause of the National Distress particularly in Manufacturing Districts* (London, Darton, Harvey and Darton), p.6.
8. Hobsbawm, E. (1962) *The Age of Revolution, 1789-1848* (London, Abacus); see Chpt. Two 'The Industrial Revolution'.
9. Heyrick, *Exposition of one Principal Cause*, p.16.
10. Thompson, E.P. (2013) *The Making of the Working Class* (London, Penguin Books).
11. Felkin, W. (1967*) Felkin's History of the Machine-Wrought Hosiery and Lace Manufacturers. Centenary Edition.* (Newton Abbot, David & Charles) p.441-2.
12. Anon, *A Brief Sketch,* p.15.
13. Heyrick, *Exposition of one Principal Cause,* p.3.
14. ibid, p.21.
15. Thompson, *The Making of the Working Class,* p.225.
16. ibid, p.225.
17. Aucott, *Elizabeth Heyrick.*
18. Temple Patterson, *Radical Leicester*.
19. ibid, p.104.
20. Heyrick, *Exposition of one principal cause,* p.8
21. ibid, p.20.
22. ibid, p.15.
23. ibid, p.8-9.
24. Heyrick, E. (1825) *On the Advantages of a High Remunerating Price for Labour* (Leicester).
25. Unions were not in active existence in Leicester until the 1820s although in an attempt to evade the Combination Laws, there was earlier a framework knitters' friendly society which took contributions from workers and sympathisers. See Temple Patterson, *Radical Leicester,* p.126.
26. Heyrick, *Exposition of one Principal Cause,* p.29-30.
27. Heyrick, E. (1819) *Enquiry into the Consequences of the Present Depreciated Value of Human Labour* in: Letters to Thos. Fowell Buxton (London, Longman & Co.), Letter the First, p.22.
28. Letter, S Coltman to Mrs S Coltman, 17 October 1819, Letters and Papers relating to the Coltman family of Leicester, ROLLR, 15D57/141.

29. Temple Patterson, *Radical Leicester,* p.139-40.
30. For full background to the dispute see Temple Patterson, *Radical Leicester,* Chapter VII.
31. Heyrick, E (1825) *A Letter of Remonstrance from an impartial public to the Hosiers of Leicester* (Leicester) p.13.
32. Heyrick, E. (1819) *Enquiry into the Consequences of the present depreciated Value of Human Labour*, in: *Letters to Thos. Fowell Burton, Esq. MD, Letter the First,* p.29.
33. See Corfield, K. (1986) 'Elizabeth Heyrick: Radical Quaker' in: Malmgreen, G. (ed.) *Religion in the Lives of English Women 1760-1930,* Chapter 3 (London, Croom Helm), footnote 109.
34. Heyrick, E (1825) *On the advantages of a high remunerating price for Labour,* (Leicester) p.4.
35. ibid, p.6.
36. ibid, p.8.
37. Heyrick, *A Letter of Remonstrance*, p. 6.
38. ibid, p.3.
39. Beale, *Hutton and Friends,* p.111.
40. ibid, p.170.
41. Letter to Mr Coltman from E Heyrick, c1824, Papers of Catherine Hutton, Miscellaneous manuscripts and letters, LB, MS168/59.
42. See Heyrick, E. (1826) *Animadversions on the late Contested Election for the Borough of Leicester* (Leicester, Cockshaw).
43. Corfield, K. (1986) 'Elizabeth Heyrick: Radical Quaker' in: Malmgreen, G. (ed.) *Religion in the Lives of English Women 1760-1930* (London, Croom Helm), p.59.
44. Thompson, *The Making of the English Working Class,* p.601.
45. Letter 'Elizabeth Heyrick to Mr Coltman, Feb 1827', Letters and papers relating to the Coltman family of Leicester, ROLLR, 15D57/194.
46. Hobsbawm, *The Age of Revolution,* see Chapter Two 'The Industrial Revolution'.

Chapter 11: 'A War with beggars! An exterminating crusade against the poor and miserable!'

1. The full title of the Act was 'An Act for the Punishment of Idle and Disorderly Persons, and Rogues and Vagabonds, in that part of Great Britain called England.'
2. For background, see Hobsbawm, *The Age of Revolution,* Chapter 4 'War'.

3. Webb, E. (2010) 'Travels and Travails' in: *Quaker Writings: An Anthology, 1650-1920,* ed. Thomas Hamm (New York, Penguin Books)
4. Stevens, S. (2013) 'Travelling Ministry' in: *The Oxford Handbook of Quaker Studies*, Chapter 19, eds S. Angell and P. Dandelion (Oxford University Press).
5. Allen, R. (2013) 'Restoration Quakerism, 1660-1691' in: *The Oxford Handbook of Quaker Studies*, Chapter 2, eds S. Angell and P. Dandelion (Oxford University Press).
6. ibid.
7. Porter, *English Society,* p.84.
8. Hutton, C. (1844) 'A Sketch of a Family of Originals, by an Original, their friend' in: *Ainsworth Magazine*, volume 5, p.56-63.
9. ibid, p.62-63.
10. Aucott, *Elizabeth Heyrick,* p.19.
11. Eccles, A. (2012) *Vagrancy in Law and Practice under the old Poor Law* (Farnham, Ashgate).
12. ibid, see Chapter 1.
13. Porter, *English Society,* p.127.
14. ibid.
15. Heyrick, E. (1824) *Protest against the Spirit and Practice of Modern Legislation as exhibited in the new Vagrant Act* (London, Harvey and Darton).
16. The editor is referring to the pamphlet entitled *Cursory remarks on the evil tendency of unrestrained cruelty; particularly on that practised in Smithfield Market* (London, Harvey and Darton) that Elizabeth Heyrick published in 1823. See Chapter Seven 'An emblem of the Wise'.
17. See 'New Vagrant Act', *Leicester Chronicle,* Saturday 31 January, 1824, p.4.
18. Temple Patterson, *Radical Leicester,* p.169-170.
19. Heyrick, *Protest against the new Vagrant Act*, p.4.
20. ibid, p.6.
21. ibid, p.9.
22. ibid, p.24. In fact, William Wilberforce was one of the 'great abolitionists' who did reportedly condemn the Act, arguing that it failed to take into account a person's individual circumstances and the reasons why they might find themselves destitute and on the streets.
23. Heyrick, E. (1824) *Immediate not gradual abolition: Or an inquiry into the shortest, safest and most effectual means of getting rid of West Indian slavery* (London, J. Hatchard & Son).

24. Heyrick, *Protest against the new Vagrant Act*, p.9.
25. ibid, p.9.
26. ibid, p.36.
27. Allen, 'Restoration Quakerism', p.32.
28. Temple Patterson, *Radical Leicester,* p.170.
29. *Victoria County History www.british-history.ac.uk/vch/leics/vol4/*, see pp.153-200 (accessed 10/2/23).
30. ibid.
31. Heyrick, *Protest against the new Vagrant Act*, p.38.
32. ibid, p.40.
33. See Chapter Ten 'The Rights of the Poor'.
34. Heyrick, *Protest against the new Vagrant Act*, p.14-15.
35. Mullett, C. (1935) 'The Historian and the Use of Pamphlets' *The Library Quarterly: Information, Community, Policy*, vol.5, no.3, p.310-311.
36. Heyrick, *Protest against the new Vagrant Act,* p.15.
37. ibid, p.16.
38. ibid, p.32.
39. See Chapter Ten 'The Rights of the Poor'.
40. Heyrick, *Protest against the new Vagrant Act*, p.34.
41. Gwyn, D. (2013) 'Quakers, Eschatology, and Time' in: *The Oxford Handbook of Quaker Studies*, Chapter 13, eds S. Angell and P. Dandelion (Oxford University Press).
42. Hamm, T. (2013) 'Hicksite, Orthodox, and Evangelical Quakerism, 1805-1887' in: *The Oxford Handbook of Quaker Studies*, Chapter 4, eds S. Angell and P. Dandelion (Oxford University Press).
43. ibid.
44. See Jenkins, 'Elizabeth Heyrick,' p.36-41.
45. 'Respected Friend? Women and Equality in the Society of Friends' *Quaker Strongroomshttps://quakerstrongrooms.org/2019/06/18/* (accessed 10/2/23).
46. See Chapter Nine 'Peace- when there is no peace'.
47. 'Respected Friend? Women and Equality in the Society of Friends' *Quaker Strongrooms, https://quakerstrongrooms.org/2019/06/18/* (accessed 10/2/23).
48. ibid.
49. Heyrick, E. (1827) *Observations on the Offensive and Injurious Effect of Corporal Punishment on the Unequal Administration of Penal Justice* (London, Hatchard and Son, Piccadilly) p.6.
50. Heyrick, *Protest against the new Vagrant Act*, p.19.

51. *Leicester Chronicle* 3rd Feb, 1827, p.3.
52. Heyrick, *Observations on Corporal Punishment*, p.18.
53. ibid.
54. ibid, p.10.
55. Macnaughton, D. (2004) 'Roscoe, William (1753-1831)' *Oxford Dictionary of National Biography, www.oxforddnb.com* (accessed 1/2/23).
56. The Prison Reform Trust (2021) *Prisons: the facts* (Bromley Briefings, London).
57. See Chapter Three '…the prettiest and the ugliest of the litter should both be preserved'.
58. Allen, *The Nathaniel Newton Foundation School,* p.14.
59. Quoted in Campbell Stewart, W. (1950) 'Punishment in Friends' Schools, 1779-1900' '*The Journal of the Friends' Historical Society,* vol.42, no.2, pp.51-66.
60. See Chapter Nine 'Peace- when there is no peace'.

Chapter 12: '...by a train of most exquisite reasoning'

1. Austen, J. (1814) *Mansfield Park* (republished in 1966 by Penguin English Library) Chapter 21 p.213.
2. Southam, B. (1995) 'The silence of the Bertrams: Slavery and the chronology of *Mansfield Park,*' *The Times Literary Supplement,* No.4794, 17 February, pp.13-14.
3. See Timeline in the Fight for the Abolition of British Slavery, pxiii. Also Hochschild, ch.21 and Walvin, ch.10.
4. Southam, 'The silence of the Bertrams', pp.13-14.
5. See Hochschild, *Bury the Chains,* Chapter 22 'Am I not a woman and a sister?'
6. See Timeline in the Fight for the Abolition of British Slavery, pxiii.
7. For a full list of the pamphlets attributed to Elizabeth Heyrick see Appendix 1.
8. See for example Heyrick, *Exposition of one Principal Cause,* written in 1817 in which she compares workers to enslaved people.
9. Heyrick, E. (1824) *Immediate, not Gradual Abolition: Or An Inquiry into the shortest, safest, and most effectual means of getting rid of West Indian Slavery*, see Appendix 2.
10. James and Shuttleworth, 'Susanna Watts and Elizabeth Heyrick'.
11. Craton, M. (1982) *Testing the Chains: Resistance to Slavery in the British West Indies* (Ithaca and London, Cornell University Press) p. 267.

12. Walvin, *A Short History of Slavery,* see p.202-3.
13. Craton, *Testing the Chains,* p.269.
14. Prince, M. (1831) 'The History of Mary Prince' in: *Three Narratives of Slavery* (Mineola, New York, Dover Publications), p.277.
15. Craton, *Testing the Chains,* p.273.
16. See 'The London Missionary Society' in: *The Christian Observer,* 1823, vol.23, p.833-836, and 'Negro Slavery' in *The Christian Observer,* 1824, vol.24, p.153-163.
17. Walvin, *A Short History of Slavery,* see Chapter 8.
18. Craton, *Testing the Chains,* p.267.
19. ibid, p. 272-3.
20. Hochschild, *Bury the Chains,* p.329.
21. Papers of the Anti-slavery Society, MS. Brit. Emp.s.20/E2/1. Bodleian Libraries, Oxford. The Society for the Mitigation and Gradual Abolition of Slavery throughout the British Dominions was founded in 1823. It was also referred to as the Society for Mitigating and Gradually Abolishing the State of Slavery throughout the British Dominions, and other variations.
22. See Chapter Five 'Never daring to think of it'.
23. Hochschild, *Bury the Chains,* p.328.
24. Craton, *Testing the Chains,* p. 274-5.
25. ibid, see Chapter 21.
26. Heyrick, *Immediate, not Gradual*, p.10.
27. For full list of pamphlets attributed to Elizabeth Heyrick, see Appendix 1.
28. Craton, *Testing the Chains,* p. 288.
29. Heyrick, E. (1824) *An Enquiry which of the two parties is best entitled to freedom? The Slave or the Slave holder?* (London, Baldwin, Cradddock and Joy; Leicester; A. Cockshaw), p.14.
30. Heyrick, *Immediate, not Gradual*, p.5.
31. ibid, p.12.
32. Heyrick, E. (1828) *Apology for Ladies' Anti-Slavery Associations* (London, Hatchard and Son; Leicester, Albert Cockshaw), p.11.
33. Blouet, Olwyn Mary (2010) 'Buxton, Sir Thomas Fowell, First Baronet' *Oxford Dictionary of National Biography, www.oxforddnb.com* (accessed 10/2/23).
34. Heyrick, E. (1819) 'Introductory Letter' *Letters to Thos. Fowell Buxton, Esq. M.D.* (London; Hurst, Rees, Orme and Brown), p.4.
35. *The History of Parliament www.historyofparliamentonline.org/volume/1820-1832/survey/vii-procedure-and-business-house.* (accessed 10/2/23).

36. *The History of Parliament https://api.parliament.uk/historic-hansard/commons/1823/may/15/abolition-of-slavery* (accessed 10/2/23).
37. Taylor, M. (2014) 'Conservative Political Economy and the Problem of Colonial Slavery, 1823-1833' *The Historical Journal*, vol 57, issue 4, pp.973-995.
38. *The History of Parliament https://api.parliament.uk/historic-hansard/commons/1823/may/15/abolition-of-slavery* (accessed 10/2/23).
39. Ellis, Charles Rose and Robert, (1824) 'West India colonies', *Quarterly Review*, 30, pp. 559-87.
40. ibid, p.569.
41. ibid, p.586.
42. Scanlan, P. (2020) *Slave Empire: How Slavery Built Modern Britain* (London, Robinson), p.282.
43. Heyrick, *Immediate, not Gradual*, p.13.
44. Taylor, *The Interest,* p.111.
45. Anon (1824) *The Hummingbird or morsels of information on the subject of slavery with various miscellaneous articles* (Leicester, Crickshaw). The journal ran for eleven months. Its publication predates the activities of the Ladies Anti-slavery Society in Birmingham (founded in 1825) and it appeared earlier than other abolitionist periodicals such as the *Anti-slavery Reporter* which began in 1825. The journal is available in the periodicals section of the Record Office of Leicestershire, Leicester & Rutland (ROLLR) and in the General Reference collection at the British Library.
46. James and Shuttleworth, 'Susanna Watts and Elizabeth Heyrick'. Literary circles overlapped so that women in Leicester became familiar with the work of women in London and the West Country. Elizabeth Coltman of the Newarke in Leicester, who wrote poetry and pamphlets as well as moral and political tracts was, for example, close friends with Mary Steele, poet and leader of a circle of West Country women writers which also included Mary Scott, little known author of the feminist poem *The Female Advocate* (1774).
47. *The Hummingbird,* vol.1, no.1, p.5.
48. ibid, p.3.
49. ibid, p.5.
50. ibid, p.12
51. James and Shuttleworth, 'Susanna Watts and Elizabeth Heyrick', p.58.
52. Midgley, *Women Against Slavery*.
53. After 1807, despite the abolition of the slave trade by Britain and some other countries, illegal trading continued for a further 60 years, much of it to the sugar plantations of Cuba and Brazil.

54. *Pity the Negro, or An address to Children on the Subject of Slavery* (Third Edition) (London, Westley, 1825), p.2-3. The pamphlet was published anonymously but is believed to have been written Charlotte Townsend. At least 14,000 copies were published.
55. ibid.
56. Dalrymple, W. (2015) 'The East India Company: The original corporate raiders' *The Guardian,* Wednesday 4 March.
57. Major, A. (2015) 'Not made by slaves': the ambivalent origins of ethical consumption https://www.opendemocracy.net/en/beyond-trafficking-and-slavery/not-made-by-slaves-ambivalent-origins-of-ethical-consumption/ (accessed 10/2/23).
58. See Chapter 8 'If we purchase the commodity, we participate in the crime'.
59. Heyrick, *Immediate, not Gradual*, p.6.
60. ibid, p.5.
61. For full list of pamphlets attributed to Elizabeth Heyrick, see Appendix 1.
62. Midgley, *Women Against Slavery.*
63. Aucott, *Elizabeth Heyrick.*
64. Leicester Auxiliary Anti-Slavery Society (1824) *An Address to the Public on the State of Slavery in the West-India Islands* (London, Ellerton and Henderson).
65. Heyrick, E (1824) *No British Slavery or an invitation to put a speedy end to it* (London, Darton and Harvey); Heyrick, E (1824) *An Appeal Not to the Government but to the People of England On the Subject of West Indian Slavery* (London, Baldwin, Craddock and Joy).
66. Heyrick, *An Appeal Not to the Government*, p.10.
67. ibid.
68. ibid, p.4. (Heyrick's capitals.)

PART V: 1820s-1830s

Chapter 13: 'Let compensation be made in the first place where it is most due'

1. Cugoano, Quobna Ottobah (1787) *Thoughts and Sentiments on the evil and wicked traffic of the slavery and commerce of the human species* (republished by Penguin Books, London, 1999), p.12-13.
2. ibid, p.98.
3. Truth, S., Jacobs, H. and Prince, M (2008) *Three Narratives of Slavery* (a new compilation of unabridged works from standard editions published by Dover Publications, New York), p.255.

4. Ferguson, M. (2004) 'Prince (married name James,) Mary (b. c1788)' *Oxford Dictionary of National Biography, www.oxforddnb.com.* For an account of the controversy that surrounded the publication of 'The History of Mary Prince' see Midgley, *Women Against Slavery*, p.86-92.
5. Walvin, *A Short History of Slavery,* p.206.
6. ibid, p.207.
7. ibid, p.210.
8. ibid, p.208.
9. Taylor, *The Interest,* p.31.
10. Heyrick, '*Immediate not Gradual,*' p.35.
11. Walvin, *A Short History of Slavery,* p.209.
12. Cugoano, *Thoughts and Sentiments*, p.98-99.
13. Taylor, *The Interest,* see Chapter 17 'The Price of Liberty'.
14. Hochschild, *Bury the Chains,* p.348.
15. Heyrick, *Immediate, not Gradual*, p.22.
16. Taylor, *The Interest,* p.267.
17. The concept of 'chattel slavery,' in which one person has total ownership of another, was developed by Europeans. See *The National Archives, https://webarchive.nationalarchives.gov.uk/ukgwa/20220201205654/ https://www.nationalarchives.gov.uk/caribbeanhistory/glossary.htm* (accessed 13/2/23).
18. Heyrick, *Immediate, not Gradual,* p.26.
19. ibid, p.19.
20. ibid, p.27.
21. ibid, p.34.
22. Heyrick, *An Enquiry which of the two parties*, p.28, capitals in original.
23. Corfield, 'Elizabeth Heyrick', p.46.
24. Leicester Auxiliary Anti-Slavery Society (1824) *An Address to the Public on the State of Slavery in the West-India Islands* (London, Ellerton and Henderson), p.11.
25. ibid.
26. Clarkson, Thomas (1823) *Thoughts on the necessity of improving the condition of the slaves in the British colonies with a view to their ultimate emancipation and on the practicability, the safety, and the advantages of the latter Measure* (London).
27. Heyrick, E. (1824)) *No British Slavery or An Invitation to the People to Put a Speedy End to it,* (London, Hatchard and Son) p.3-4. In fact, not all slave-holders were white; William Ellison who had been born into slavery in the American South, purchased his first slaves in 1820 and though they experienced discrimination blacks owning blacks

continued up to the Civil War. See *https://historyengine.richmond.edu/episodes/view/6699.*

28. Olusoga, *Black and British,* p. 258.
29. Taylor, *The Interest,* p, 113.
30. ibid.

Chapter 14: 'Finish the great work'

1. Townsend, 'Extracts from the Letters of Thomas Clarkson,' in: *Scrapbook on Negro Slaves,* March 30th 1825, BLO, MSS.Brit.Emp.s.4, p.115.
2. Hochschild, *Bury the Chains,* quoted on p.327.
3. Midgley, C (2004) 'Townsend (nee Jesse) Lucy (1781-1847)' *Oxford Dictionary of National Biography, www.oxforddnb.com* (accessed 13/2/23).
4. Minutes 1825-1852, Records of the Birmingham Ladies Negro's Friend Society for the Relief of Negro Slaves, LB, MS 3173/1/1.
5. This woman shared the same name as an older relative, who was born Mary Falmer, was also Birmingham based, and married to the banker Charles Lloyd. She had been Elizabeth's correspondent in 1806. She died in about 1821. [See Chapter Nine 'Peace- when there is no peace'].
6. Reports, Records of the Birmingham Ladies Negro's Friend Society for the Relief of Negro Slaves, LB, MS 3173/2/1.
7. Midgley, C. (2004) 'Townsend (nee Jesse) Lucy (1781-1847)' *Oxford Dictionary of National Biography, www.oxforddnb.com* (accessed 13/2/23).
8. Reports, Records of the Birmingham Ladies Negro's Friend Society for the Relief of Negro Slaves, LB, MS3173/2/1, p.16.
9. The Society went through several name changes during its existence. After slavery had been abolished, it changed from the 'Female Society for the Relief of British Negro Slaves' to 'The Ladies' Negro's Friend Society' and later, to the 'Female Society for Birmingham'.
10. Aucott, *Elizabeth Heyrick*, p.29.
11. Midgley, *Women Against Slavery.* Chapter 4 'Anti-slavery in the Fabric of Women's Lives'.
12. Records of the Birmingham Ladies Negro's Friend Society for the Relief of Negro Slaves, LB, MS3173.
13. See Chapter Nine 'Peace, when there is no peace'.
14. Walvin, J. (2018) 'The Slave Trade, Quakers, and the Early Days of British Abolition' in Carey, B. & Plank, G. (eds.) *Quakers and Abolition* (Urbana, Chicago and Springfield, University of Illinois Press) p.177

15. Reports, Records of the Birmingham Ladies Negro's Friend Society for the Relief of Negro Slaves, LB, MS3173/2/1, p.14.
16. Abstract of the Cash Account, Reports, Records of the Birmingham Ladies Negro's Friend Society for the Relief of Negro Slaves, LB, MS3173/2/1, p.33.
17. According to the website *www.measuringworth.com,* a simple purchasing power calculator obtains this relative value by multiplying £80.00 by the percentage increase in the RPI from 1825 to 2021.
18. Midgley, *Women Against Slavery,* p.115.
19. Reports, Records of the Birmingham Ladies Negro's Friend Society for the Relief of Negro Slaves, LB, MS3173/2/1, p.3-4.
20. Midgley, C. (2004) 'Lloyd (nee Honeychurch) Mary (1795-1865)' *Oxford Dictionary of National Biography, www.oxforddnb.com* (accessed 13/2/23).
21. See Chapter Seven '…an Emblem of the Wise'.
22. James and Shuttleworth, 'Susanna Watts and Elizabeth Heyrick', p.68.
23. See Chapter Seven '…an Emblem of the Wise'.
24. James and Shuttleworth, ibid.
25. See Chapter Eight 'If we purchase the commodity we participate in the crime'
26. Midgley, 'Townsend (nee Jesse) Lucy.'
27. Hochschild, *Bury the Chains,* p.326.
28. Minute Book, Records of the Birmingham Ladies Negro's Friend Society for the Relief of Negro Slaves, 1825-1852, LB, MS3173/1/1, p.50.
29. William Cowper (1731-1800) was friends with John Newton (1725-1807) who had been active in the slave trade but had later regretted his involvement and supported William Wilberforce in the abolition campaign. Cowper wrote a number of anti-slavery poems including 'The Negro's Complaint' which was often quoted by Martin Luther King during the twentieth-century civil rights movement.
30. See Chapter Eight 'If we purchase the commodity we participate in the crime'.
31. See Chapter Five 'Never daring to think of it.'
32. Watts, S. (c1817-1839), *Scrapbook,* ROLLR, DE8170, p.303.
33. Hurwitz, E. (1973) *Politics and the Public Conscience*, p.88-89.
34. Later, Newton regretted his involvement in the slave trade, became an abolitionist and a supporter of William Wilberforce. See D. Bruce Hindmarsh (1996) *John Newton and the English Evangelical tradition: between the conversions of Wesley and Wilberforce* (Oxford, Clarendon Press).

35. Corfield, 'Elizabeth Heyrick: Radical Quaker', p.44. See also Chapter Eight 'If we purchase the commodity, we participate in the crime.'
36. Quoted in Twells, A. (2018) 'Rawson (née Read) 1801-1887' *Oxford Dictionary of National Biography, www.oxforddnb.com* (accessed 13/2/23).
37. Heyrick, E. (1828) *Appeal to the Hearts and Consciences of British Women* (Leicester, A. Cockshaw) p.3.
38. Wollstonecraft, M. (1792) *A Vindication of the Rights of Woman* Chapter Two, (London, Vintage Books). Abridged edition published in 2015.
39. Heyrick, *Appeal to Hearts and Consciences*, p.3.
40. Hochschild, *Bury the Chains*, p.325.
41. Heyrick, *Appeal to Hearts and Consciences*, p.16.
42. Vickery, *The Gentleman's Daughter,* p.9.
43. Whelan, *Other British Voices*, ch.6 For example, see Coltman, E. (1811) 'Letter VII' in *Familiar Letters addressed to Children and Young Persons of Middle Rank,*' (London, printed for the author), pp.27-32.
44. James and Shuttleworth, 'Susanna Watts and Elizabeth Heyrick'.
45. See Chapter Five 'Never daring to think of it.'
46. 'The Wish,' in *The Hummingbird or morsels of information on the subject of slavery* (Leicester, A. Crickshaw) vol.1, no.8, July 1825, p.248.
47. Letter from Elizabeth Heyrick to Lucy Townsend, Dec. 28th 1826, BLO, *MSS.Brit.Emp.s.*5, p.102.
48. Hochschild, A. (2006) *Bury the Chains: The British Struggle to Abolish Slavery* (London, Pan Macmillan), p.327.
49. See Chapter Six 'All the Work of a Moment'.
50. The Corn Laws were tariffs on imported food that were enforced between 1815 and 1846 and were designed to keep corn prices high. They enhanced the profits and power associated with land ownership. For background reading, see Hobsbawm, E. (1962) *The Age of Revolution 1789-1848* (London, Weidenfeld and Nicholson Ltd., London) Part 1.
51. See *Victoria County History https://www.british-history.ac.uk/vch/leics/vol4/pp110-152* (accessed 13/2/23).
52. Heyrick, E. (1826) *Animadversions on the Late Contested Election for the Borough of Leicester* (Leicester, Albert Crockshaw), p.14-15.
53. 'The First Report of the Female Society for the Relief of British Negro Slaves', 1826, Records of the Birmingham Ladies Negro Friend Society for the Relief of Negro Slaves, Library of Birmingham MS 3173/2/1, p.12.
54. Midgley, *Women Against Slavery.* See Chapter 3 'Cement of the Whole Anti-slavery Building'.

55. ibid. See Chapter 5 'Perspectives, Principles and Policies.'
56. ibid.
57. Anon (1862) *A Brief Sketch of the Life and Labours of Mrs Elizabeth Heyrick* (Leicester, Crossley and Clarke) p.20.
58. Knutsford, Viscountess (1900) *Life and Letters of Zachary Macaulay* (London, Edward Arnold) p.433.
59. Beale, *Hutton and Friends,* p.207.
60. ibid, p.106.
61. Minutes of meeting held on 8 April 1830. Records of the Birmingham Ladies Negro's Friend Society for the Relief of Negro Slaves, LB, MS 3173/1/1.
62. The current building in Great Queen Street is still a masonic meeting place and is the third to be erected on this site. It was designed in classic art deco style between 1927 and 1933 as a memorial to Freemasons killed on active service during World War I.
63. Stephen, G. (1854) *Anti-slavery Recollections: in a series of letters addressed to Mrs Beecher Stowe* (London, Thomas Hatchard) p.120.
64. Taylor, *The Interest,* p.172.
65. Stephen, *Anti-slavery Recollections,* p.122.
66. Minute Book 20th Jan 1829-5 Dec 1832, Archive of the Anti-slavery Society, BLO, MSS.Brit.Emp.s.20/E2/3, p.49.
67. Midgley, *Women Against Slavery,* p.115.

Chapter 15: 'A burning passion for justice'

1. Letter from her sister to Miss Coltman, 1831, Letters and Papers relating to the Coltman family of Leicester, ROLLR, 15D57/214.
2. Stephen, *Anti-slavery Recollections*. Just months afterwards, the Representation of the People Act was passed in Parliament and a series of major changes to the voting system in England and Wales were introduced which eventually resulted in the election of more liberal and progressive representatives.
3. Letter from Samuel to his wife, 1831. Letters and Papers relating to the Coltman family of Leicester, ROLLR, 15D57/215.
4. Turner, M. (2010) 'A Good Death' in: *Quaker Writings: An Anthology, 1650-1920,* ed. T. Hamm, *(New York, Penguin Classics)*, p.195.
5. Letter from Samuel to his wife, 1831. Letters and Papers relating to the Coltman family of Leicester, ROLLR, 15D57/215.
6. Beale, *Hutton and Friends,* p.213.

7. *Leicester Journal*, Friday October 21, 1831, p.3.
8. *Leicester Chronicle*, Saturday 22 October 1831, p.3.
9. Temple Patterson, *Radical Leicester,* p. 171. When the chapel closed in 1921, the remains of those who had been buried there were moved to a communal grave in Welford Road Cemetery.
10. Letter from Samuel to his wife, 1831. Letters and Papers relating to the Coltman family of Leicester, ROLLR, 15D57/215.
11. Samuel's wife, Mrs Anne Coltman, assisted with the transcription of his memoirs in three volumes. In addition, a collection of family letters was carefully transcribed by his sister Mary Ann Coltman who dedicated them to her great nephew on the understanding that they should never pass out of the family's hands. Much of this material is also held at ROLLR in: Coltman S. *Time's Stepping Stones- or some memorial of four generations of a family by an octogenarian of the same,* 3 vols., 1772-1857, M1153, p.2.
12. Letter from Samuel Coltman to John Coltman, 23 Oct 1841. Letters and Papers relating to the Coltman family of Leicester, ROLLR, 15D57/243.
13. Beale, *Hutton and Friends,* p.215-6.
14. ibid.
15. 'The Late Mrs Heyrick' in: *Leicester Chronicle,* Saturday 29 October, 1831, p.3.
16. Corfield, 'Elizabeth Heyrick: Radical Quaker,' p.48.
17. 'The Free Labour Movement', *The Slave,* August 1853, no.32.
18. Beale, *Hutton and Friends,* p.216-7.
19. Thanks to Melissa Atkinson for her observations.
20. Allen, D.E. (2004) 'Gibson, George Stacey (1818-1883)' *Oxford Dictionary of National Biography, www.oxforddnb.com* (accessed 13/2/23).
21. See Chapter Nine 'Peace- when there is no peace.'
22. Gross, I. (1980) 'The Abolition of Negro Slavery and British Parliamentary Politics 1832-3' *The Historical Journal,* vol. 23, no.1, pp.63-85.
23. ibid.
24. See Chapter Thirteen 'Let Compensation be made in the first place where it is most due'.
25. Aucott, *Susanna Watts.*
26. Midgley, *Women Against Slavery.* See Chapter 6 'The Transatlantic Sisterhood.'
27. Beale, *Hutton and Friends,* p.210-11.

28. 'Anti-Slavery Meeting' *The Scotsman,* Saturday 24 October, 1846, p.3.
29. *The Liberator,* vol. 1 no.1, Saturday January 1, 1831, p.1.
30. Dhillon, M. (1966) *Benjamin Lundy and the Struggle for Negro Freedom* (Urbana and London, University of Illinois Press). As a young man, Lundy had first encountered slaves in a town called Wheeling, Illinois, where he had been shocked to see dozens of ragged men, chained and handcuffed, being driven through the streets with horse whips and bludgeons, as they made their way to new plantations down the Ohio and the Mississippi. Brought face to face with the brutality of the institution, according to his biographer, Lundy now made a vow to follow in the Quaker anti-slavery tradition.
31. ibid, p.68.
32. ibid, p.146.
33. 'Immediate not Gradual Abolition of Slavery' in: *Genius of Universal Emancipation,* December 1824, no.3 Vol. IV, p.34.
34. 'MRS H.B. STOWE' *The Anti-slavery Reporter,* vol 1, no.7 New Series, July 1, 1853, p.148-151.
35. See Chapter Eight 'If we purchase the commodity, we participate in the crime'.
36. Whelan, T. (2015) 'Mary Steel, May Hays and the Convergence of Women's literary Circles in the 1790s' *Journal for Eighteenth-Century Studies*, vol. 38, no.4, pp.511-524.
37. ibid.
38. See Chapter Eleven 'A War with beggars! An exterminating crusade against the poor and miserable!'
39. See Chapter Six 'All the work of a moment'.
40. Beale, *Hutton and Friends,* p.231-239.
41. Private family papers. Volume the First, 'A portion of the correspondence of Elizabeth Cartwright afterwards Elizabeth Coltman'.
42. See Chapter Ten 'The Rights of the Poor'
43. Coltman, S, *Time's Stepping Stones - or some memorial of four generations of a family by an octogenarian of the same,* 3 vols., 1772-1857, ROLLR, M1153, p.177.
44. ibid. p.149.
45. Halbersleben, K. (1993) *Women's Participation in the British Anti-slavery movement 1824-1865* (Lewiston, Edwin Mellen Press)
46. Midgley, *Women Against Slavery.*
47. Taylor, *The Interest,* p.272.

Select Bibliography

I Unpublished Sources

Family Papers

Three volumes of transcribed letters and diary extracts are held in a private family collection to which the author has had generous and unrestricted access.

Archive Collections

Full archival references to material used in the chapters can be found in the Endnotes. Below is a key to abbreviations used.

The Record Office for Leicestershire, Leicester, and Rutland (ROLLR), Wigston Magna.
University of Leicester (UL), Leicester.
The Library of Birmingham (LB), Birmingham.
The Library of the Religious Society of Friends (LSF), London.
The Bodleian Library (BLO), Oxford.
The British Library (BL), London.
Borthwick Institute for Archives, University of York, (BIA), York.
Victoria and Albert Museum (V&A).

II Published Sources

Elizabeth Heyrick's pamphlets were all published by her in her lifetime and are listed in Appendix 1.

Key Newspapers and Periodicals

Leicester Chronicle
Leicester Journal
Leicestershire Historian
Anti-slavery Reporter
The Friend, the Quaker Magazine.

Websites

Where specific reference is made in the chapters to a website page, the full URL is given in the Endnotes. The most frequently consulted websites are listed below:

Oxford Dictionary of National Biography
http://www.oxforddnb.com

British History Online
http://www.british-history.ac.uk

Measuring Worth
http://www.measuringworth.com

Centre for the Study of the Legacies of British Slavery
https://www.ucl.ac.uk/lbs/

The Record Office for Leicestershire, Leicester and Rutland
http://www.recordoffice.org.uk

British Library
https://www.bl.uk

National Archives
https://www.nationalarchives.gov.uk

Birmingham City Archives
https://www.birmingham.gov.uk/archives

Victoria County History
https://www.history.ac.uk/research/victoria-county-history

Brycchan Carey, author
https://www.brycchancarey.com/

Books and Academic Articles

Where specific reference is made to published texts in the chapters, full bibliographical details are given in the Endnotes where there are also some suggestions for further reading.

Appendix 1

Pamphlets by Elizabeth Heyrick (née Coltman)

Elizabeth Heyrick published her pamphlets anonymously and at her own expense. Her work has often been conflated with that of another writer, Elizabeth Coltman (1761-1838) also from Leicester. This list therefore includes only the publications that can be most reliably attributed to our Elizabeth Heyrick (1769-1831).

1809	*A Christmas box for the advocates of bull baiting* (1809) *Bull baiting: a village dialogue between Tom Brown and John Sims* (1809)
1817	*Exposition of one principal cause of the national distress, particularly in manufacturing districts; with some suggestions for its removal* (1817)
1819	*Enquiry into the consequences of the present depreciated value of human labour, etc.* in Letters to Thomas Fowell Buxton, Esq. M.P. (1819)
1823	*Cursory remarks on the evil tendency of unrestrained cruelty; particularly on that practised in Smithfield Market* (1823)
1824	*Protest against the spirit and practice of Modern Legislation as exhibited in the New Vagrant Act* (1824) *Immediate not gradual abolition; or an inquiry into the shortest, safest, and most effectual means of getting rid of West Indian slavery* (1824) *An Enquiry which of the two parties is best entitled to freedom? The slave or the slave holder? From an impartial examination of the conduct of each party at the bar of public justice* (1824)

	No British slavery; or an invitation to the people to put a speedy end to it (1824) *An appeal not to the government but to the people of England on the subject of West Indian slavery* (1824)
1825	*On the advantages of a high remunerating price for labour* (1825) *A letter of remonstrance from an impartial public to the hosiers of Leicester* (1825)
1826	*Animadversions on the late Contested Election for the Borough of Leicester* (1826) *Appeal to the Electors of the United Kingdom on the Choice of a New Parliament* (1826) *Letters on the Necessity of A Prompt Extinction of British Colonial Slavery chiefly addressed to the more influential classes. To which are added thoughts on Compensation* (1826)
1827	*Observations on the Offensive and Injurious Effect of Corporal Punishment, on the Unequal administration of Penal Justice, and on the Pre-eminent Advantages of the Mild and Reformatory over the Vindictive System of Punishment*
1828	*An Appeal to the Hearts and Consciences of British Women (1828)* *Apology for Ladies' Anti-slavery Associations* (1828)
1830	*Letters of a Recluse* (1830)

Appendix 2

Heyrick E. (1824) *Immediate Not Gradual Abolition or, An Inquiry into the Shortest, Safest, and Most Effectual Means of Getting Rid of West Indian Slavery.*

IMMEDIATE,

NOT GRADUAL

ABOLITION;

OR,

AN INQUIRY

INTO THE SHORTEST, SAFEST, AND MOST EFFECTUAL MEANS OF GETTING RID OF

WEST INDIAN SLAVERY.

by E. Heyrick

LONDON:

SOLD BY

HATCHARD AND SON, PICCADILLY; SEELEY AND SON, FLEET STREET; SIMPKIN AND MARSHALL, STATIONERS' COURT; HAMILTON, ADAMS, AND CO. PATERNOSTER ROW; J. AND A. ARCH, CORNHILL; W. DARTON, HOLBORN HILL; W. PHILLIPS, GEORGE YARD, LOMBARD STREET; HARVEY AND DARTON, GRACECHURCH STREET.

MDCCCXXIV.

IMMEDIATE,

NOT GRADUAL

ABOLITION,

&c. &c. &c.

IT is now seventeen years since the *Slave Trade* was abolished by the Government of this country—but *Slavery* is still perpetuated in our West India colonies, and the horrors of the Slave Trade are aggravated rather than mitigated. By making it felony for British subjects to be concerned in that inhuman traffic, England has only transferred her share of it to other countries. She has, indeed, by negociation and remonstrance, endeavoured to persuade them to follow her example.—But has she succeeded?—How should she, whilst there is so little consistency in her conduct? Who will listen to her pathetic declamations on the injustice and cruelty of the Slave Trade—whilst she rivets the chains upon her own slaves, and subjects them to all the injustice and cruelty which she so eloquently deplores when her own interest is no longer at stake? Before we can have any rational hope of prevailing on our guilty neighbours to abandon this atrocious commerce—to relinquish the gain of oppression,—the wealth obtained by rapine and violence,—by the deep groans, the bitter anguish of our unoffending fellow creatures;—we must purge ourselves from these pollutions;—we must break the iron yoke from off the neck of *our own slaves*,—and let the wretched captives in our own islands go free. Then, and not till then, we shall speak to the surrounding nations with the *all-commanding eloquence of sincerity and truth*,—and our persuasions will be backed by the *irresistible argument of consistent example*. But to invite others to be just and merciful whilst we grasp in our own hands the rod of oppression,—to solicit others to relinquish the wages of iniquity whilst we are putting them into our own pockets—what is it but cant and hypocrisy? Do such preachers of justice and mercy ever make converts? On the contrary, do they not render themselves ridiculous and contemptible?

But let us, *individually*, bring this great question closely home to our own bosoms. We that hear, and read, and approve, and applaud the powerful appeals, the irrefragable arguments against the Slave Trade, and against slavery,—are we *ourselves* sincere, or hypocritical? Are *we* the true friends of justice, or do we only cant about it?—To which party do *we* really belong?—to the friends of emancipation, or of perpetual slavery? Every individual belongs to one party or the other; not speculatively, or professionally merely, but practically. The perpetuation of slavery in our West India colonies, is not an abstract question, to be settled between the Government and the Planters,—it is a question in which we are *all* implicated;—we are all guilty,—(with shame and compunction let us admit the opprobrious truth) of supporting and perpetuating slavery. The West Indian planter and the people of this country, stand in the same moral relation to each other, as the thief and the receiver of stolen goods. The planter refuses to set his wretched captive at liberty,—treats him as a beast of burden,—compels his reluctant unremunerated labour under the lash of the cart whip,—why?—because WE furnish the stimulant to all this injustice, rapacity, and cruelty,—by PURCHASING ITS PRODUCE. Heretofore, it may have been thoughtlessly and unconsciously,—but now this palliative is removed;—the veil of ignorance is rent aside;—the whole nation must now divide itself into the *active supporters*, and the *active opposers* of slavery;—there is no longer any ground for a neutral party to stand upon.

The state of slavery, in our West Indian islands, is now become notorious;—*the secret is out*;—the justice and humanity, the *veracity* also, of slave owners,—is exactly ascertained;—the credit due to their assertions, that their slaves are better fed, better clothed,—are more comfortable, more *happy* than our English peasantry, is now universally understood. The tricks and impostures practised by the colonial assemblies, to hoodwink the people,—to humbug the Government,—and to bamboozle the *saints* (as the friends of emancipation are scornfully termed)—have all been detected—and the cry of the nation has been raised, from one end to the other, against this complicated system of knavery and imposture,—of intolerable oppression, of relentless and savage barbarity.

But is all this knowledge to end in exclamations, in petitions and remonstrances?—Is there nothing to be *done*, as well as said? Are there no tests to prove our sincerity,—no sacrifices to be offered in confirmation of our zeal?—Yes, there is *one*, (but it is in itself so small and insignificant that it seems almost burlesque to dignify it with the name of sacrifice)—it is ABSTINENCE FROM THE USE OF WEST INDIAN PRODUCTIONS, *sugar*, especially, in the cultivation of which slave labour is chiefly occupied. Small, however, and insignificant as the sacrifice may appear,—it would, at once, give the death blow to West Indian slavery. When there was no longer a market for the productions of *slave labour*, then, and *not till then*, will the slaves be emancipated.

Many had recourse to this expedient about thirty years ago, when the public attention was so generally roused to the enormities of the Slave Trade. But when the trade was abolished by the British legislature, it was too readily concluded that the abolition of slavery, in the British dominions, would have been an inevitable consequence, this species of abstinence was therefore unhappily discontinued.

" But (it will be objected) if there be no market for West Indian produce, the West Indian proprietors will be ruined, and the slaves, instead of being benefited, will perish by famine." Not so,—the West Indian proprietors understand their own interest better. The market though shut to the productions of *slave labour*, would still be open to the productions of *free labour*,—and the planters are not such devoted worshippers of slavery as to make a voluntary sacrifice of their own interests upon her altar;—they will not doom the soil to perpetual barrenness rather than suffer it to be cultivated by free men. It has been abundantly proved that voluntary labour is more productive,—more advantageous to the employer than compulsory labour. The experiments of the venerable and philanthrophic Joshua Steele have established the fact beyond all doubt :—But the planter shuts his eyes to such facts, though clear and evident as the sun at noon day. None are so blind as those who *will* not see. The conviction then must be *forced* upon these infatuated men. It is often asserted, that slavery is too deeply rooted an evil to be eradicated by the exertions of any principle less potent and active than *self interest*—if so, the resolution to abstain from West Indian produce, would bring this potent and active principle into the fullest operation,—would *compel* the planter to set his slaves at liberty.*

But were such a measure to be ultimately injurious to the interest of the planter—that consideration ought not to weigh a feather in the scale against emancipation. The slave has a *right* to his liberty, a right which it is a crime to withhold—let the consequences to the planters be what they may. If I have been deprived of my rightful inheritance, and the usurper,

* It has been ascertained that the abstinence of *one tenth* of the inhabitants of this country from West Indian sugar would abolish West Indian slavery.

6

because he has long kept possession, asserts his *right* to the property of which he has defrauded me; are my just claims to it at all weakened by the boldness of his pretensions, or by the plea that restitution would impoverish and involve him in ruin? And to what inheritance, or birth-right, can any mortal have pretensions so just, (until forfeited by crime) as to liberty? What injustice and rapacity can be compared to that which defrauds a man of his best earthly inheritance,—tears him from his dearest connexions, and condemns him and his posterity to the degradation and misery of interminable slavery?

In the great question of emancipation, the interests of *two* parties are said to be involved,—the interest of the slave and that of the planter. But it cannot for a moment be imagined that these two interests have an equal right to be consulted, without confounding all moral distinctions, all difference between real and pretended, between substantial and assumed claims. With the interest of the planters, the question of emancipation has (properly speaking) nothing to do. The right of the slave, and the interest of the planter, are distinct questions; they belong to separate departments, to different provinces of consideration. If the liberty of the slave can be secured not only without injury but with advantage to the planter, so much the better, certainly;—but still the liberation of the slave ought ever to be regarded as an independent object; and if it be deferred till the planter is sufficiently alive to his own interest to co-operate in the measure, we may for ever despair of its accomplishment. The cause of emancipation has been long and ably advocated. Reason and eloquence, persuasion and argument have been powerfully exerted; experiments have been fairly made,—facts broadly stated in proof of the impolicy as well as iniquity of slavery,—to little purpose; even the *hope* of its extinction, with the concurrence of the planter, or by any enactment of the colonial, or British legislature, is still seen in very remote perspective,—so remote, that the heart sickens at the cheerless prospect. All that zeal and talent could display in the way of argument, has been exerted in vain. All that an accumulated mass of indubitable evidence could effect in the way of conviction, has been brought to no effect.

It is high time, then, to resort to other measures,—to ways and means more summary and effectual. Too much time has already been lost in declamation and argument,—in petitions and remonstrances against *British* slavery. The cause of emancipation calls for something more decisive, more efficient than words. It calls upon the real friends of the poor degraded and oppressed African to bind themselves by a solemn engagement, an irrevocable vow, to participate no longer in the crime of keeping him in bondage. It calls upon them to "wash their

7

own hands in innocency;"—to abjure for ever the miserable hypocrisy of pretending to commiserate the slave, whilst, by purchasing the productions of his labour they *bribe* his master to keep him in slavery. The great Apostle of the gentiles declared, that he would "eat no flesh whilst the world stood, rather than make his Brother to offend." Do you make a similar resolution respecting West Indian produce. Let your resolution be made conscientiously, and kept inviolably;—let no plausible arguments which may be urged against it from without,—no solicitations of appetite from within, move you from your purpose,—and in the course of a few months, slavery in the British dominions will be annihilated.

"Yes, (it may be said) if *all* would unite in such a resolution,—but what can the abstinence of a few individuals, or a few families do, towards the accomplishment of so vast an object?"—It can do wonders. Great effects often result from small beginnings. Your resolution will influence that of your friends and neighbours;—each of them will, in like manner, influence their friends and neighbours;—the example will spread from house to house,—from city to city,—till, *among those who have any claim to humanity,* there will be but one heart, and one mind,—one resolution,—one uniform practice. Thus, *by means the most simple and easy, would West Indian slavery be most safely and speedily abolished.*

"But, (it will be objected) it is not an *immediate,* but a *gradual* emancipation, which the most enlightened and judicious friends of humanity call for, as a measure best calculated, in their judgment, to promote the real interests of the *slave,* as well as his master; the former, not being in a condition to make a right use of his freedom, were it suddenly restored to him." This, it must be admitted, appears not only the general, but almost universal sentiment of the abolitionists;—to oppose it therefore, may seem a most presumptuous, as well as hopeless attempt. But truth and justice are stubborn and inflexible;—they yield neither to numbers or authority.

The history of emancipation in St. Domingo, and of the conduct of the emancipated slaves for thirty years subsequent to that event (as detailed in Clarkson's admirable pamphlet, on the necessity of improving the condition of our West Indian slaves,) is a complete refutation of all the elaborate arguments which have been artfully advanced to discredit the design of *immediate* emancipation. No instance has been recorded in these important annals, of the emancipated slaves (not the *gradually,* but the *immediately* emancipated slaves) having abused their freedom. On the contrary, it is frequently asserted in the course of the narrative, that the negroes continued to work upon all the plantations as quietly as before emancipation. Through the whole of Clarkson's diligent and candid investigations of the conduct of emancipated slaves, comprising a body of more than 500,000 persons,—under a great variety of circumstances, —a considerable proportion of whom had been *suddenly* emancipated—*with all the vicious habits of slavery upon them;* many of them *accustomed to the use of arms;* he has not, throughout this vast mass of emancipated slaves, found a *single instance of bad behaviour,* not even a refusal to work, or of disobedience to orders; much less, had he heard of frightful massacres, or of revenge for past injuries, even when they had it amply in their power. Well might this benevolent and indefatigable abolitionist arrive at the conclusion, "that emancipation, (why did he not say *immediate* emancipation?) was not only practicable, but practicable without danger." All the frightful massacres and conflagratious which took place in St. Domingo, in 1791 and 1792, *occurred during the days of slavery.* They originated too, not with the slaves, but with the white and coloured planters,—between the royalists, and the revolutionists, who, for purposes of mutual vengeance, called in the aid of the slaves. Colonel Malenfant, in his history of the emancipation, written during his residence in St. Domingo, *ridicules the notion that the negroes would not work without compulsion,*—and asserts, that in one plantation, more immediately under his own observation, on which more than four hundred negroes were employed, *not one in the number refused to work after* their emancipation.

In the face of such a body of evidence, the detaining our West Indian slaves in bondage, is a continued acting of the same atrocious injustice which first kidnapped and tore them from their kindred and native soil, and robbed them of that sacred unalienable right which no considerations, how plausible soever, can justify the withholding. We have no right, on any pretext of expediency or pretended humanity, to say—"because you have been made a slave, and thereby degraded and debased,—therefore, I will continue to hold you in bondage until you have acquired a capacity to make a right use of your liberty." As well might you say to a poor wretch, gasping and languishing in a pest house, "here will I keep you, till I have given you a capacity for the enjoyment of pure air."

You admit, that the *vices* of the slave, as well as his miseries,—his intellectual and moral, as well as corporeal degradation are consequent on his slavery;—remove the cause then, and the effect will cease. Give the slave his liberty,—in the sacred name of justice, give it him at once. Whilst you hold him in bondage, he will profit little from your plans of amelioration. He has not, by all his complicated injuries and debasements, been disinherited of his *sagacity;*—this will teach him to give no credit to your admonitory lessons—your Christian instructions will be lost upon him, so long as he both knows and feels that his instructors are grossly violating their own lessons.

The enemies of slavery have hitherto ruined their cause by the senseless cry of *gradual* emancipation. It is marvellous that the *wise* and the *good* should have suffered themselves to have been imposed upon by this wily artifice of the slave holder, —for with him must the project of gradual emancipation have first originated. The slave holder knew very well, that his prey would be secure, so long as the abolitionists could be cajoled into a demand for *gradual* instead of *immediate* abolition. He knew very well, that the contemplation of a *gradual* emancipation, would beget a *gradual indifference to emancipation itself.* He knew very well, that even the *wise* and the *good,* may, by habit and familiarity, be brought to endure and tolerate almost any thing. He had caught the poet's idea, that—

"Vice is a monster of such frightful mien,
"As to be hated, need but to be seen;
"But, seen too oft, *familiar with her face,*
"*We first endure, then pity, then embrace.*"

He caught the idea, and knew how to turn it to advantage.—He knew very well, that the faithful delineation of the horrors of West Indian slavery, would produce such a general insurrection of sympathetic and indignant feeling; such abhorrence of the oppressor, such compassion for the oppressed, as must soon have been fatal to the whole system. He knew very well, that a strong moral fermentation had begun, which, had it gone forward, must soon have purified the nation from this foulest of its corruptions;—that the cries of the people for emancipation, would have been too unanimous, and too importunate for the Government to resist, and that slavery would, long ago, have been exterminated throughout the British dominions. Our example might have spread from kingdom to kingdom,—from continent to continent,—and the slave trade, and slavery, might, by this time, have been abolished—all the world over:—"A sacrifice of a sweet savour," might have ascended to the Great Parent of the Universe;—"His kingdom might have come, and his will (thus far) have been done on earth, as it is in Heaven."

But this GRADUAL ABOLITION, has been the grand marplot of human virtue and happiness;—the very master-piece of satanic policy. By converting the cry for *immediate*, into *gradual* emancipation, the prince of slave holders, "transformed himself, with astonishing dexterity, into an angel of light,"—and thereby—"deceived the very elect."—He saw very clearly, that if public justice and humanity, especially, if *Christian* justice and humanity, could be brought to demand only a *gradual* extermination of the enormities of the slave system;—if they could be brought to *acquiesce*, but for one year, or for one month, in the slavery of our African brother,—in robbing

10

him of all the rights of humanity,—and degrading him to a level with the brutes;—that then, they could imperceptibly be brought to acquiesce in all this for an unlimited duration. He saw, very clearly, that the time for the extermination of slavery, was precisely that, when its horrid impiety and enormity were *first distinctly known and strongly felt.* He knew, that every moment's unnecessary delay, between the discovery of an imperious duty, and the setting earnestly about its accomplishment, was dangerous, if not fatal to success. He knew, that strong excitement, was necessary to strong effort;—that intense feeling was necessary to stimulate intense exertion;—that, as strong excitement, and intense feeling are generally transient, in proportion to their strength and intensity,—the most effectual way of crushing a great and virtuous enterprize,—was to gain time,—to defer it to "a more convenient season," when the zeal and ardour of the first convictions of duty had subsided;—when our sympathies had become languid;—when considerations of the difficulties and hazards of the enterprize, the solicitations of ease and indulgence should have chilled the warm glow of humanity,—quenched the fervid heroism of virtue;—when familiarity with relations of violence and outrage, crimes and miseries, should have abated the horror of their first impression, and, at length induced indifference.

The father of lies, the grand artificer of fraud and imposture, transformed himself therefore, on this occasion, pre-eminently, "into an angel of light"—and deceived, not the unwary only, the unsuspecting multitude,—but the wise and the good, by the plausibility, the apparent force, the justice, and above all, by the *humanity* of the arguments propounded for *gradual* emancipation. He, is the subtilest of all reasoners, the most ingenious of all sophists, the most eloquent of all declaimers.—He, above all other advocates, "can make the worst appear the better argument;" can, most effectually pervert the judgment and blind the understanding,—whilst they seem to be most enlightened and rectified. Thus, by a train of most exquisite reasoning, has he brought the abolitionists to the conclusion,—that the interest of the poor, degraded, and oppressed *slave,* as well as that of his master, will be best secured by his *remaining in slavery.* It has indeed, been proposed to mitigate, in some degree, the miseries of his interminable bondage, but the blessings of *emancipation,* according to the propositions of the abolitionists in the last session of Parliament, were to be reserved for his *posterity* alone,—and every idea of *immediate* emancipation is still represented, not only as impolitic, enthusiastic and visionary, but as highly injurious to the slave himself, —and a train of supposed apt illustrations is continually at hand, to expose the absurdity of such a project. "Who (it is asked) would place a sumotuous banquet before a half-famished

11

wretch, whilst his powers of digestion were so feeble that it would be fatal to partake of it?—Who would bring a body benumbed and half frozen with cold, into sudden contact with fervid heat? Who would take a poor captive from his dungeon, where he had been immured whole years, in total darkness, and bring him at once into the dazzling light of a meridian sun? No one, in his senses, certainly. All these transitions from famine to plenty,—from cold to heat,—from darkness to light, must be gradual in order to be salutary. But must it therefore follow, by any inductions of common sense, that emancipation out of the gripe of a robber or an assassin,—out of the jaws of a shark or a tiger, must be gradual? Must, it, therefore, follow, that the wretched victim of slavery must always remain in slavery?—that emancipation must be *so* gradual, that the blessings of freedom shall never be tasted by him who has endured all the curses of slavery, but be reserved for his posterity alone?

There is something unnatural, something revolting to the common sense of justice, in reserving all the sweets of freedom for those who have never tasted the bitter cup of bondage,—in dooming those who have once been compelled to drink it, to drain it to the very dregs. Common equity demands that relief should be administered first to those who have suffered most;—that the healing balm of mercy should be imparted first to those who have smarted most under the rod of oppression: that those who have borne the galling yoke of slavery, should first experience the blessings of liberty. The cause of emancipation loses more than half its interest, when the public sympathy is diverted from its natural channel,—turned from the *living* victims of colonial bondage to their unborn progeny.

It is utterly astonishing, with such an object as West Indian slavery before us, rendered palpable, in all its horrors, almost to our very senses, by a multitude of indubitable facts, collected from various sources of the highest authority, all uniting in the same appalling evidence;—with the sight of our fellow-creatures in bondage so rigorous,—in moral and physical degradation so abject;—under a tyranny so arbitrary, wanton and barbarous;—it is utterly astonishing, that our compassion and sympathy should be so timid and calculating,—so slow and cautious.

Under the contemplation of *individual* suffering, comparatively trifling, both in nature and duration, our compassion is prompt and quick in its movements,—our exertions, spontaneous and instinctive;—we go the shortest way to work, in effecting the relief of the sufferer. But, in emancipating *eight hundred thousand* of our fellow creatures and fellow subjects from a worse than Egyptian bondage, we advance towards the object, by a route, the most indirect and circuitous; we petition Parliament, year after year, for *gradual* emancipation:—to what purpose?

Are we gaining or losing ground by these delays? Are we approaching nearer or receding farther from the attainment of our object? The latter, it is too evident, is, and must be the case. The evil principle is more subtle and active in its various operations, than the good principle. The advocates of slavery, are more alert and successful in insinuating into the public mind, doubts and fears, coldness and apathy on the subject of emancipation, than the abolitionists are in counteracting such hostile influence;—and the desertions from the anti-slavery standard in point of zeal and activity, if not in numbers, since the agitation of the question in Parliament last year, are doubtless very considerable.

Should the numerous petitions to Parliament be ultimately successful;—should the prayer for gradual emancipation be granted; still, how vague and indefinite would be the benefit resulting from such success. Should some specific time be appointed by government, for the final extinction of colonial slavery;—that period, we have been informed from high authority, will not be an early one. And who can calculate the tears and groans, the anguish and despair;—the tortures and outrages which may be added, during the term of that protracted interval, to the enormous mass of injuries already sustained by the victims of West Indian bondage? Who can calculate the aggravated accumulation of guilt which may be incurred by its active agents, its interested abettors and supporters? Why then, in the name of humanity, of common sense, and common honesty, do we petition Parliament, year after year, for a gradual abolition of this horrid system,—this complication of crime and misery? Why petition Parliament *at all*, to do that for us, which, were they ever so well disposed, we can do more speedily and more effectually for ourselves?

It is no marvel that *slave holders*, should cry out against immediate emancipation, as they have done against all propositions for softening the rigors of colonial slavery. "*Insurrection of all the blacks,—massacre of all the whites.*"—are the bug-bears which have been constantly conjured up, to deter the British Parliament from all interference between the master and his slave. The panic was the same, the outcry just as violent, when an attempt was made about forty years ago, to abate the horrors of the middle passage, by admitting a little more air into the suffocating and pestilent holds of the slave ships; and a noble duke, besought Parliament *not to meddle with the alarming question.** Confident predictions, from this quarter, of rebellion and bloodshed, have, almost uniformly followed every proposition to restrain the power of the oppressor and to mitigate the sufferings of the oppressed.

See the Debate on this subject in 1823.

13

It is therefore no wonder, that West Indian proprietors, and slave holders, should exclaim against immediate emancipation; that they should tell us, the slaves are so *depraved* as well as degraded, as to be utterly incapacitated for the right use of freedom;—that emancipation, instead of leading them into habits of sober contented industry, would be inevitably followed by idleness, pillage, and all sorts of enormities;—in short, *that they would rise in a mass, and massacre all the white inhabitants of the islands.*

That *slave holders* should say, and really believe all this, is perfectly natural;—it is no wonder at all that they should be full of the most groundless suspicions and terrors;—for tyrants are the greatest of all cowards.—" The wicked fleeth when no man pursueth;"—he is terrified at shadows,—and shudders at the spectres of his own guilty imagination.

But that the *abolitionists* should have caught the infection,—should be panic-struck;—that the friends of humanity,—the wise and the good—should be diverted from their purpose by such visionary apprehensions;—that they should " fear where no fear is;"—should swallow the bait, so manifestly laid to draw them aside from their great object;—that they should be so credulous, so easily imposed upon—is marvellous.

The simple enquiry, what is meant by emancipation? might have dissipated at once all these terrible spectres of rapine and murder. Does emancipation from slavery imply emancipation from law? Does emancipation from lawless tyranny,—from compulsory unremunerated labour, under the lash of the cart whip, imply emancipation from all responsibility and moral restraint? Were slavery in the British colonies extinguished,—the same laws which restrain and punish crime in the *white* population, would still restrain and punish crime in the *black* population. The danger arising from inequality of numbers would be more than counteracted by the wealth, influence, and the armed force, possessed by the former. But independent of such considerations, the oppressed and miserable, corrupt as is human nature, do not naturally become savage and revengeful when their oppressions and miseries are removed. As long as a human being is bought and sold,—regarded as goods and chattels, — compelled to labour without wages, — branded, chained, and flogged at the caprice of his owner; he will, of necessity, as long as the feeling of pain,—the sense of degradation and injury remain, he will, unless he have the spirit of a Christian martyr, be vindictive and revengeful. " Oppression (it is said) will make (even) a wise man, mad." But will the liberated captive, when the iron yoke of slavery is broken;—when his heavy burdens are unbound,—his bleeding wounds healed, his broken heart bound up; will he then scatter vengeance and destruction around him?

14

. Should the wretched African find the moment for *breaking his own chains,—and asserting his own freedom*,—he may well be expected to take terrible vengeance,—to push the law of retaliation to its utmost extreme. But, when presented with his freedom,—when the sacred rights of humanity are restored to him, would that be the moment for rage, for revenge and murder? To *polished* and *Christianized* Europeans, such abuses of liberty may appear natural and inevitable, since their own history abounds with them. But the history of negro emancipation abundantly proves that no such consequences are to be apprehended from the poor *uncultivated* and *despised* African.

" But, to demand *immediate* emancipation, however safe, however just and desirable in itself, would (we are told) be most *impolitic*,—for it would never be granted;—by striving to obtain too much, you would lose all. You must go cautiously and gradually to work. A very powerful interest and a very powerful influence are against you. You must try to conciliate instead of provoke the West Indian planters;—to convince them that their own interest is concerned in the better treatment and gradual emancipation of their slaves, or your object will never be accomplished."

But you will strive and labour in vain;—you will reason, however eloquently, however forcibly, in the ears of the " deaf adder." The moral and rational perceptions of the *slave holder*, are still more perverted than those of the slave;—oppression, is more debasing and injurious to the intellect of the oppressor, than that of the oppressed. The gains of unrighteousness,—familiarity with injustice and cruelty, have rendered the slave holder, more obstinately, more incurably blind and inaccessible to reason, than the slave. And what justice or restitution would there be in the world, were unlawful possessions never to be reclaimed till there was a disposition in the possessor *voluntarily* to relinquish them,—till he was convinced that it was his *interest* to part with them?

The interests and the prejudices of the West Indian planters, have occupied much too prominent a place in the discussion of this great question. The abolitionists have shewn a great deal too much politeness and accommodation towards these gentlemen. With reference to them, the question is said, to be a very *delicate* one. (Was ever the word delicacy so preposterously misapplied?)—It is said, to be beset with difficulties and dangers.—Yes, the parties interested,—*criminally* interested, protest that the difficulties are insurmountable,—the dangers tremendous. But those difficulties and dangers have been proved to be visionary and futile, the offspring of idle, or of hypocritical fears. A little *temporary* pecuniary loss, would be the mighty amount of all the calamities which emancipation would entail upon its virulent and infuriated opposers.* And is that a consideration to stand in competition with the liberation of *eight hundred thousand* of our fellow creatures from the heavy yoke of slavery! Must hundreds of thousands of human beings continue to be disinherited of those inherent rights of humanity, without which, life becomes a curse, instead of a blessing; must they continue to be roused and stimulated to uncompensated labour, night as well as day, during a great part of the year, by the impulse of the cart whip, that a few *noble lords* and *honourable gentlemen* may experience no privation of expensive luxury,—no contraction of profuse expenditure,—no curtailment of state and equipage! Must the scale in which is placed the just claims, the sacred rights of *eight hundred thousand British subjects*, be made to kick the beam, when weighed in the balance against pretensions so comparatively light and frivolous!

Among the West Indian proprietors, there are doubtless, individuals of high character and respectability, whose education and circumstances may, nevertheless, disqualify them from taking a strictly impartial view of colonial slavery. Such, of course, must be exempt from the just odium,—the reprobation, which belongs to the general body, as far as they have rendered their own character notorious by their own declarations,—by the speeches they have published, and the decrees they have issued;—by the virulent abuse, the rage and calumny which they have heaped upon the abolitionists;—by the alternations of fawning servility and insolent threatening, with which they at one time "prostrate themselves at the foot of the throne;"—at another, protest, in the tone of defiance, not to say rebellion, against British interference with colonial legislation. Towards these gentlemen, there has been extended a great deal too much delicacy and tenderness. They are *culprits*, in the strictest sense of the word,—and as such, they ought to be regarded, notwithstanding their rank and consequence, by every honest impartial moralist. They have received too long, the gains of oppression;—too long have they fattened on the spoils of humanity.

It matters not at all, how, or when, the planter acquired his pretended right to the slave;—whether by violence or robbery,—by purchase or by inheritance. His claim always was, and always will be, ill-founded, because it is opposed to nature, to reason, and to religion. It is also illegal, as far as legality has any foundation of justice, divine or human, to rest upon. His plea for protection against the designs of the abolitionists, on the ground that his property has been embarked in this nefari-

* The account of the London Meeting of West Indian Planters, which took place in February last, perfectly justifies the application of these epithets.

ous speculation, on the faith of Parliament,—in the confidence that no change would be effected in the laws which sanction the enormous injustice and wickedness of slavery, is childish and futile. Are not commercial speculations of every kind, subject to perpetual vicissitudes and revolutions? Are not human laws perpetually undergoing new modifications and changes in accommodation to the ever-varying circumstances of the times, —to increasing light and civilization? It is absurd to imagine that the progress of humanity, of moral and political improvement, is to be arrested, because some individual perquisites, derived from institutions of brutal ignorance and barbarism, would be curtailed. A great deal more reasonably might the industrious artizan, whose daily subsistence depends on his daily labour,—whose only property is his labour—and who, in many cases, has no means, like the West Indian capitalist, of transferring it from one channel to another;—with a great deal more reason might he exclaim and cry out for protection against all mechanical improvements, which diminish labour, which deprive thousands of the labouring classes of their wonted resources, and drive them to beggary.

But if the West Indian gentlemen fail to obtain *protection* against the designs of the abolitionists, then, they demand *compensation*, in the event of the emancipation of their slaves, to the immense amount of *sixty four millions*. And is *compensation* demanded in no other quarter?—or, if not demanded, is it no where else due? If compensation be demanded as an act of justice to the slave holder, in the event of the liberation of his slaves;—let justice take her free, impartial course;—let compensation be made in the first instance, where it is most due; —let compensation be first made to the *slave*, for his long years of uncompensated labour, degradation and suffering. It is in *this* quarter, that justice cries aloud for *compensation*,—and if our attention is turned, but for a moment, to these two substantial and well authenticated claims,—the demands of the *slave holder*; (even had they been couched in terms less arrogant and insulting,) will become not a little questionable.

Experience has already sufficiently evinced the fallacy of the notion, of the superior policy of aiming at gradual, instead of immediate emancipation, on the ground of its meeting with less opposition; for the planters have shewn themselves just as much enraged at the idea of *gradual*, as of immediate emancipation. They appear indeed, either incapable of perceiving, or determined to confound all distinction between them;—for, in the bitterness of their invectives, they accuse the *gradual* abolitionists of endeavouring to bring upon their heads all the calamities and destruction which they formerly deprecated as the inevitable consequence of *immediate* emancipation.

On this great question, the spirit of accommodation and conciliation has been a spirit of delusion. The abolitionists have lost, rather than gained ground by it;—their cause has been weakened, instead of strengthened. The great interests of truth and justice are betrayed, rather than supported, by all softening qualifying concessions. Every iota which is yielded of their rightful claims, impairs the conviction of their rectitude, and, consequently, weakens their success. Truth and justice, make their best way in the world, when they appear in bold and simple majesty;—their demands are most willingly conceded, when they are most fearlessly claimed.

Were the *immediate* freedom of the slave demanded, because in the first instance, it was unlawfully and violently wrested from him!—because, ever since, it has been most unjustly and cruelly withheld from him; because it is his unalienable right, which he holds by a divine charter, which no human claims can disannul:—were the immediate abolition of slavery, in the *British dominions*, demanded, because slavery, is in direct opposition to the spirit of the *British constitution*, to the spirit and letter of the Christian religion,—to every principle of humanity and justice;—because, as long as it is suffered to exist, it must remain the fruitful source of the most atrocious crimes, the most cruel sufferings; because, as long as it is suffered to exist, its abettors and supporters, passive as well as active, *(now that their eyes are wide open to its enormities)* must lie under the divine malediction, and experience, sooner or later, the certain and awful visitations of retributive justice,—the fearful accomplishment of that solemn declaration,—"With what measure ye mete, it shall be measured to you again:" — Demands so evidently just,—such plain appeals to reason and conscience,—to law and equity;—such serious reference to Divine authority,—to future retribution;—would be more successful,—would be better calculated to keep alive the public sympathy,—would lead to more unwearied exertions,—to greater sacrifices,—than the slow, cautious, accommodating measures now proposed by the abolitionists;—than any timorous suggestions of expediency,—any attempts to conciliate the favour, or to disarm the opposition of West Indian slave holders.

When an obvious and imperative duty is encumbered with considerations which do not properly belong to it; its obligations, instead of being enforced, are enfeebled; its motives, instead of being concentrated, are divided and scattered; and the duty, if not entirely neglected, will be but languidly and partially performed. We make slow progress in virtue, lose much time in labour, when, instead of going boldly forward in its straight and obvious path, we are continually enquiring how far we may proceed in it without difficulty and without opposition.

Had the abolitionists preserved a single eye to their great object;—had they kept it distinct and separate from all extraneous considerations;—had they pursued it by a course more direct, through means more simple;—had they confided more in the goodness of their cause, and dreaded less the opposition of its adversaries;—had they depended more upon divine, and less upon human support—their triumphs, instead of their defeats, would, long since, have been recorded. Surely their eyes must at length be opened;—they must perceive that they have not gone the right way to work,—that the apprehension of *losing all, by asking too much*,—has driven them into the danger of losing all, by having asked *too little*;—that the spirit of compromise and accommodation has placed them nearly in the situation of the unfortunate man in the fable, who, by trying to please every body, pleased nobody, and lost the object of his solicitude into the bargain.

It had been well, for the poor oppressed African, had the asserters of his rights entered the lists against his oppressors, with more of the spirit of Christian combatants, and less of worldly politicians;—had they remembered, through the whole of the struggle, that it was a conflict of sacred duty, against sordid interests,—of right against might;—that it was, in fact, an *holy war*,—an attack upon the strong holds, the deep intrenchments of the very powers of darkness; in which courage would be more availing than caution;—in which success was to be expected, less from prudential or political expedients, than from that all-controling power, which alone gives efficacy to human exertions,—which often defeats the best concerted schemes of human sagacity and accomplishes his great purposes through the instrumentality of the simplest agency. Had the labours of the abolitionists been begun and continued on Divine, instead of human reliance, *immediate* emancipation would have appeared just as attainable as *gradual* emancipation. But, by substituting the latter object for the former, under the idea that its accomplishment was more probable, less exposed to objection;—and by endeavouring to carry it, through considerations of interest, rather than obligations of duty; they have betrayed an unworthy diffidence in the cause in which they have embarked;—they have converted the great business of emancipation into an object of political calculation;—they have withdrawn it from Divine, and placed it under human patronage;—and disappointment and defeat, have been the inevitable consequence.

If the deadly root of slavery be ever extirpated out of British soil, it will be by such exertions as are prompted by duty rather than interest. We cannot sufficiently admire the great wisdom and goodness of those providential arrangements which have, in the general course of events, so inseparably connected our duty with our interest;—but with regard to the broad and palpable distinctions between right and wrong, virtue and vice;—the more simple and direct the reference to the will of our Divine Lawgiver, and that of his vicegerent, conscience,—the more determined will be our resolution,—the more decisive our conduct.—" How shall I do this great wickedness and sin

19

against God"—will be the most influential of all considerations. And the solemn inquiry, pressed home to the conscience, how an enlightened and Christian government,—how an enlightened and Christian community, can, in any way, encourage or sanction such a complicated system of iniquity as that of slavery,—"the greatest practical blunder, as well as the greatest calamity, that has ever disgraced and afflicted human nature,"—without sharing its guilt, and, if there be a righteous Governor of the universe, its punishment also?—will be followed up by propositions more consistent and energetic, than such as aim only at its *gradual* extermination.

The very able mover of the question in Parliament last year, proposed that our colonial slavery should be suffered—"to expire of itself,—to die a natural death.—But a natural death, it never will die.—It must be crushed at once, or not at all. While the abolitionists are endeavouring *gradually* to enfeeble and kill it by inches, it will gradually discover the means of reinforcing its strength, and will soon defy all the puny attacks of its assailants.

In the mean time, let the abolitionists remember,—while they are reasoning and declaiming and petitioning Parliament for gradual emancipation,—let them remember, that the miseries they deplore remain unmitigated,—the crimes they execrate are still perpetuated;—still the tyrant frowns—and the slave trembles;—the cart-whip still plies at the will of the inhuman driver—and the hopeless victim still writhes under its lash. The ameliorating measures *recommended* by Parliament, to the colonial legislators, are neglected and spurned. The bad passions of the slave holder are exasperated and infuriated by interference, and vengeance falls, with accumulated weight, on the slave. It had been better for him, had no efforts been made for his emancipation, than that they should ultimately fail, or be feebly exerted—the interval of suspense, will be an interval of restless perturbation,—of aggravated tyranny in the oppressor,—of aggravated suffering to the oppressed. *Unsuccessful opposition, to crimes of every description, invariably increases their power and malignity.*

An *immediate* emancipation then, is the object to be aimed at;—it is more wise and rational,—more politic and safe, as well as more just and humane,—than gradual emancipation. The interest, moral and political, temporal and eternal, of all parties concerned, will be best promoted by *immediate* emancipation. The sooner the planter is obliged to abandon a system which torments him with perpetual alarms of insurrection and massacre,—which keeps him in the most debasing moral bondage,—subjects him to a tyranny, of all others, the most injurious and destructive—that of sordid and vindictive passions;—the sooner he is obliged to adopt a more humane and more *lucrative* policy in the cultivation of his plantations;—the sooner the overlaboured, crouching slave, is converted into a free labourer,—

his compulsory, unremunerated toil, under the impulse of the cart whip, exchanged for cheerful, well recompensed industry, —his bitter sufferings for peaceful enjoyment,—his deep execration of his merciless tyrants, for respectful attachment to his humane and equitable masters ;—the sooner the Government and the people of this country purify themselves from the guilt of supporting or tolerating a system of such monstrous injustice, productive of such complicated enormities ;—the sooner all this mass of impolicy, crime and suffering is got rid of—the better.

It behoves the advocates of this great cause then, to take the most direct, the most speedy and effectual means of accomplishing their object. If any can be devised more direct, more speedy and effectual, or less exceptionable in its operation than that which has been suggested,—let it be immediately adopted; but let us no longer compromise the requisitions of humanity and justice, for those of an artful and sordid policy ;—let there be no betraying of the cause by needless delay ;—delay is always dangerous ;—on this momentous question, (humanly speaking) it will be fatal, if much longer protracted. The public sympathy is already declining,—people are becoming tired of the subject,—they grow listless and impatient when it is introduced ;—they tell you, " they wish to hear no more of it,—their minds are made up,—no advantage can be gained by farther discussion,—the subject must now be left to Parliament." Alas! and *how* has Parliament disposed of it? How has it realized the *very modest* hopes, indulged by the abolitionists, in consequence of its declarations in favour of gradual abolition, a year ago? By its recent decisions, the great work of emancipation appears to retrograde instead of advance. The bullying of the slave holders, is said to have proved completely triumphant. The royal proclamation just issued, is rightly denominated a *hope extinguisher*, to the wretched slave population. Well may the abolitionists express their disappointment, on finding the present measures of Government, fall so far short of the expectations, which the promises of last session had excited. Well may the right honourable secretary be charged with, " having done nothing, or worse than nothing; with being satisfied, at most, to see his pledge in favour of a whole archipelago, reduced to a single island ; while a law is still to prevail in every island of the West Indies, except *Trinidad*, which authorises a female negro, to be stripped, in the presence of her father, husband or son, and flogged with a cart whip ! !"

There were some, who anticipated these results ; cheerless and melancholy as they are, they are such as might reasonably have been expected from the proposition for *gradual* emancipation,—and if persisted in, it will assuredly end, in *no emancipation*. The time is critical. The *general* interest, in this great subject, is evidently on the wane,— and it should be remembered, that even the most humane and susceptible,—

those who are most under the influence of true Christian principle, are not always wound up to such a pitch of disinterested and ardent zeal, as is requisite to cope with such a host of interested and powerful opponents, as are the West Indian proprietors and slave holders. Those, who are "called to glory and virtue,"—invited, to labour, in the Divine vineyard,—are admonished, to "work whilst it is day,—for the night cometh, in which no man can work;"—whilst they have light, they are admonished to "walk in the light, lest darkness come upon them." Mental darkness, and spiritual night, steal fast upon those, who, when an imperious duty is presented to them,—when sufficient ability is imparted for its accomplishment,—falter and procrastinate.

If the great work of emancipation be not *now* accomplished,—humanly speaking, it may be despaired of, as far as our agency is concerned. The rising generation may furnish no such zealous, devoted advocates, as a Clarkson, a Wilberforce, and a Buxton. If the clear light, the full information, they have so generally diffused:—the deep interest and sympathy they have so generally excited, produce no other results than those at present contemplated by the abolitionists;—this country may fall under the curse of being judicially hardened and blinded, in consequence of having been softened and enlightened to so little purpose;—and the emancipation of *eight hundred thousand British slaves!* may be effected through other means and other agency, which, when once roused into action, may realize all those terrific scenes of insurrection and carnage which the imagination of the planter has so often contemplated.

Since the preceding pages were written, the sentences passed upon the insurgents of Demerara and Kingston have reached us. Some, had been hung, others, had received corporeal punishment—to what extent—let those who have ears to hear, and hearts to feel, deeply ponder. Some had received, others, were yet to receive—ONE THOUSAND LASHES,—AND WERE CONDEMNED TO BE WORKED IN CHAINS DURING THE RESIDUE OF THEIR LIVES!! The horrid work, has probably, by this time been completed, human interposition therefore, with respect to these individual victims of WEST INDIAN JUSTICE will now be of no avail.

But shall such sentences as these, be suffered to pass the ordeal of public opinion? Shall they be established as precedents for future judgments, on future insurgents? Forbid it—every feeling of humanity—in *every bosom*. Let every principle of virtue which distinguishes the human from the brute creation,—the professors of the benignant, compassionate religion of Christ, from the savage and blood-thirsty worshippers of Moloch,—raise one united, determined and solemn protest against the repetition of these barbarities, which blaspheme the sacred name of justice,—and seem to imprecate Almighty vengeance.

22

Will the inhabitants of this benevolent, this *Christian* country, *now* want a stimulant to rouse their best exertions,—to nerve their resolutions against all participation with these human blood-hounds? Will the British public *now* want a "spirit stirring" incentive to prohibit, and to interdict,—henceforth, and for ever,—the merchandize of slavery? Let the produce of slave labour,—henceforth, and for ever,—be regarded as "*the accursed thing*," and refused admission into our houses;—or let us renounce our Christian profession, and disgrace it no longer, by a selfish, cold-hearted indifference which, under such circumstances, would be reproachful to savages.

What was the offence which brought down this frightful vengeance on the heads of these devoted victims? What horrible crime could have instigated man to sentence his fellow man, to a punishment so tremendous?—to doom his brother to undergo the protracted torture of a THOUSAND LASHES?—to have his quivering flesh mangled and torn from his living body?—and to labour through life under the galling and ignominious weight of chains? It was insurrection. But in what cause did they become insurgents? Was it not in that cause, which, of all others, can best *excuse*, if it cannot *justify* insurrection? Was it not in the cause of self-defence from the most degrading, intolerable oppression?

But what was the *immediate* occasion of this insurrection? What goaded these poor wretches on to brave the dreadful hazards of rebellion? One of them, now hanging in chains at Demerara, was sold and separated from his wife and family of ten children, after a marriage of eighteen years,—*and thereby made a rebel.* Another was a slave of no common intellect, whose wife, the object of his warmest affections, was torn from his bosom, and forced to become the mistress of an overseer. His domestic happiness thus destroyed for ever, he became, (how should it have been otherwise?) disaffected and desperate. Such provocations, added to their common and every day wrongs, seem beyond human endurance, and might instigate "the very stones to mutiny."

How preposterously partial and inconsistent are we in the extension of our sympathy, our approbation and our assistance towards the oppressed and miserable! We extol the resistance of the *Greeks*,—we deem it heroic and meritorious. We deem it an act of virtue,—of *Christian charity*, to supply *them* with *arms* and *ammunition*, to enable them to *persist in insurrection.* Possibly, in the longest list of munificent subscribers to these *Greek* insurgents, the names of some noble lords and honourable gentlemen may be found—who sanction and approve the visitation of WEST INDIAN SLAVE INSURGENTS, with the GIBBET, and the infliction of ONE THOUSAND LASHES!!

But let us, whose moral perceptions are unblinded by interest or prejudice,—whose charity is unwarped by partiality or hypocrisy;—let *us* pursue a more rational and consistent course.

23

Let us not overlook our own urgent duties in the pursuit of such as are less imperative. Let us *first—mind our own business,*—" pluck the beam out of our own eye." Let us *first* extend the helping hand, to those who have the *first* claim to our assistance. Let us *first* liberate our own slaves—which we may do, without furnishing them with *arms* or *ammunition. Then,* we shall have *clean hands,*—and the Divine blessing may *then* be expected to crown our exertions for the redemption of other captives.

Should the weak objection, still haunt some inconsiderate reader, of the little good, which can reasonably be expected to result from *individual* abstinence from West Indian produce; let him reflect, that the most wonderful productions of human skill and industry; the most astonishing effects of human power have been accomplished by combined exertions, which, when individually and separately considered, appear feeble and insignificant. Let him reflect, that the grandest objects of human observation consist of small agglomerated particles; that the globe itself is composed of atoms too minute for discernment; that extended ages consist of accumulated moments. Let him reflect, that greater victories have been achieved by the combined expression of *individual opinion,* than by fleets and armies; that greater moral revolutions have been accomplished by the combined exertion of *individual resolution,* than were ever effected by acts of Parliament.

The hydra-headed monster of slavery, will never be destroyed by other means, than the united expression of *individual opinion,* and the united exertion of *individual resolution.* Let no man restrain the expression of the one, or the exertion of the other, from the apprehension that his single efforts will be of no avail. The greatest and the best work must have a *beginning,*—often, it is a very small and obscure one. And though the example in question should not become *universal,* we may surely hope that it will become general.

It is too much, to expect that the matter will be taken up—(otherwise, than to make a jest of it) by the thoughtless and the selfish: what proportion these bear to the considerate and the compassionate, remains to be ascertained. By *these,* we may reasonably expect that it *will* be taken up, with resolution and consistency. By Christian societies of every denomination,—pre-eminently by that, which has hitherto stood foremost in the great cause of abolition. By the great body of the Catholics too, who attach so *much merit* to abstinence and self-denial;—and by all the different Protestant professors, (who are at all sincere in their profession) of the one religion of universal compassion;—which requires us " *to love our neighbour as ourselves,*"—this testimony against slavery may be expected to be borne with scrupulous and conscientious fidelity.

Think, but for a moment, at what a trifling sacrifice the redemption of *eight hundred thousand of our fellow creatures from* *the lowest condition of degradation and misery may be accomplished.* Abstinence from *one single article* of luxury would annihilate West Indian slavery!! But *abstinence* it cannot be called;—we only need substitute *East* India, for *West* India sugar,—and the British atmosphere would be purified at once, from the poisonous infection of slavery. The antidote of this deadly bane; for which we have been so many years in laborious but unsuccessful search, is most simple and obvious,—too simple and obvious, it should seem, to have been regarded. Like Naaman, of old, who expected to be cured of his leprosy, by some grand and astonishing evolution, and disdained to wash, as he was directed, in the obscure waters of ~~Damascus~~;—we look for the abolition of British slavery, not to the simple and obvious means of its accomplishment, which lie within our own power,—but through the slow and solemn process of Parliamentary discussion,— through the "pomp and circumstance" of legislative enactment;—most absurdly remonstrating and petitioning *against* that system of enormous wickedness, which we voluntarily tax ourselves to the annual amount of two millions sterling, to *support!!**

That abstinence from West Indian sugar alone, would sign the death warrant of West Indian slavery, is morally certain. The gratuity of two millions annually, is acknowledged by the planters, to be insufficient to bolster up their tottering system,—and they scruple not, to declare to Parliament, that they must be ruined, if the protecting duties, against East India competition, be not augmented.

One, concluding word, to such as may be convinced of the duty, but may still be incredulous as to the *efficacy* of this species of abstinence, from the apprehension that it will never become sufficiently general to accomplish its purpose. Should your example *not* be followed;—should it be utterly unavailing towards the attainment of its object;—still, it will have its own abundant reward:—still, it will be attended with the consciousness of sincerity and consistency,—of possessing "*clean hands*,—of having "no fellowship with the workers of iniquity;" still, it will be attended with the approbation of conscience,—and doubtless, with that of the Great Searcher of hearts,—who regarded with favourable eye, the mite cast by the poor widow, into the treasury, and declared, that a cup of cold water only, administered in Christian charity, "shall in no wise lose its reward."

* Every reader may not be aware, that such is the amount of duty laid on *East* India, to keep up the unnatural price of *West* India sugar.

Knight and Bagster, 14, Bartholomew Close, London.

Index

Adams, John (John Coltman's step-nephew), 35
An Address to the People of Great Britain, on the Propriety of Abstaining from West Indian Sugar and Rum (William Fox), 76–7
Advocacy approaches, 34
African and Asiatic Society, 129
Aikin, Reverend John, 6
Ainsworth's Magazine, 103
America, 145–7
'Am I not a Man and a Brother?', 75
'Am I not a Woman and a Sister?', 132
Anglo-French Wars, 44–5, 80
Anti-Slavery Society *see* Society for the Mitigation and Gradual Abolition of Slavery Throughout the British Dominions
Anti-Slavery Society, Ladies' *see* Female Society for the Relief of British Negro Slaves, Birmingham
Apprenticeship, former slave, 126
The Art of Cookery Made Plain and Simple (Hannah Glasse), 73
Attack on Joseph Whetstone's house, 28–30
Babington MP, Thomas (abolitionist), 41–3, 133
Baptist Magazine, 137
Barbauld, Anna (poet), 6
The Benevolent Planters (musical play), 46
Benezet, Anthony (abolitionist), xxvii
Berry, Reverend Charles, 142–3, 149–50
Blood sports, 67–9
Bonsall, Derbyshire, 67–8
Book society, Leicester, 62, 66
Boston Tea Party, 77
Bow Bridge school, 86–7
Boycotts, consumer, 77–9
Brookes (slave ship), 39, 41, 75
Brookhouse, Joseph (inventor), 31–2, 35
Brougham, Henry (politician), 137
Bull-baiting, 67–71
Bunyan, John (poet), 2
Buxton, Thomas Fowell (abolitionist), 117

Capper, Mary (Quaker), 89
Cartwright, Elizabeth *see* Coltman, Elizabeth (EH's mother)
Chapone, Hester (writer), 56, 59, 63
The Christian Observer (journal), 114, 137
Clapham Sect, 43

Clarkson, John (abolitionist), 44–5, 77
Clarkson, Thomas (abolitionist), 40–1, 128, 130
Cockfighting, 3
Collingwood, Captain Luke, 37
Coltman, Elizabeth (EH's mother), 8–16, 23–4, 41, 55–6, 86–7, 91–2
Coltman, Elizabeth (Elizabeth Heyrick) *see* Heyrick, Elizabeth
Coltman, Elizabeth (no relation), 65, 67
Coltman, John (EH's brother), 19–21, 56–7, 96–7, 99, 121–2
Coltman, John (EH's father), 8–16, 28–32, 32–3, 35, 44–5, 91
Coltman, Joseph (EH's grandfather), 29–30
Coltman, Mary Ann (EH's sister), 4, 49, 67, 140–1, 148–9
Coltman, Rowland (EH's brother), 21–2, 52
Coltman, Samuel (EH's brother), 2–3, 4, 7–9, 19–21, 99, 121–2, 140–2
Combination Acts 1799 and 1800, 98
Compensation for slave owners, 126–7
Corn Laws, 95
Cowper, William (poet), 73, 132–3
Crown and Anchor tavern, London, 150
Cruelty to animals, 67–72
Cugoano, Quobna Ottobah (former slave), 75, 124–6
Cumberland, Richard (playwright), xxiv

Dame schools, 19
Deaths aboard ship, slave, 38–40
Death sentence, 94–5
Demerara, West Indies, 112–16, 127
Depression (melancholia), 60, 80, 84–5
Dissenters, 5–6, 32
Dodsley, Robert (bookseller), 7
Duelling, 56
Duty on East India Company sugar, 120–1, 125

East India Company, 120–1, 125
Edinburgh Review, 98
Elections, Leicester Borough, 136–7
Elections unrepresentative, 100
Ellis, Charles (pro-slavery advocate), 117–18
Emancipation Act 1833 *see* Slavery Abolition Act 1833
Enclosure, 31
Equiano, Olaudah (former slave), 37–8, 40
Evangelical Magazine, 24
Evans, William (reformer), 136–7

Fashion, late 18th century, 21
Female Society for the Relief of British Negro Slaves, Birmingham, 34, 130–2
Fieldhouse, Mrs (Elizabeth Cartwright's friend), 9–10, 16–17
Fox, William (radical), 76–7
Framework knitters, 30–2, 94–6
Freetown, Sierra Leone, 44
Fry, Elizabeth (née Gurney), 81

Gallowtree Gate, Leicester, 141
Gambling, 54
Gaol fees, 81
Gardiner, William (Nonconformist), 3, 19, 33, 51
Garrison, William Lloyd (abolitionist), 145–6
Genius of Universal Emancipation (newspaper), 147
Gibson, George Stacey (Quaker), 145
Granville Town *see* Freetown, Sierra Leone
Great Meeting chapel, Leicester, 5
The Guinea Voyage (James Stanfield), 75
Gurney, Martha (writer), 76
Gurney, Priscilla (Quaker minister), 81–2
Guyana, West Indies, 112

Hall, Reverend Robert, 5
Hays, Mary (writer), 65–6
Herrick, Robert (poet), 51
Hesperides (Robert Herrick), 51
Heyrick, Elizabeth:
born, 2
childhood anecdotes, 18
artist, 22
admonished by her mother, 23–4
starts writing, 35, 67
religious conviction, 42–3
courted by John Heyrick, 48–50
marries, 50
marriage under strain, 51–7
reaction to husband's death, 57–60
against cruelty to animals, 67–72
stops bull-baiting contest, 67–8
urges boycott of sugar, 78–9
and Quakerism, 81–90
prison visiting, 81–2
and William Tuke, 84–7
works in Esther Tuke's school, 86
assists beggars, 86, 103
sets up Bow Bridge school, 86–7
and Lindley Murray, 87–8
joins Leicester Quakers, 89–90
sympathy with Luddites, 94–5
compares workers' lot to that of slaves, 96–7
campaigns for living wages, 96–100
censures brother John, 99–101
and vagrancy, 102–107
opposes gradual emancipation, 115–16, 125–7
decries brutal treatment after Demerara uprising, 116–17
writes for *The Hummingbird,* 119–20, 135–6
opposes compensation for slave owners, 126–7
establishes Leicester Ladies Anti-Slavery Society, 130–1
addresses women in struggle for abolition, 134–5
last letter (to sister Mary Ann), 140
extolled by William Garrison, 146
records in brother Samuel's memoirs destroyed, 148–9
suffers from depression (melancholia), 60, 80, 84, 136, 149
silhouette, xix–xxiv, 144–5

dies, 140–2
pamphlets, 191–2
An Appeal Not to the Government But to the People of England ..., 46
An Enquiry which of the two parties is best entitled to freedom?, 127–8
Animadversions on the Late Contested Election for the Borough of Leicester, 137
Bull-baiting: A Christmas Box ..., 69–70
Bull-baiting: a Village Dialogue ..., 69
Exposition of one Principal Cause of the National Distress ..., 95
Immediate not Gradual abolition ..., 112, 121, 126, 192
Letter of remonstrance from an impartial public to the Hosiers of Leicester, 99
No British Slavery ..., 46
Protest Against the Spirit and Practice of Modern Legislation ..., 104
Heyrick, John (EH's husband), 48–50, 53, 56, 57
Heyrick, William (EH's brother-in-law), 81, 128
Hogarth, William (painter), xxviii
Honeychurch, Mary *see* Lloyd, Mary (friend of EH)
Hosiery trade, 30–2
The Hummingbird (periodical), 119–20, 135–6
Hurwitz, Edith (writer), 133
Hutton, Catherine (novelist), 9, 17, 36–7, 39, 51–2, 82, 99

The Interesting Narrative of the Life of Olaudah Equiano, 40

Kauffman, Angelica (artist), 21–2
Kibworth, Leicestershire, 6
King's Head Tavern, London, 114, 116
Klockenbrink, Deborah (Rowland Page's relative), 10, 14–15

Ladies' Anti-Slavery Society, 130–1
Leicester, 2–3, 32, 64, 136–7
Leicester Auxiliary Anti-Slavery Society, 121, 128
Leicester Chronicle, 141–2, 148
Leicester Ladies Anti-Slavery Society, 130–1
Letters from an American Farmer (J. Hector St John de Crèvecœur), 36–7
Letters on the Improvement of Mind (Hester Chapone), 56
*The Liberato*r (journal), 145–7
Liberty's Daughters (Mary Beth Norton), 77–8
Lloyd, Mary (friend of EH), 89, 130–2
London Yearly [Quaker] Meeting, 108
Luddites, 94–5
Lundy, Benjamin (abolitionist), 147

Macaulay, Zachary (abolitionist), 41–2, 45, 114, 129, 137
Maddock, Reverend Henry, 70
Mansfield, Chief Justice Lord, 38
Mansfield Park (Jane Austen), 111

Marginalisation of women, 62–3, 66
Matlock, Derbyshire *see* Coltman, Elizabeth (EH's mother)
Medallions, slave, 132
Melancholia *see* depression (melancholia)
Memoirs of Emma Courtney (Mary Hays), 65–6
Middle Passage slave trade, 38–40
Mills, Hannah (asylum deceased), 85
Mitcham Road Barracks, Croydon, 53
A Modest Proposal (Jonathan Swift), 107
Monthly Magazine (Dissenters' journal), 92
Moody, Thomas (pro-slavery advocate), 118
More, Hannah (writer), 45–7, 75
The Morning Dream (William Cowper), 132–3
Murray, Governor (of Demerara), 114
Murray, Lindley (grammarian), 87–8

Nathaniel Newton Foundation School, Hartshill, 19–20
Newton, John (slave trader), 134

Page, Rowland (John Coltman's uncle), 6, 9–10, 20–1
Paine, Thomas (activist), 33, 76
Pamela (Samuel Richardson), 22–4
Penal system, 81–2
Perry, Isabella (EH's pupil), 88
Peterloo Massacre, 97–9
Petitions, 40–1
Phillips, Richard (bookseller), 33–4, 92
Pity for Poor Africans (William Cowper), 73
Post in 1760s, 8–9
Pownall, Henry (lawyer), 138
Priestley, Dr Joseph (theologian), 2, 5
Prince, Mary (former slave), 113, 124–5
Prison visiting, 81–2
Property, slaves as, 126–7
Province of Freedom *see* Sierra Leone
Punishment, corporal, 108–10

Quakerism, 19–20, 81–90, 102–103
Quamina (slave), 113

Reid, Mary (EH's friend), 48, 50–1
Religious divide, 4–5
Revolution, French, 33–4, 53, 76–8
Rights of Man (Thomas Paine), 33, 76
Riots, anti-machine spinning, 28–32
Roscoe, William (penal reformer), 109–10
Rothley Temple, Leicestershire, 41–2

Sadler, Reverend Mr (Elizabeth Cartwright's fiancé), 13, 15–16
St Domingo, Dominican Republic, 128
Sancho, Ignatius (abolitionist), 24–5
Scrapbook on Negro Slaves (Lucy Townsend), 130

Sharp, Granville (abolitionist), xxvi, 38, 43–4
Shenstone, William (writer), 7
Sierra Leone, 43–5
Slare, Dr Frederick, 74
The Slave (journal), 143
Slavery Abolition Act 1833, 126, 145
Slavery, a poem (Hannah More), 45–6, 75
Slave Trade Act 1807, 89
Smithfield Market, London, 71
Smith, John (missionary), 113–16
Society for the Mitigation and Gradual Abolition of Slavery Throughout the British Dominions, 114, 125, 138–9
Society for the Purpose of Effecting the Abolition of the Slave Trade, 40–1, 75
Society of Friends, Religious *see* Quakerism
Somerset Ruling, xxvi–xxvii, 38
Sons of Africa, 75
Spence, Joseph (scholar), 7
Stanfield, James (publisher), 75
Stephen, George (Anti-slavery Society member), 138
Sterne, Laurence (author), 22, 24–5
Stowe, Harriet Beecher (writer), 147
Sugar, 73–5, 120–1, 125
Surrey (nonconformist) Chapel, 147–8
Swift, Jonathan (satirist), 107

Testing the Chains (Michael Craton), 115
The Retreat, York, 85–6
Thompson, Dr Gilbert, 85
Throsby, Reverend Robert, 62
Toleration Act 1688, 103
To The Sympathetic: An African Picture (John Heyrick), 54
Townsend, Charlotte (writer), 120–1
Townsend, Lucy (abolitionist), 130, 132, 136, 138
Treaty of Paris, 76
Trinity Lane School, York, 86
Tuke, Ann (prison reformer), 86
Tuke, Esther (EH's friend), 84, 86
Tuke, William (mental illness reformist), 84–7

Unitarianism, 2
Uprising in Demerara, 115–16

Vagrancy Act 1824, 102–106, 110
A Vindication of the Rights of Woman (Mary Wollstonecraft), 59, 65, 78–9

A Walk Through Leicester (Susanna Watts), 64
Waltire, John (lecturer), 34
War of Independence, American, 43, 76
Watts, Susanna (poet), 62–5, 78, 119, 133, 143–4
Way, Reverend Lewis, 88
Wedgwood, Josiah (potter), 75
Wesley, John (preacher), 2
The West Indian (Richard Cumberland), xxiv–xxvi, 75
Wheatley, Phyllis (slave and author), xxviii
Whetstone, Joseph (John Coltman's business partner), 28–9
Wigston Magna, Leicestershire, 31

Wilberforce, William (abolitionist), 41, 42, 89, 129, 133
Wilmot-Horton, Robert (pro-slavery advocate), 118
Wollstonecraft, Mary (writer), 59–60, 78–9
Worthington, Reverend Hugh, 5

Wuthering Heights (Emily Brontë), xxvi

York, 84

Zong (slave ship), 37–8